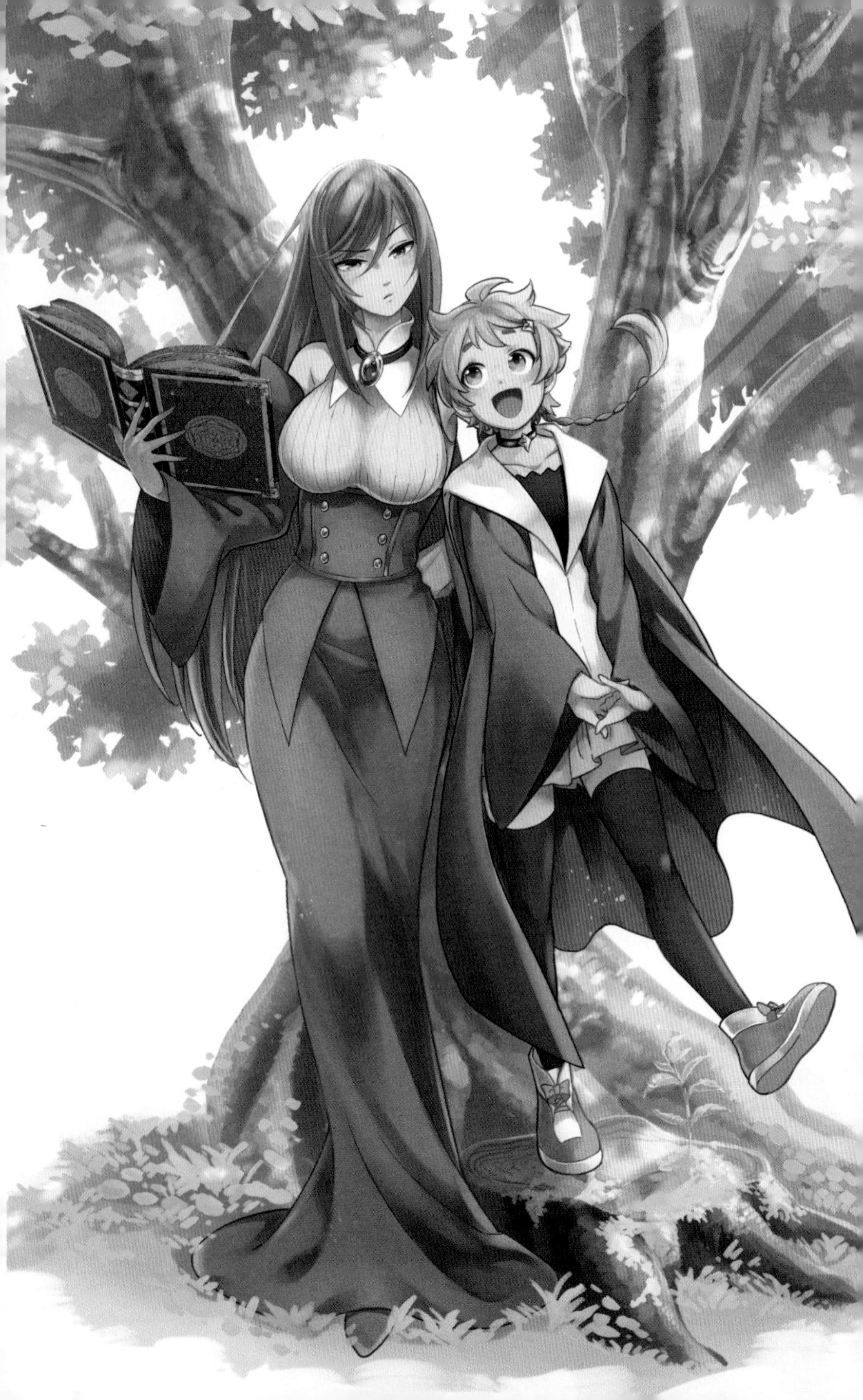

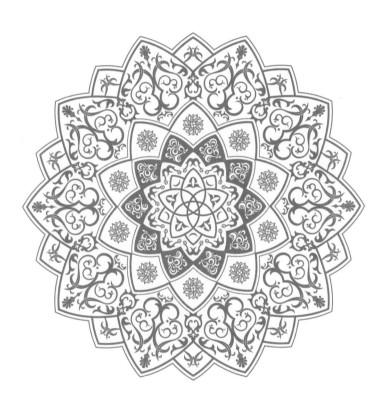

The Witches' Marriage

1

studio HEADLINE

CONTENTS

✦

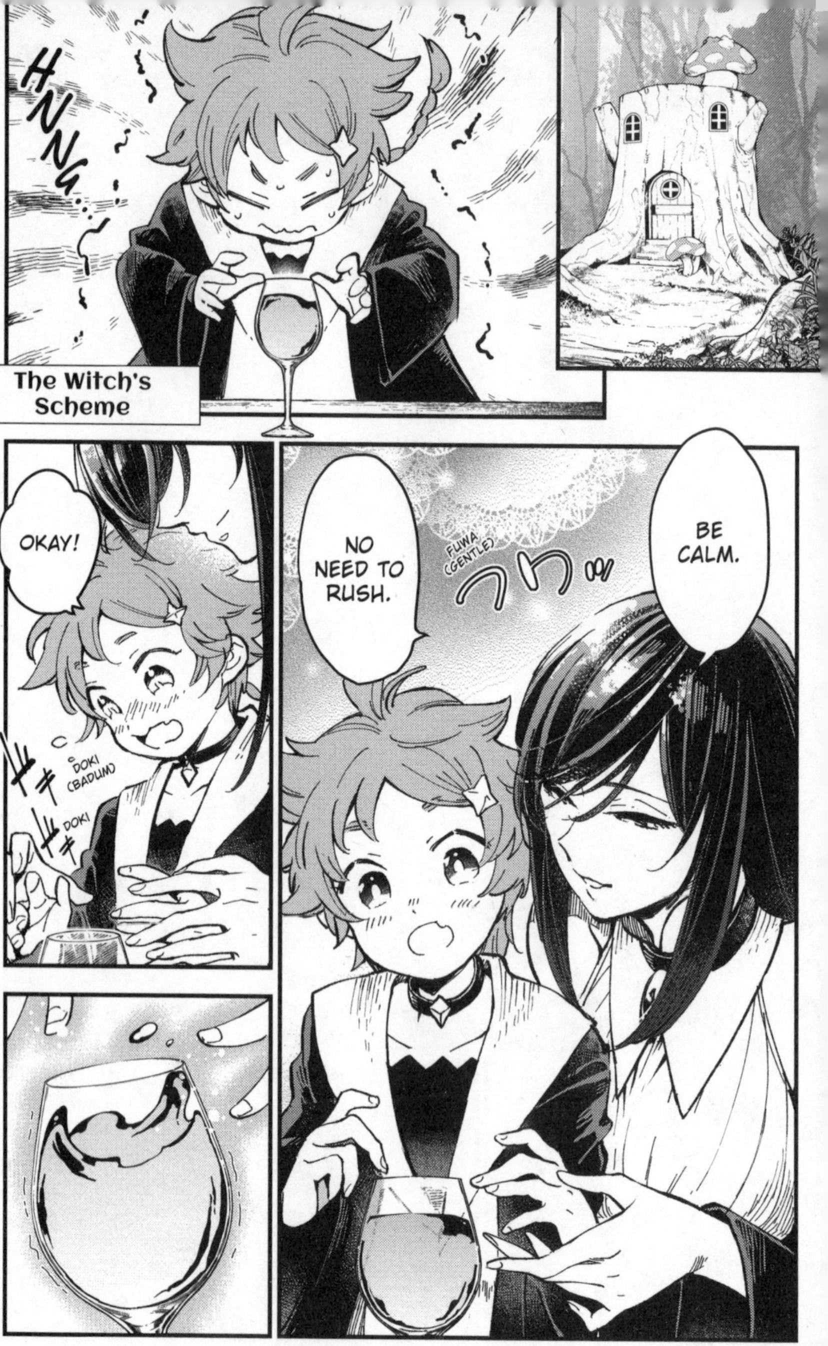
HNNG...
The Witch's Scheme
BE CALM.
FUWA (GENTLE)
NO NEED TO RUSH.
OKAY!
DOKI (BADUM)
DOKI

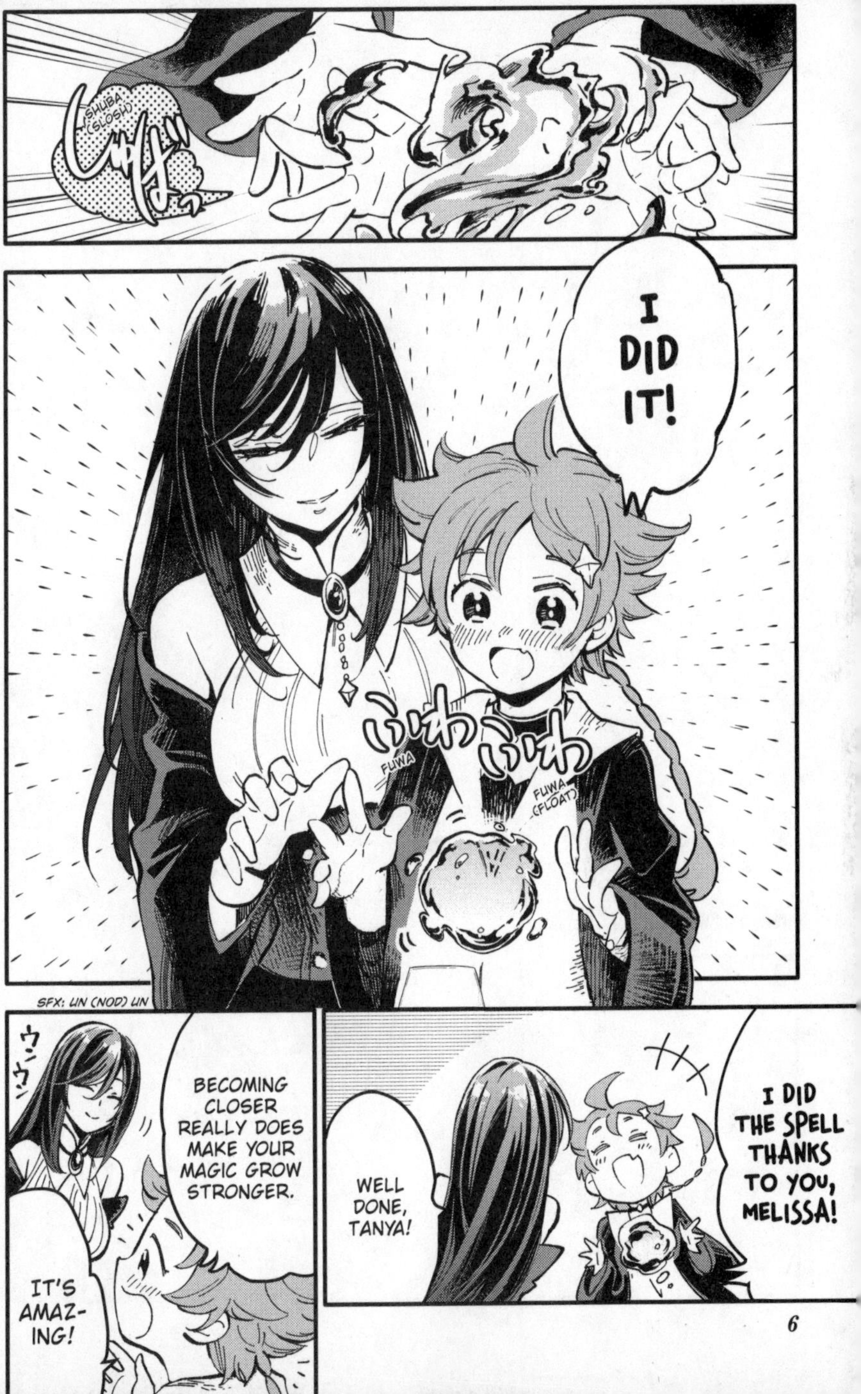
しゅばっ
SHUBA (SLOSH)
I DID IT!
ふわふわ
FUWA
FUWA (FLOAT)
I DID THE SPELL THANKS TO YOU, MELISSA!
WELL DONE, TANYA!
SFX: UN (NOD) UN
ウンウン
BECOMING CLOSER REALLY DOES MAKE YOUR MAGIC GROW STRONGER.
IT'S AMAZ-ING!

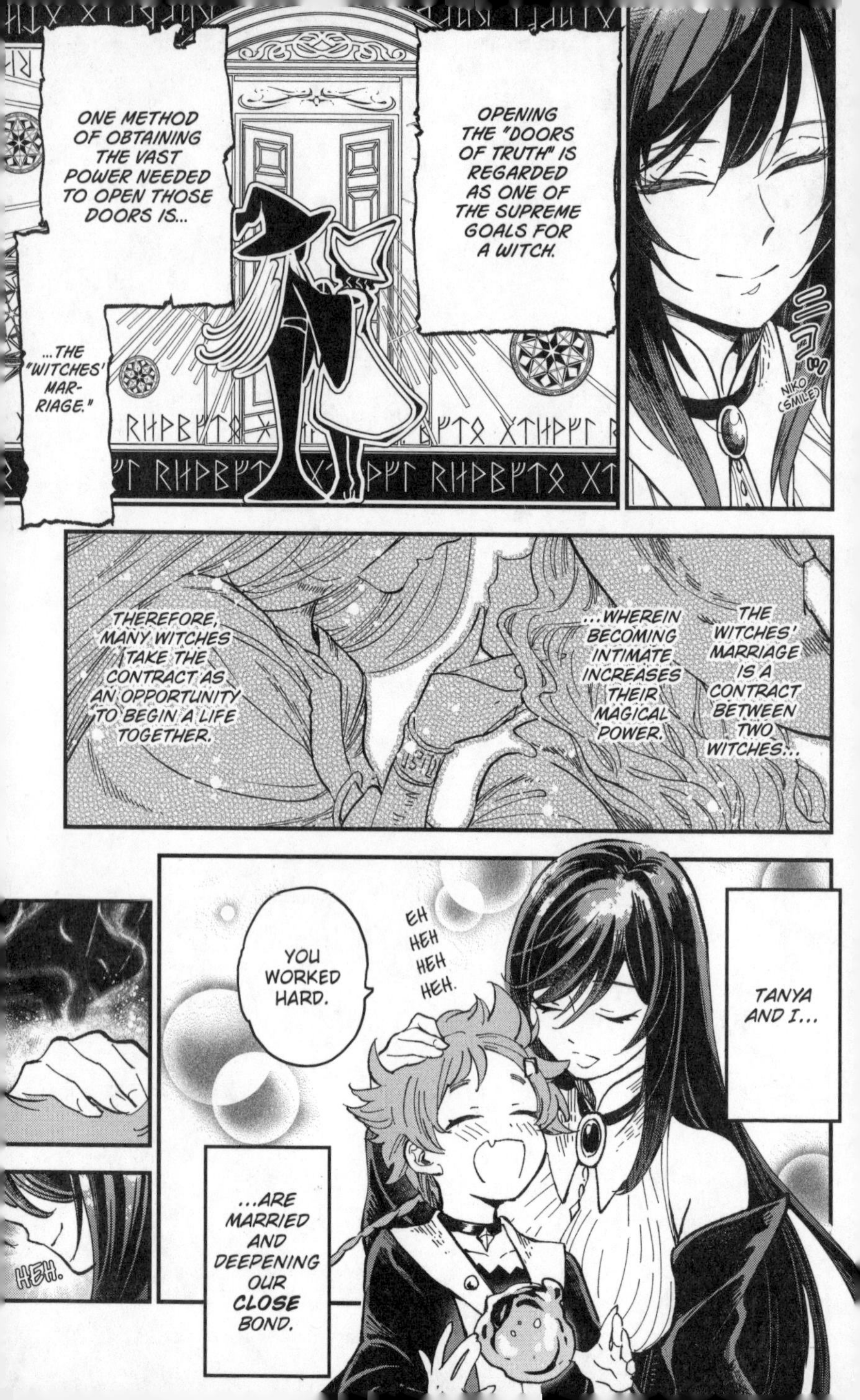
NIKO (SMILE)
OPENING THE "DOORS OF TRUTH" IS REGARDED AS ONE OF THE SUPREME GOALS FOR A WITCH.
ONE METHOD OF OBTAINING THE VAST POWER NEEDED TO OPEN THOSE DOORS IS...
...THE "WITCHES' MAR-RIAGE."
THE WITCHES' MARRIAGE IS A CONTRACT BETWEEN TWO WITCHES...
...WHEREIN BECOMING INTIMATE INCREASES THEIR MAGICAL POWER.
THEREFORE, MANY WITCHES TAKE THE CONTRACT AS AN OPPORTUNITY TO BEGIN A LIFE TOGETHER.
TANYA AND I...
EH HEH HEH HEH.
YOU WORKED HARD.
...ARE MARRIED AND DEEPENING OUR **CLOSE** BOND.
HEH.

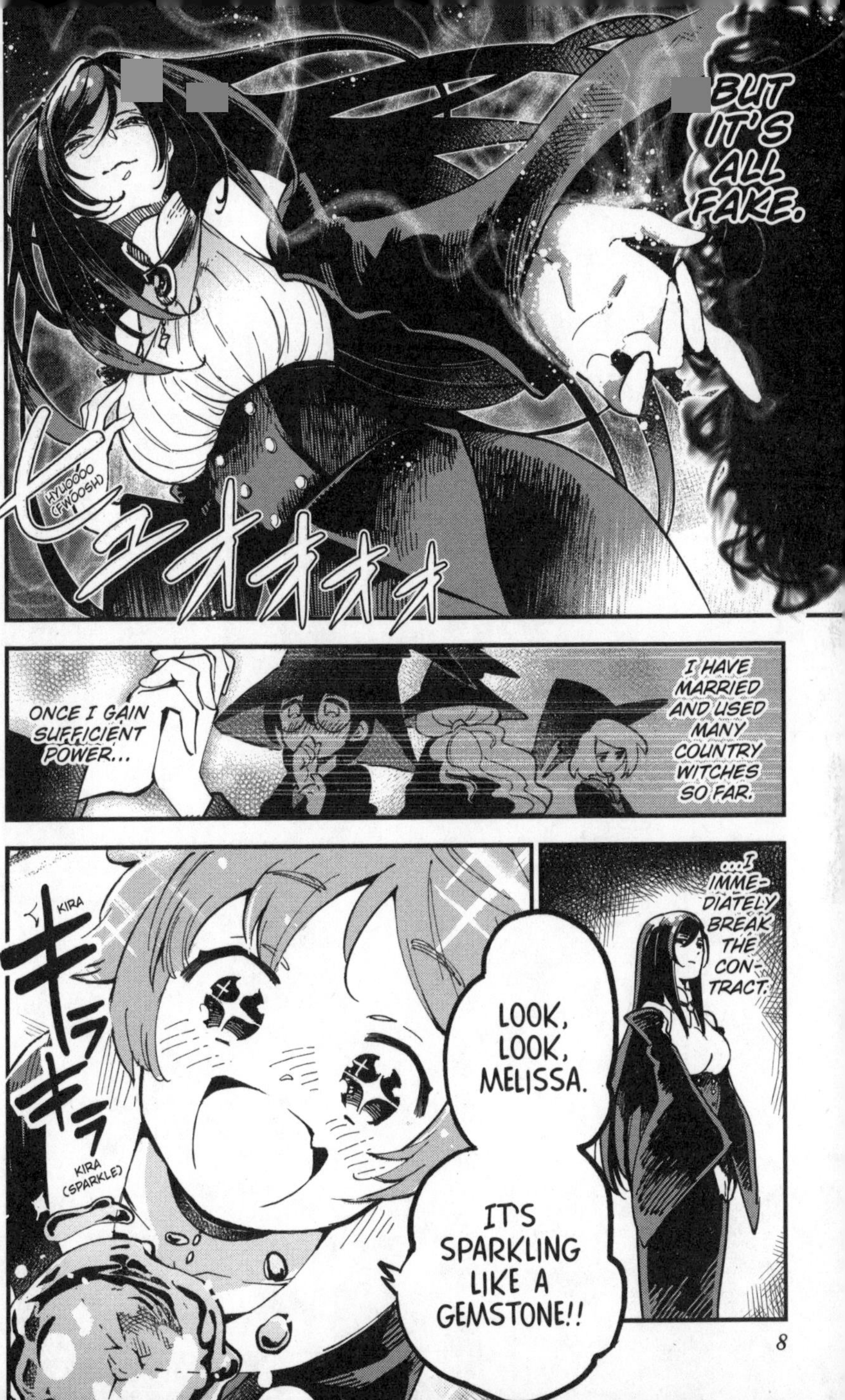
BUT IT'S ALL FAKE.
HYUOOOO (FWOOSH)
I HAVE MARRIED AND USED MANY COUNTRY WITCHES SO FAR.
ONCE I GAIN SUFFICIENT POWER...
...I IMMEDIATELY BREAK THE CONTRACT.
KIRA
KIRA (SPARKLE)
LOOK, LOOK, MELISSA.
IT'S SPARKLING LIKE A GEMSTONE!!

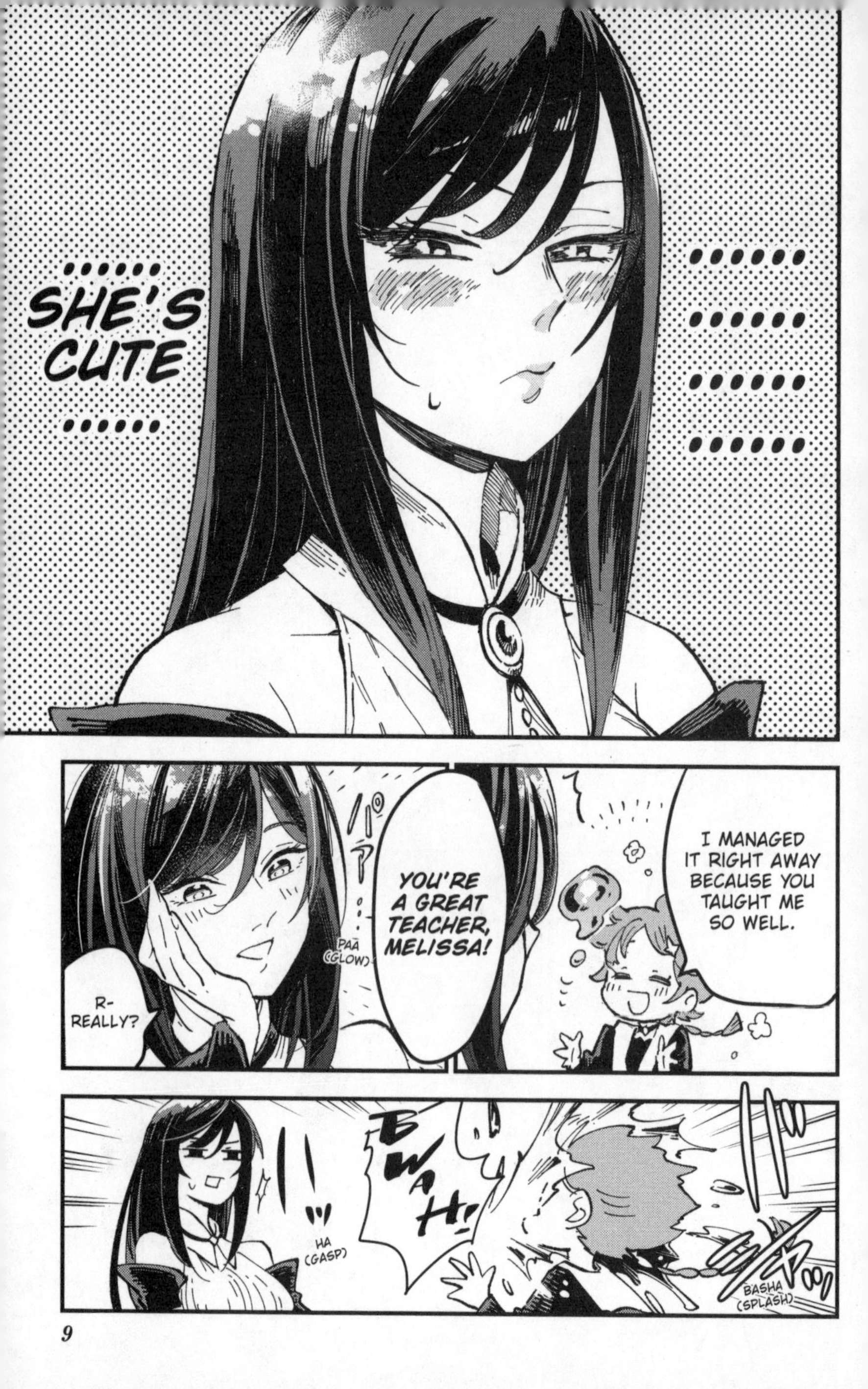

....
......SHE'S CUTE......
I MANAGED IT RIGHT AWAY BECAUSE YOU TAUGHT ME SO WELL.
YOU'RE A GREAT TEACHER, MELISSA!
PAA (GLOW)
R-REALLY?
BASHA (SPLASH)
BWAH!
HA (GASP)

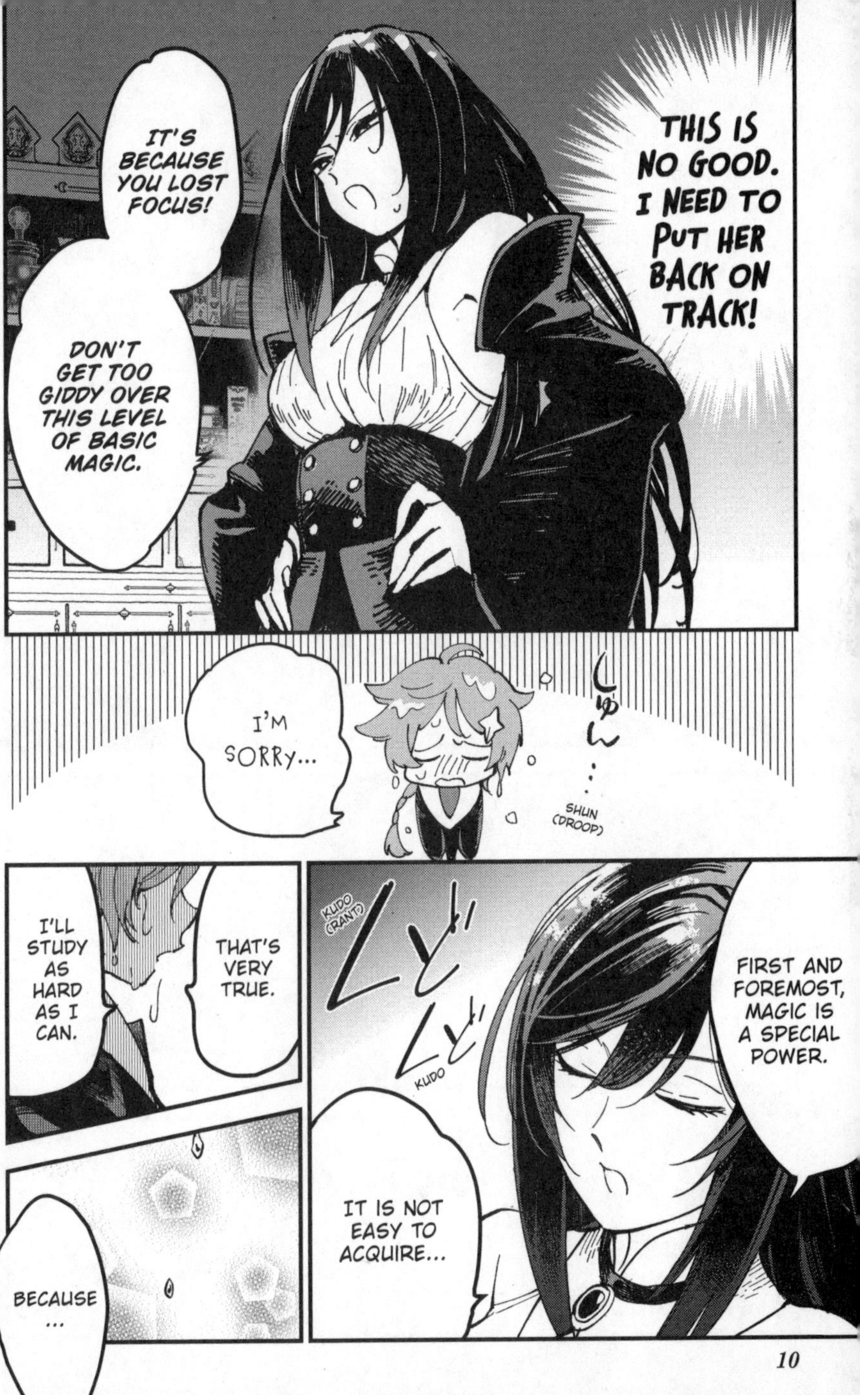
THIS IS NO GOOD. I NEED TO PUT HER BACK ON TRACK!
IT'S BECAUSE YOU LOST FOCUS!
DON'T GET TOO GIDDY OVER THIS LEVEL OF BASIC MAGIC.
しゅん…
SHUN (DROOP)
I'M SORRY...
FIRST AND FOREMOST, MAGIC IS A SPECIAL POWER.
KUDO (RANT)
KUDO
IT IS NOT EASY TO ACQUIRE...
THAT'S VERY TRUE.
I'LL STUDY AS HARD AS I CAN.
BECAUSE ...

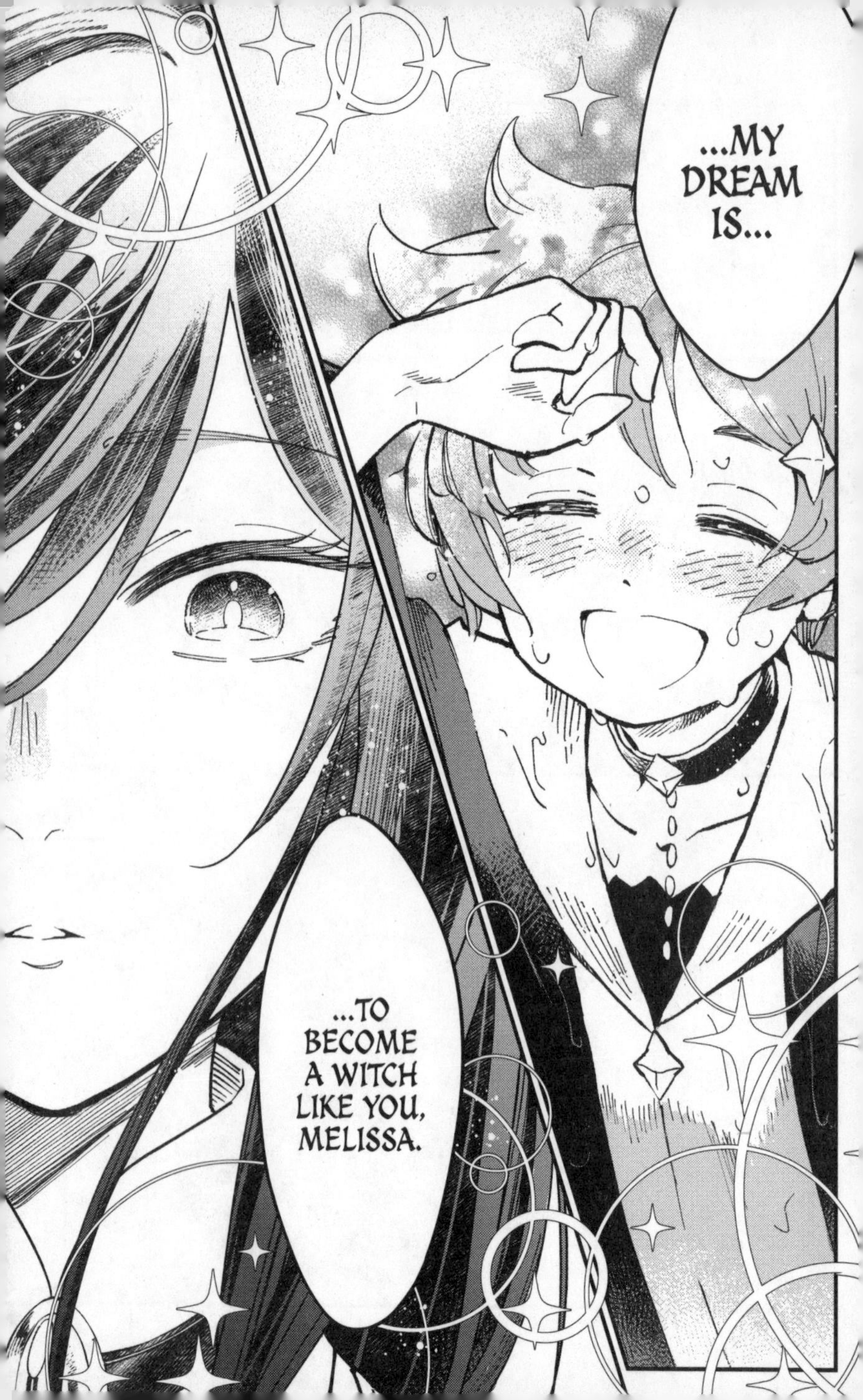
...MY DREAM IS...
...TO BECOME A WITCH LIKE YOU, MELISSA.

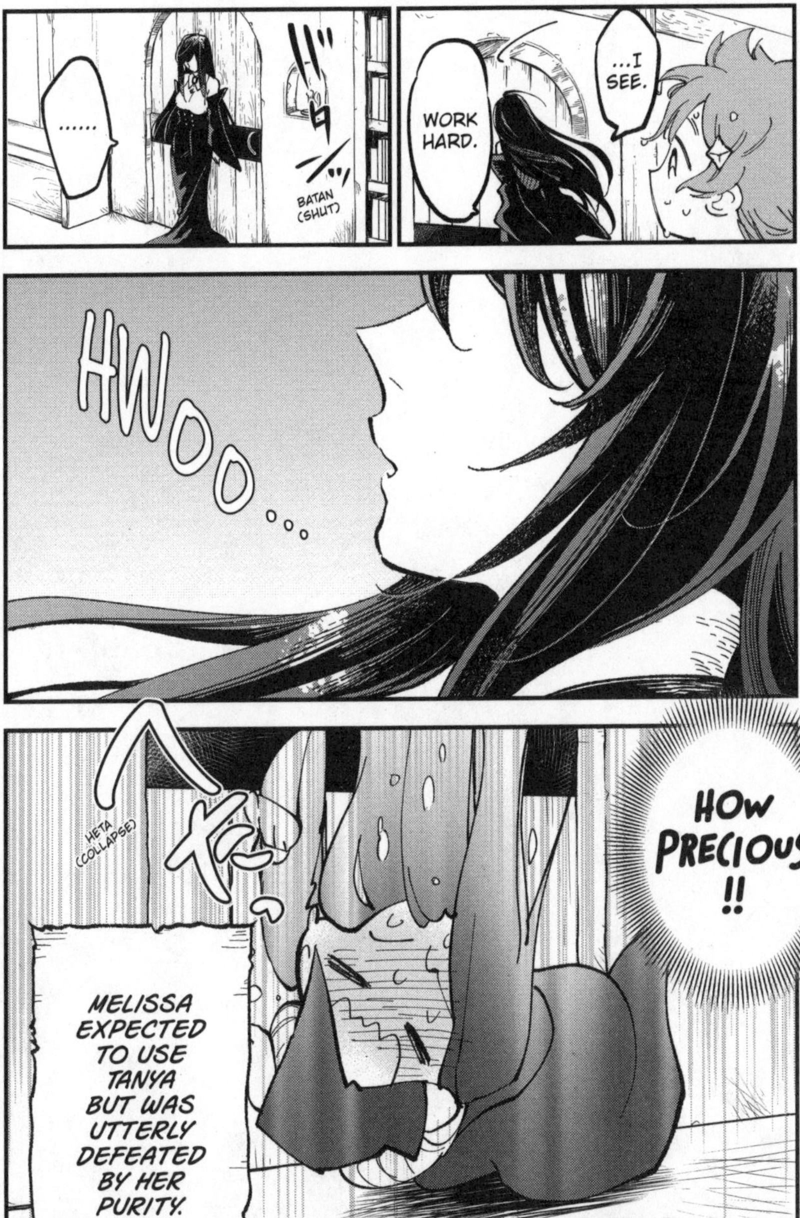
...I SEE.
WORK HARD.
BATAN (SHUT)
......
HWOO...
HOW PRECIOUS!!
HETA (COLLAPSE)
MELISSA EXPECTED TO USE TANYA BUT WAS UTTERLY DEFEATED BY HER PURITY.

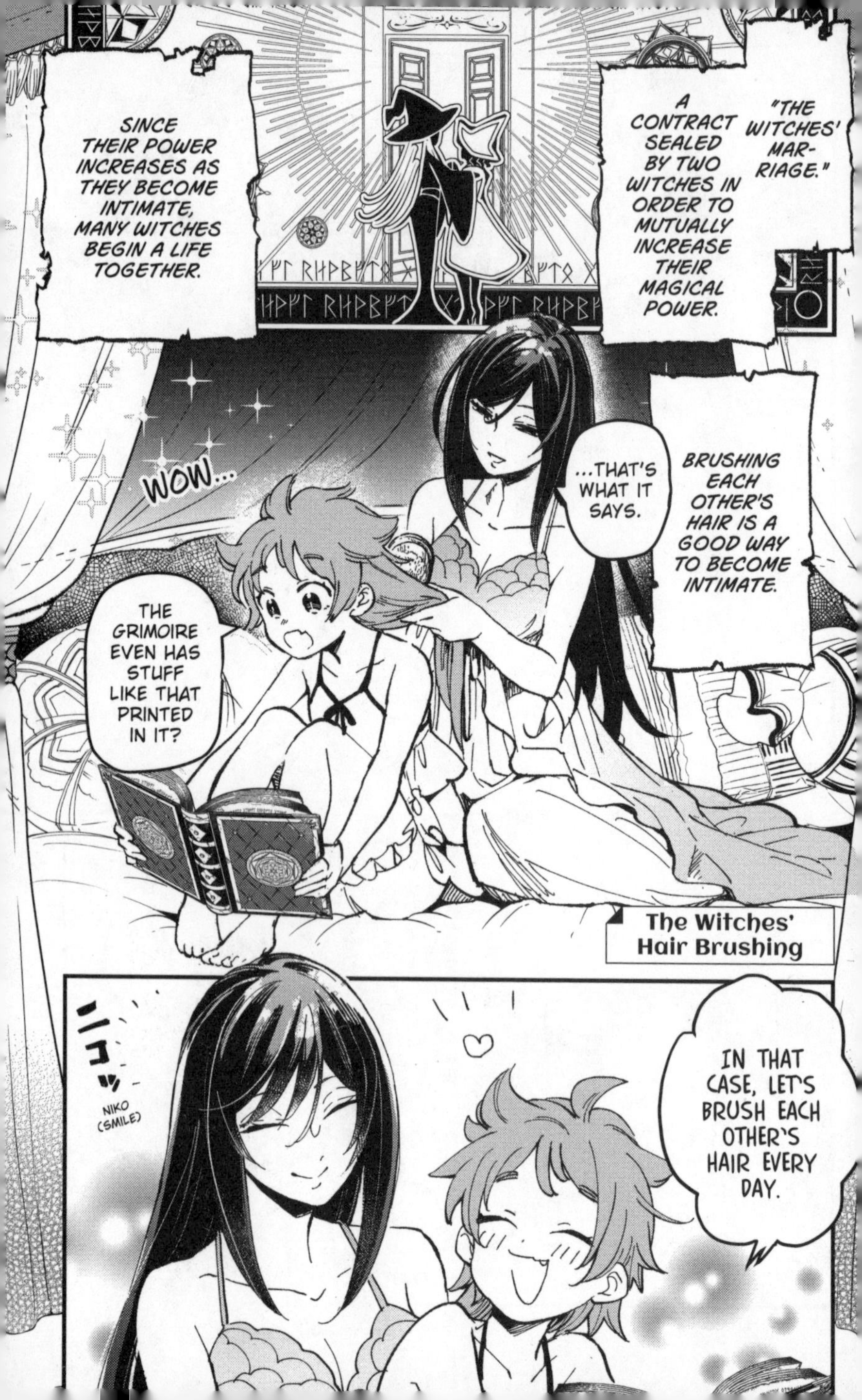
"THE WITCHES' MARRIAGE."
A CONTRACT SEALED BY TWO WITCHES IN ORDER TO MUTUALLY INCREASE THEIR MAGICAL POWER.
SINCE THEIR POWER INCREASES AS THEY BECOME INTIMATE, MANY WITCHES BEGIN A LIFE TOGETHER.
BRUSHING EACH OTHER'S HAIR IS A GOOD WAY TO BECOME INTIMATE.
...THAT'S WHAT IT SAYS.
WOW...
THE GRIMOIRE EVEN HAS STUFF LIKE THAT PRINTED IN IT?
The Witches' Hair Brushing
IN THAT CASE, LET'S BRUSH EACH OTHER'S HAIR EVERY DAY.
NIKO (SMILE)

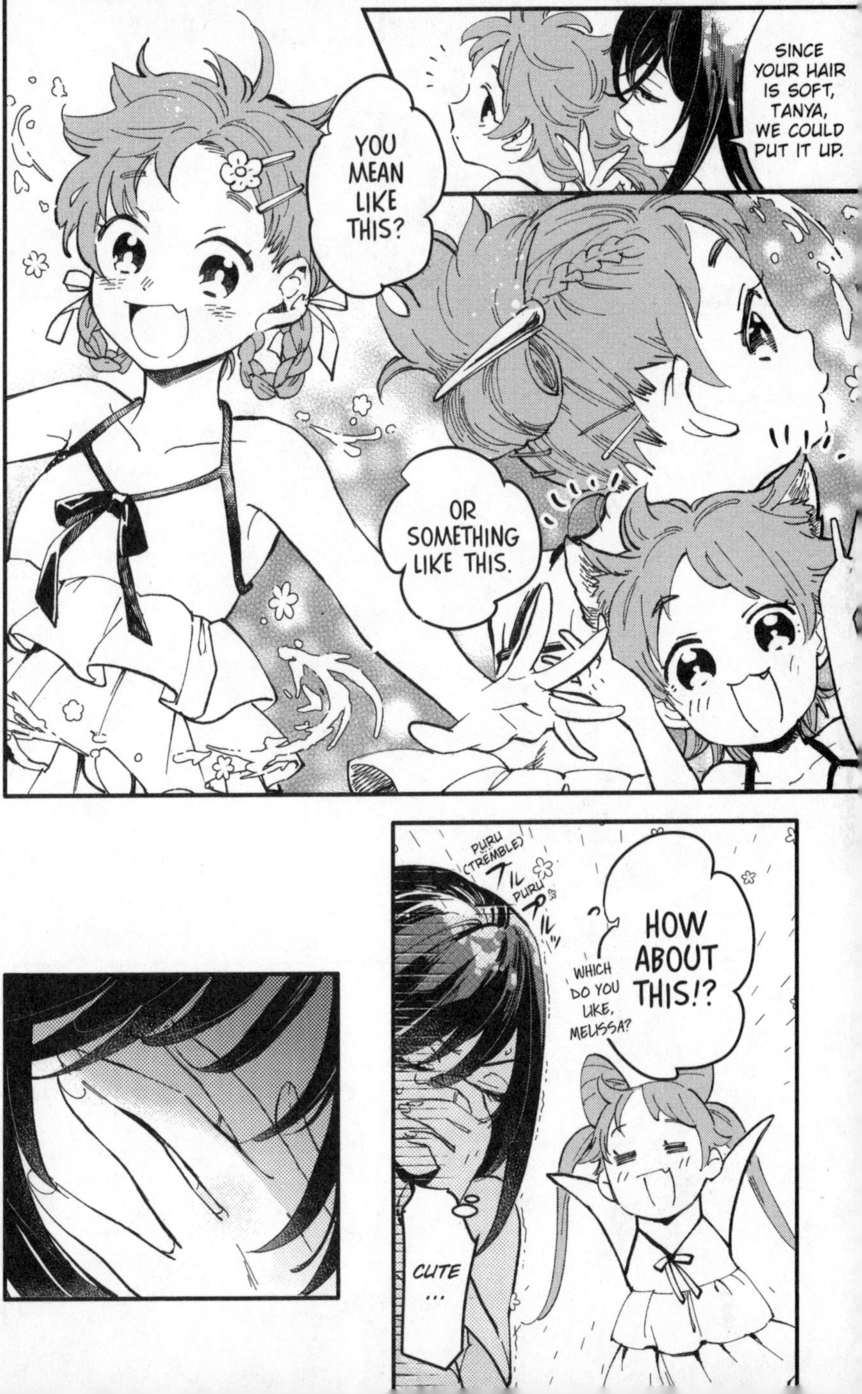
SINCE YOUR HAIR IS SOFT, TANYA, WE COULD PUT IT UP.
YOU MEAN LIKE THIS?
OR SOMETHING LIKE THIS.
PURU (TREMBLE)
PURU
HOW ABOUT THIS!?
WHICH DO YOU LIKE, MELISSA?
CUTE ...

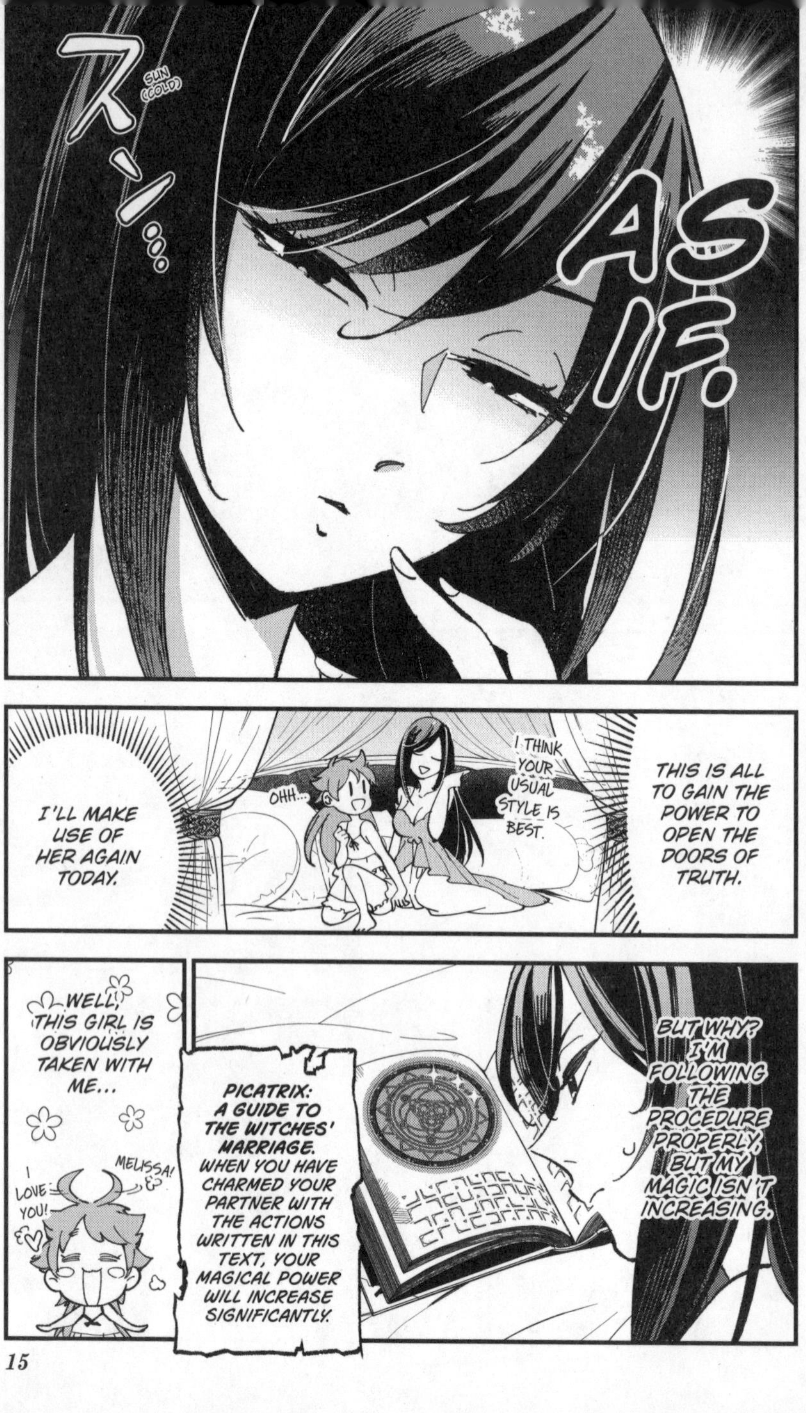
AS IF.
スン…
SUN (COLD)
THIS IS ALL TO GAIN THE POWER TO OPEN THE DOORS OF TRUTH.
I THINK YOUR USUAL STYLE IS BEST.
OHH...
I'LL MAKE USE OF HER AGAIN TODAY.
BUT WHY? I'M FOLLOWING THE PROCEDURE PROPERLY, BUT MY MAGIC ISN'T INCREASING.
PICATRIX: A GUIDE TO THE WITCHES' MARRIAGE. WHEN YOU HAVE CHARMED YOUR PARTNER WITH THE ACTIONS WRITTEN IN THIS TEXT, YOUR MAGICAL POWER WILL INCREASE SIGNIFICANTLY.
WELL, THIS GIRL IS OBVIOUSLY TAKEN WITH ME...
MELISSA!
I LOVE YOU!

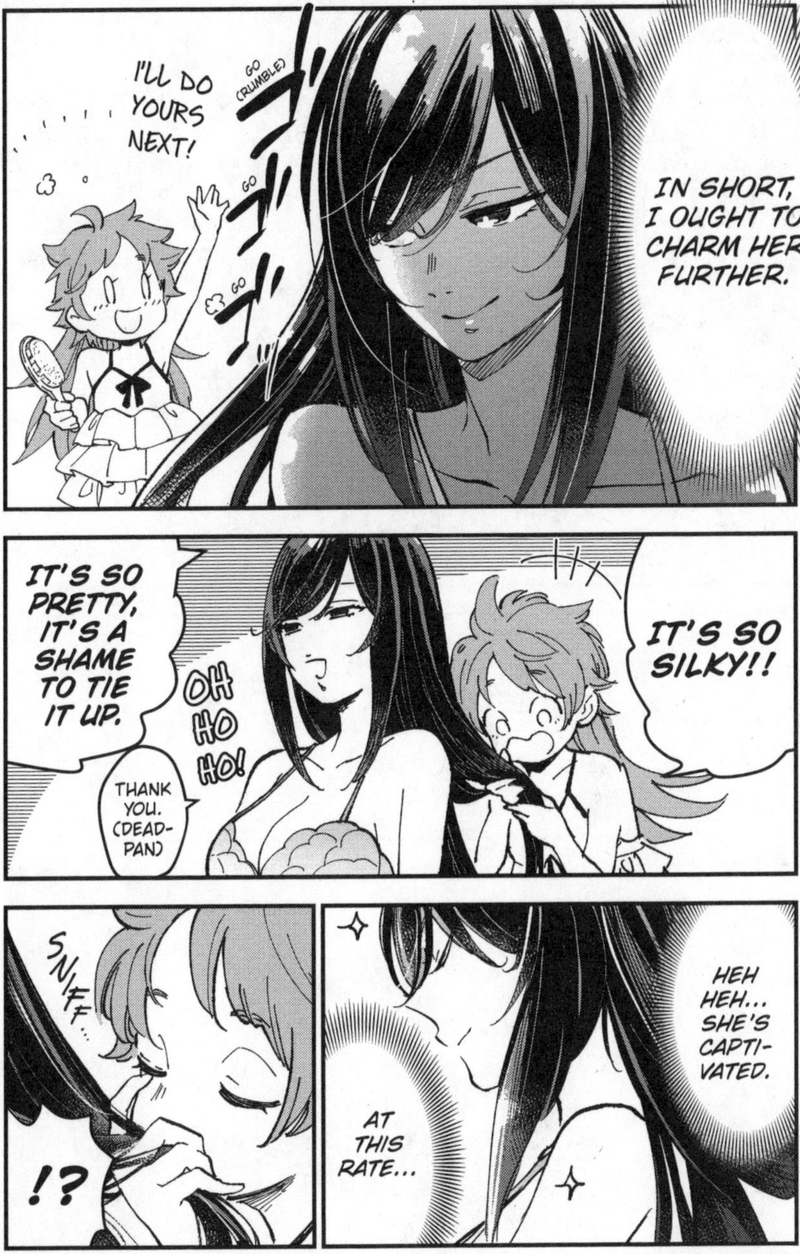
IN SHORT, I OUGHT TO CHARM HER FURTHER.
GO (RUMBLE)
GO
GO
I'LL DO YOURS NEXT!
IT'S SO SILKY!!
IT'S SO PRETTY, IT'S A SHAME TO TIE IT UP.
OH HO HO!
THANK YOU. (DEADPAN)
HEH HEH... SHE'S CAPTIVATED.
AT THIS RATE...
SNIFF...
!?

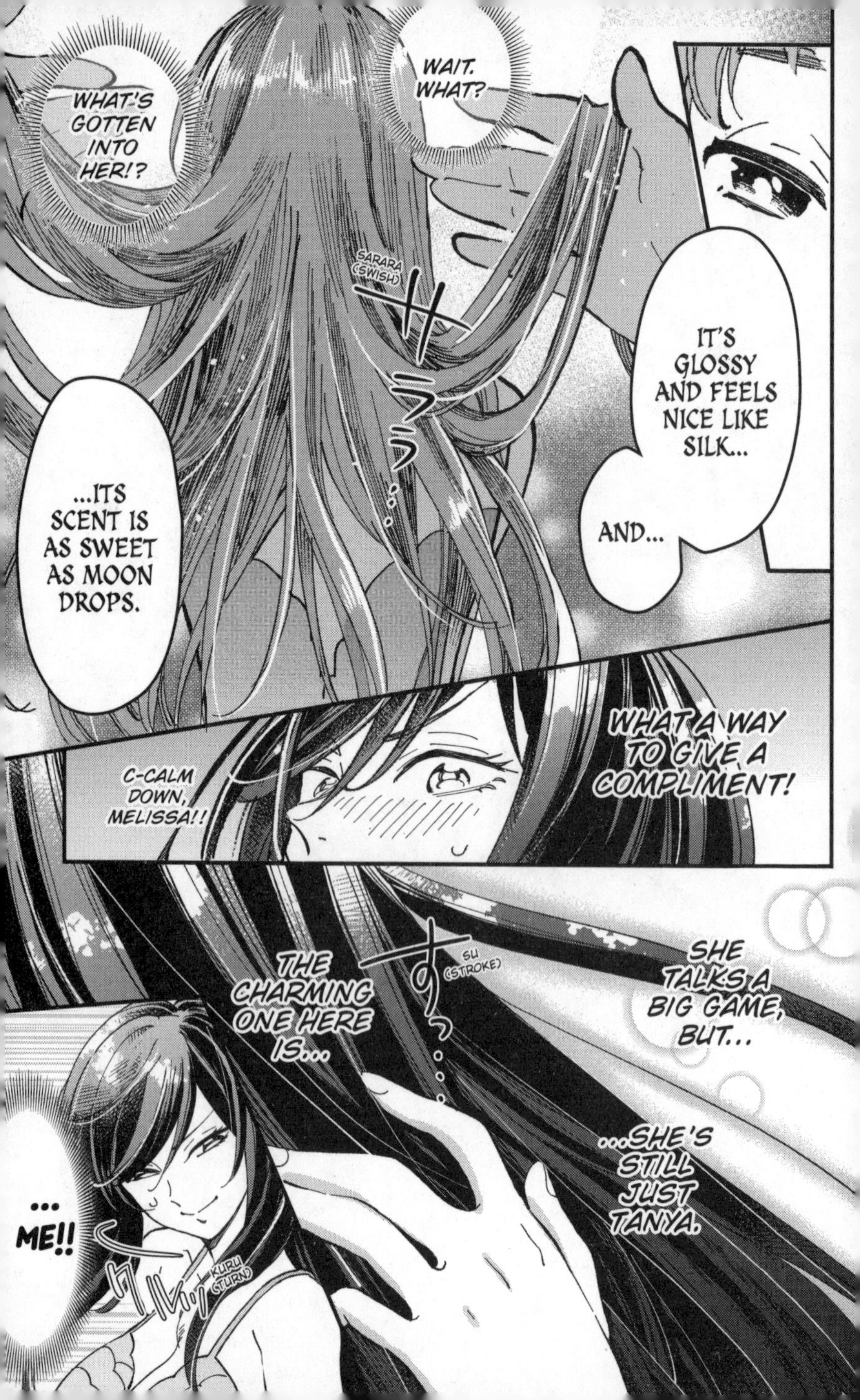
WAIT. WHAT?
WHAT'S GOTTEN INTO HER!?
IT'S GLOSSY AND FEELS NICE LIKE SILK...
AND...
SARARA (SWISH)
...ITS SCENT IS AS SWEET AS MOON DROPS.
WHAT A WAY TO GIVE A COMPLIMENT!
C-CALM DOWN, MELISSA!!
SHE TALKS A BIG GAME, BUT...
...SHE'S STILL JUST TANYA.
SU (STROKE)
THE CHARMING ONE HERE IS...
...ME!!
KURU (TURN)

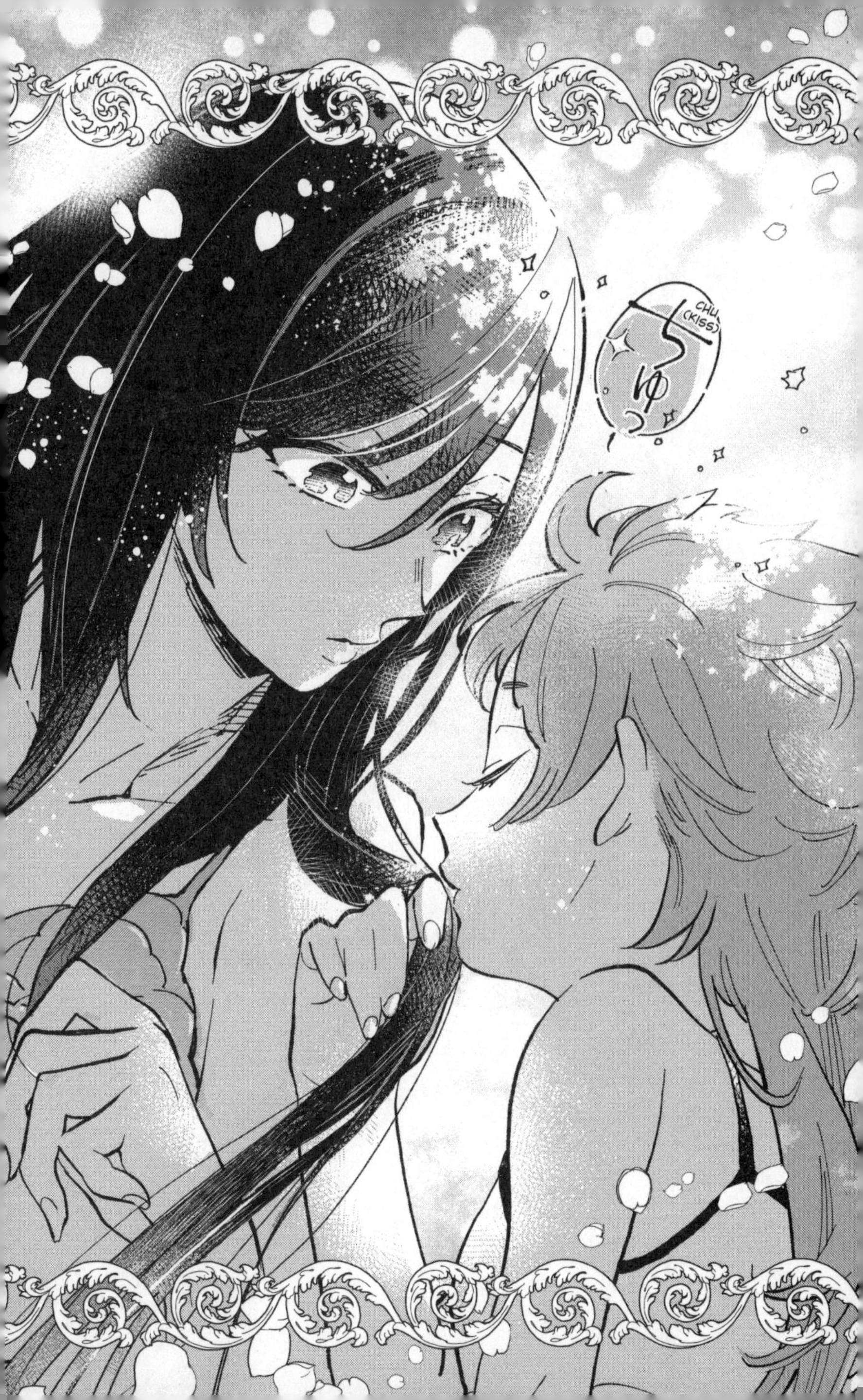
ちゅっ
CHU (KISS)

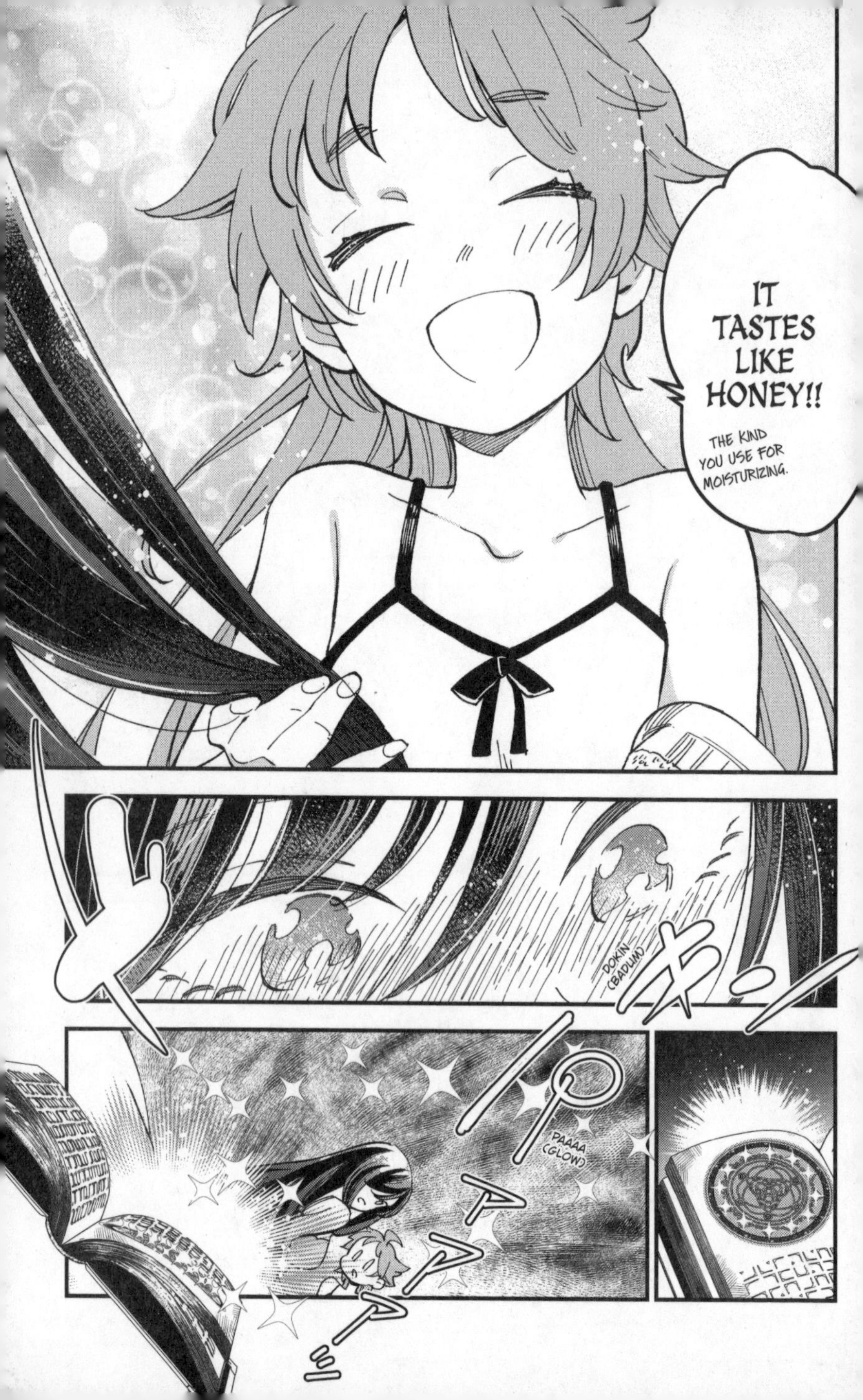
IT TASTES LIKE HONEY!!
THE KIND YOU USE FOR MOISTURIZING.
DOKIN (BADUM)
PAAAA (GLOW)

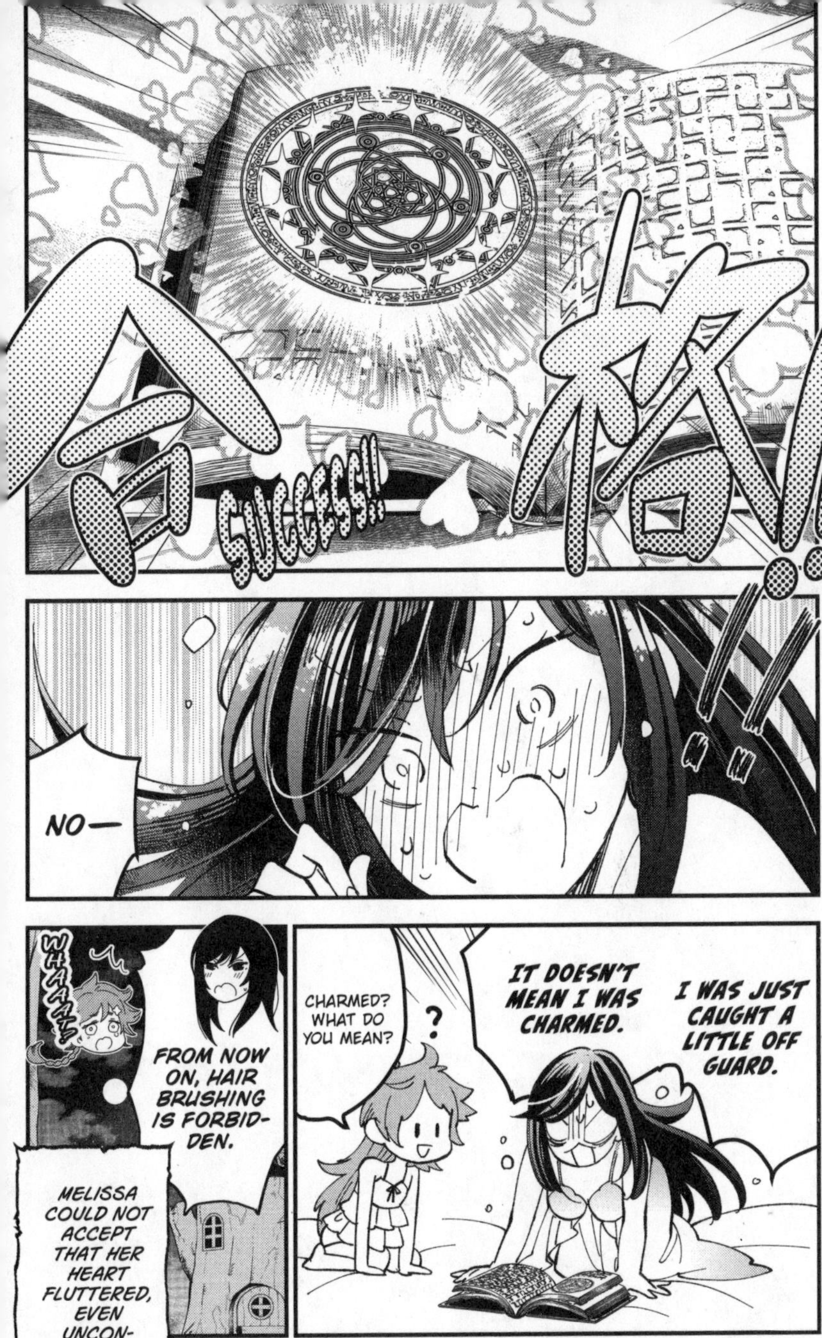

合格!!
SUCCESS!!
NO—
I WAS JUST CAUGHT A LITTLE OFF GUARD.
IT DOESN'T MEAN I WAS CHARMED.
CHARMED? WHAT DO YOU MEAN?
?
WHAAAA!
FROM NOW ON, HAIR BRUSHING IS FORBID-DEN.
MELISSA COULD NOT ACCEPT THAT HER HEART FLUTTERED, EVEN UNCON-SCIOUSLY.

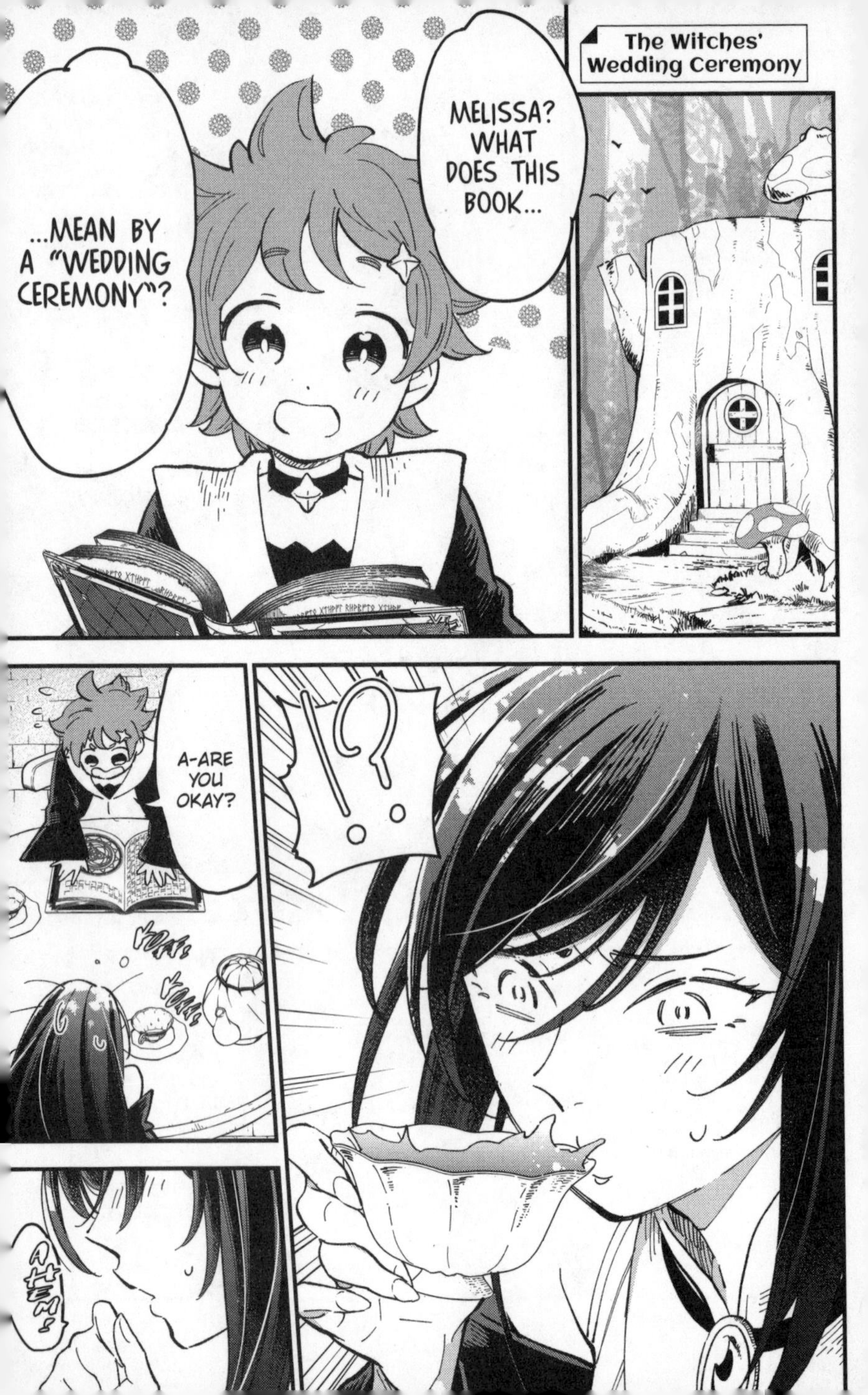
The Witches' Wedding Ceremony
MELISSA? WHAT DOES THIS BOOK...
...MEAN BY A "WEDDING CEREMONY"?
!?
A-ARE YOU OKAY?
AHEM!

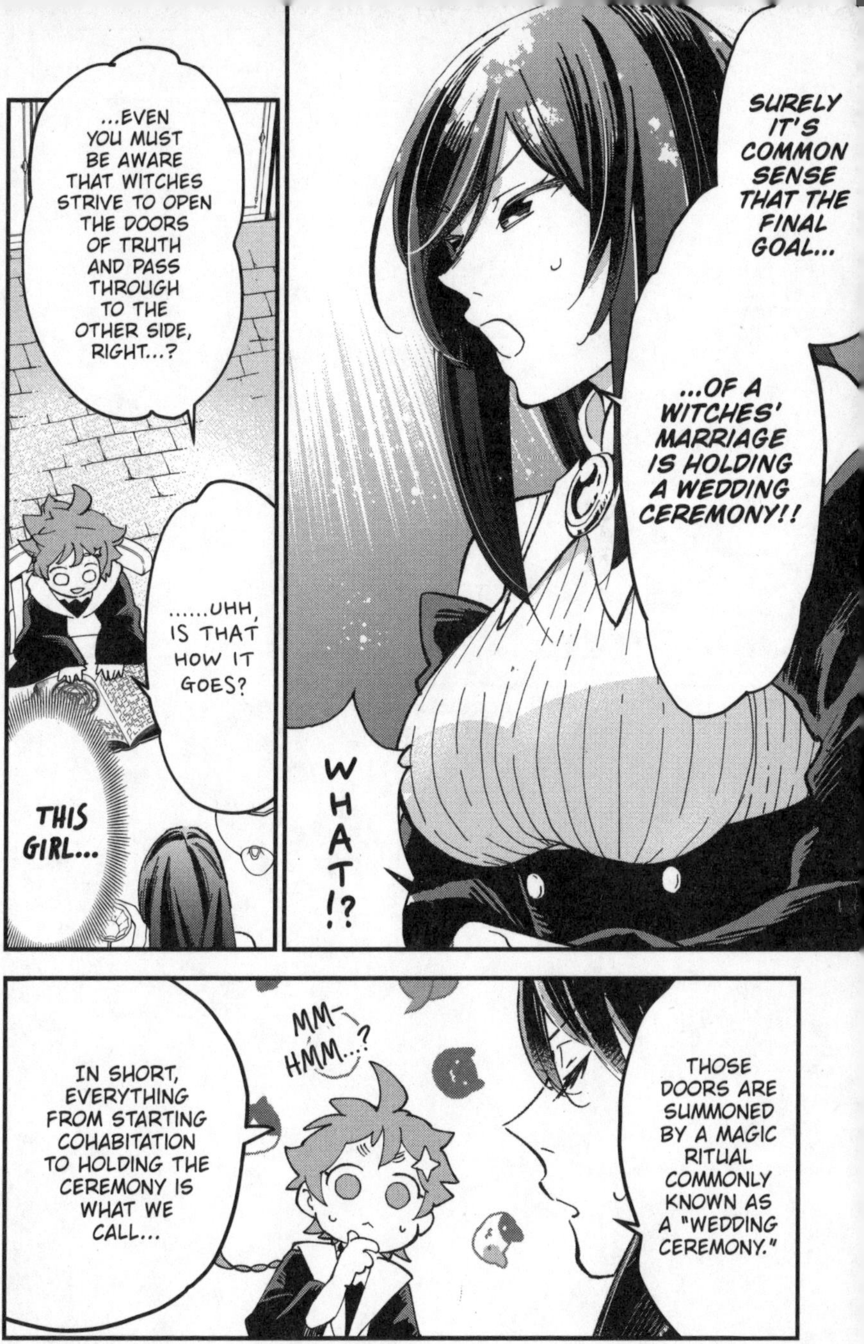
SURELY IT'S COMMON SENSE THAT THE FINAL GOAL...
...OF A WITCHES' MARRIAGE IS HOLDING A WEDDING CEREMONY!!
WHAT!?
...EVEN YOU MUST BE AWARE THAT WITCHES STRIVE TO OPEN THE DOORS OF TRUTH AND PASS THROUGH TO THE OTHER SIDE, RIGHT...?
......UHH, IS THAT HOW IT GOES?
THIS GIRL...
THOSE DOORS ARE SUMMONED BY A MAGIC RITUAL COMMONLY KNOWN AS A "WEDDING CEREMONY."
MM-HMM...?
IN SHORT, EVERYTHING FROM STARTING COHABITATION TO HOLDING THE CEREMONY IS WHAT WE CALL...

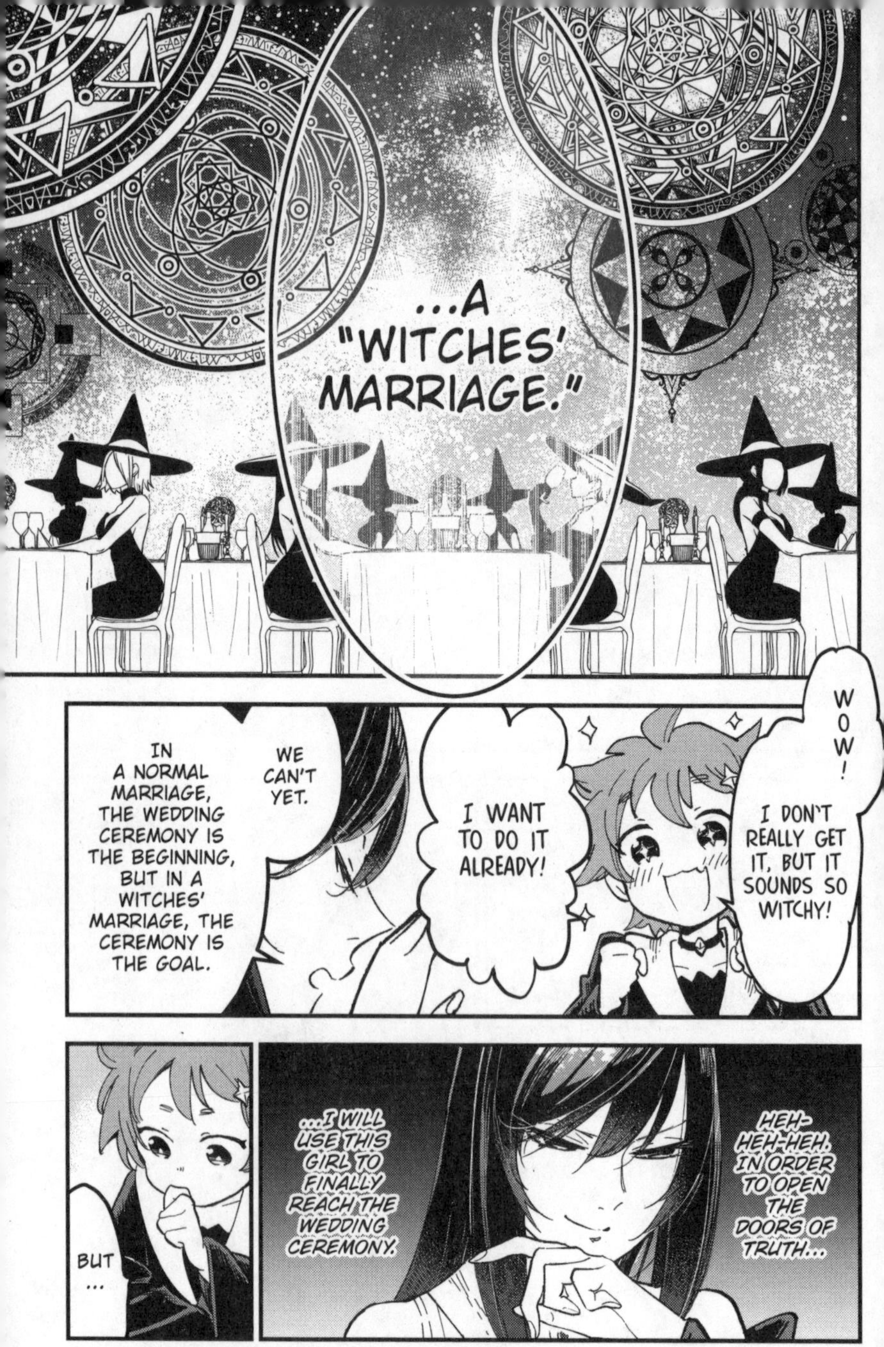
...A "WITCHES' MARRIAGE."
WOW!
I DON'T REALLY GET IT, BUT IT SOUNDS SO WITCHY!
I WANT TO DO IT ALREADY!
WE CAN'T YET.
IN A NORMAL MARRIAGE, THE WEDDING CEREMONY IS THE BEGINNING, BUT IN A WITCHES' MARRIAGE, THE CEREMONY IS THE GOAL.
HEH-HEH-HEH. IN ORDER TO OPEN THE DOORS OF TRUTH...
...I WILL USE THIS GIRL TO FINALLY REACH THE WEDDING CEREMONY.
BUT ...

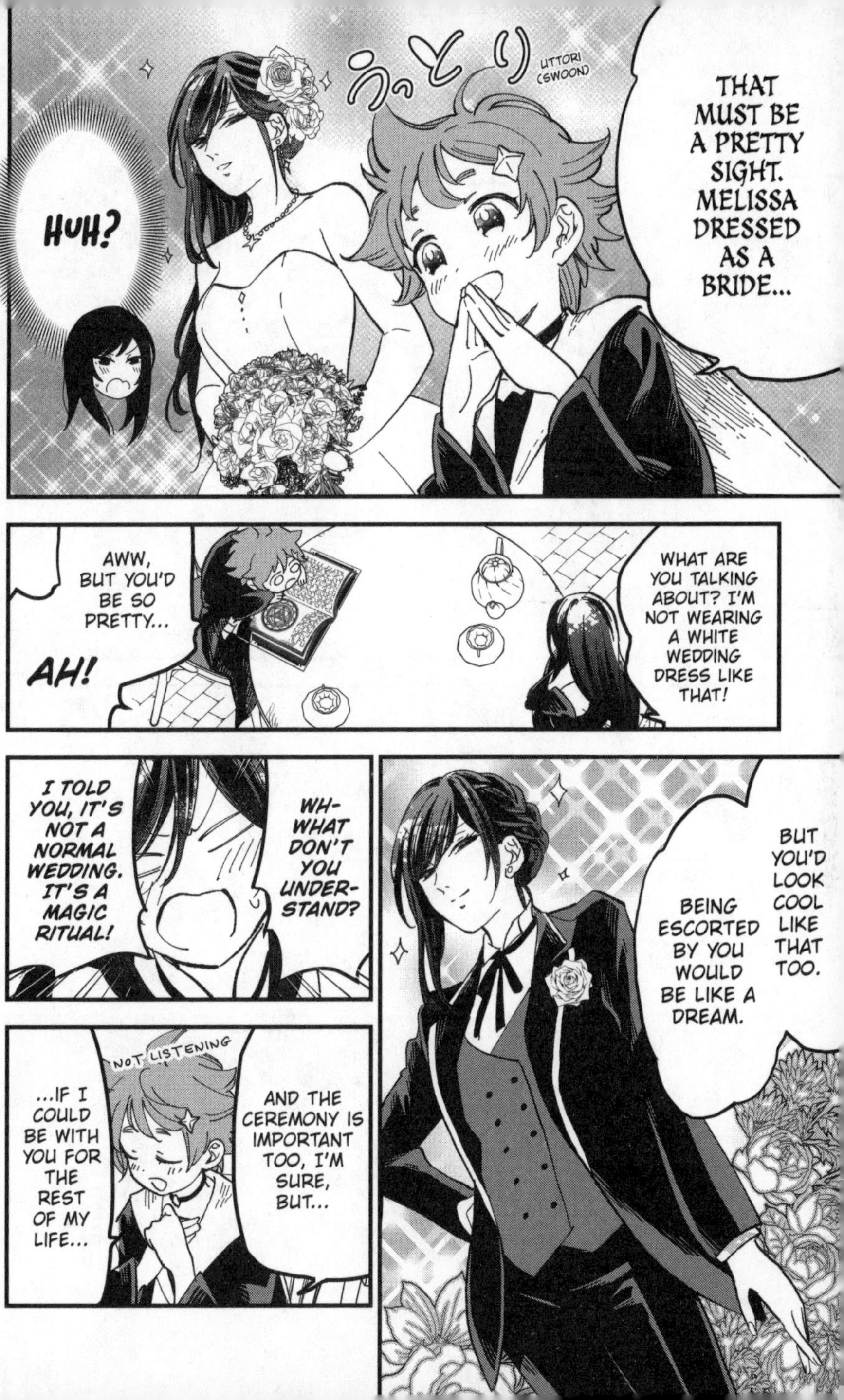
THAT MUST BE A PRETTY SIGHT. MELISSA DRESSED AS A BRIDE...
UTTORI (SWOON)
HUH?
WHAT ARE YOU TALKING ABOUT? I'M NOT WEARING A WHITE WEDDING DRESS LIKE THAT!
AWW, BUT YOU'D BE SO PRETTY...
AH!
BUT YOU'D LOOK COOL LIKE THAT TOO.
BEING ESCORTED BY YOU WOULD BE LIKE A DREAM.
WH-WHAT DON'T YOU UNDERSTAND?
I TOLD YOU, IT'S NOT A NORMAL WEDDING. IT'S A MAGIC RITUAL!
NOT LISTENING
AND THE CEREMONY IS IMPORTANT TOO, I'M SURE, BUT...
...IF I COULD BE WITH YOU FOR THE REST OF MY LIFE...

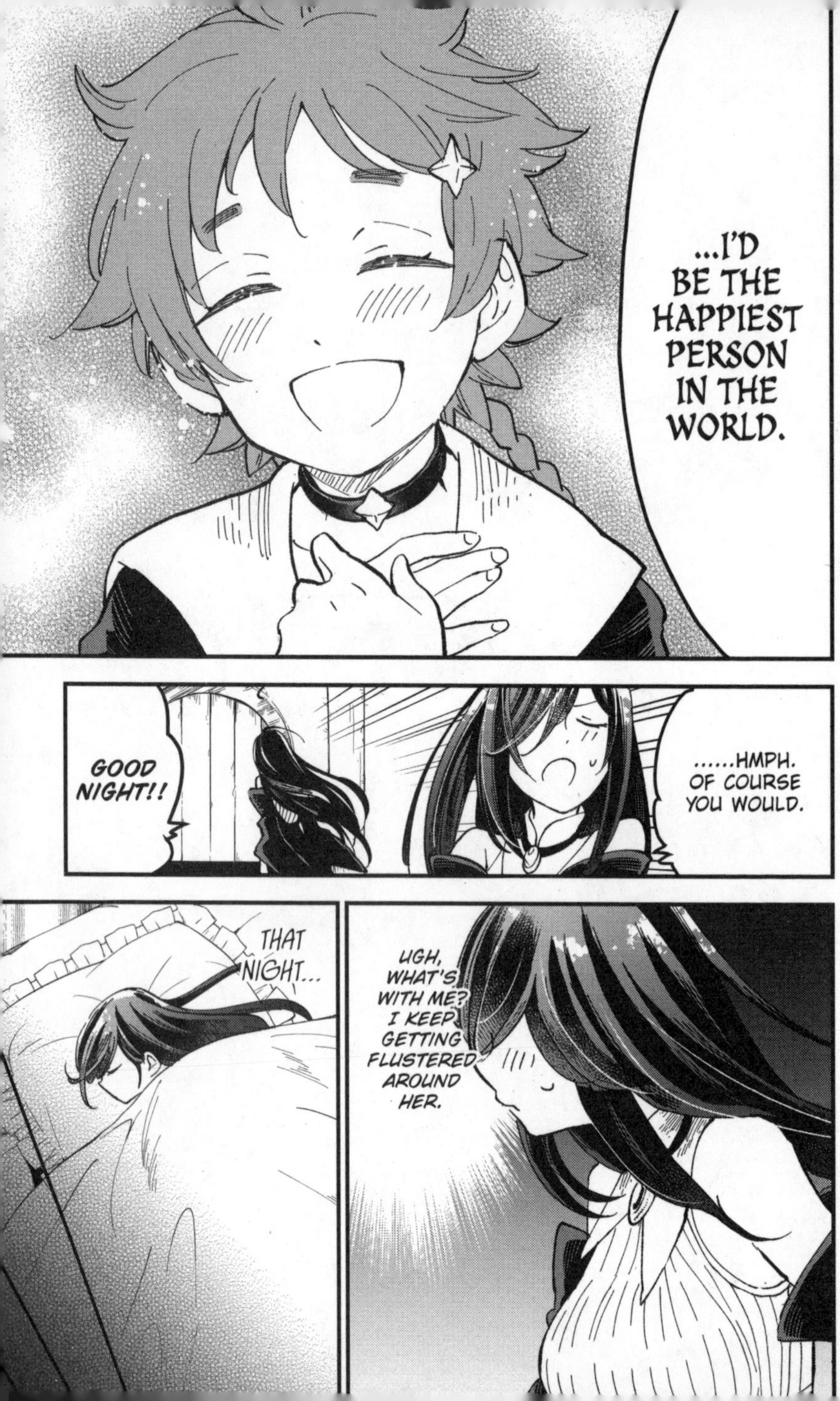
...I'D BE THE HAPPIEST PERSON IN THE WORLD.
......HMPH. OF COURSE YOU WOULD.
GOOD NIGHT!!
UGH, WHAT'S WITH ME? I KEEP GETTING FLUSTERED AROUND HER.
THAT NIGHT...

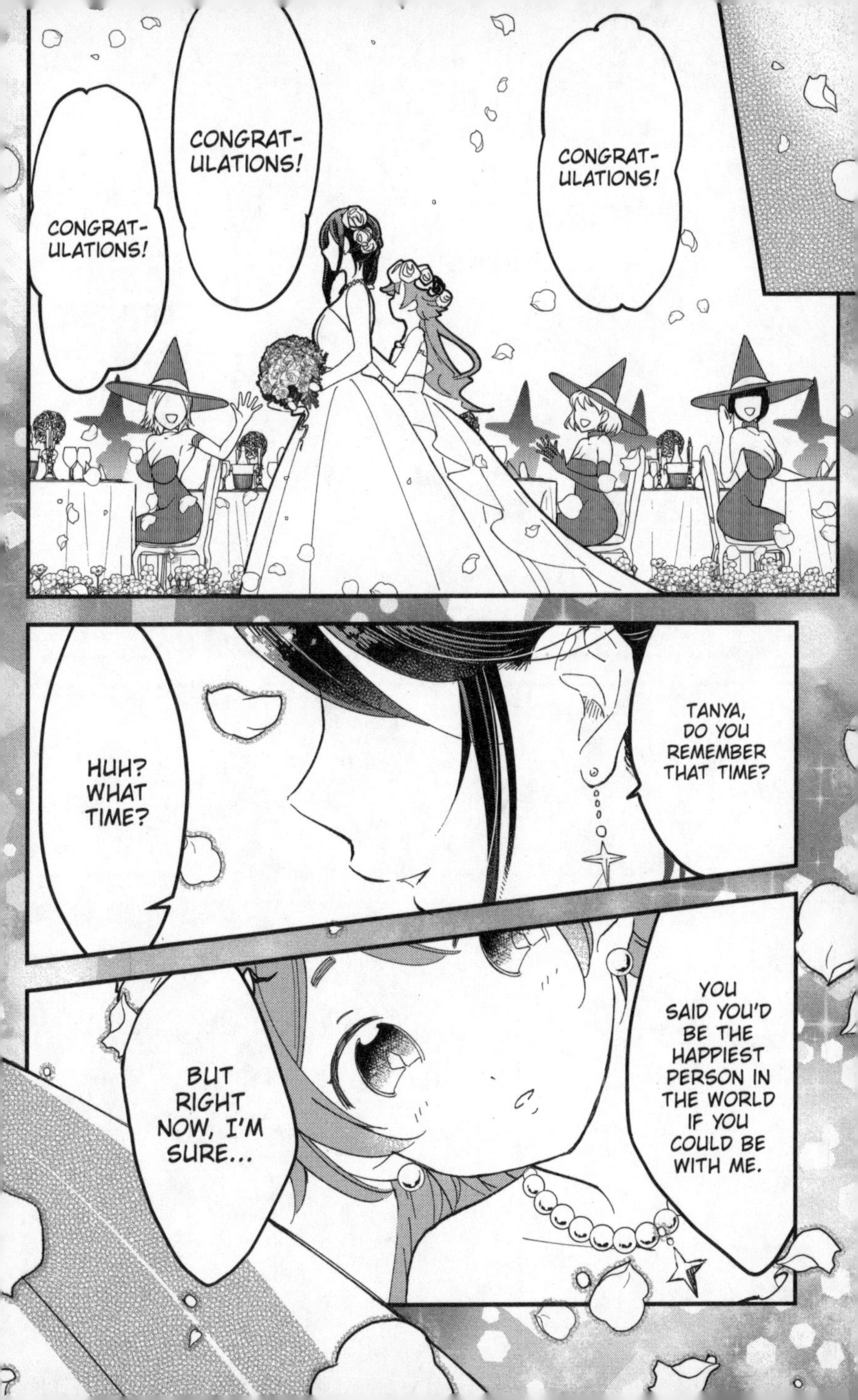
CONGRAT-ULATIONS!
CONGRAT-ULATIONS!
CONGRAT-ULATIONS!
TANYA, DO YOU REMEMBER THAT TIME?
HUH? WHAT TIME?
YOU SAID YOU'D BE THE HAPPIEST PERSON IN THE WORLD IF YOU COULD BE WITH ME.
BUT RIGHT NOW, I'M SURE...

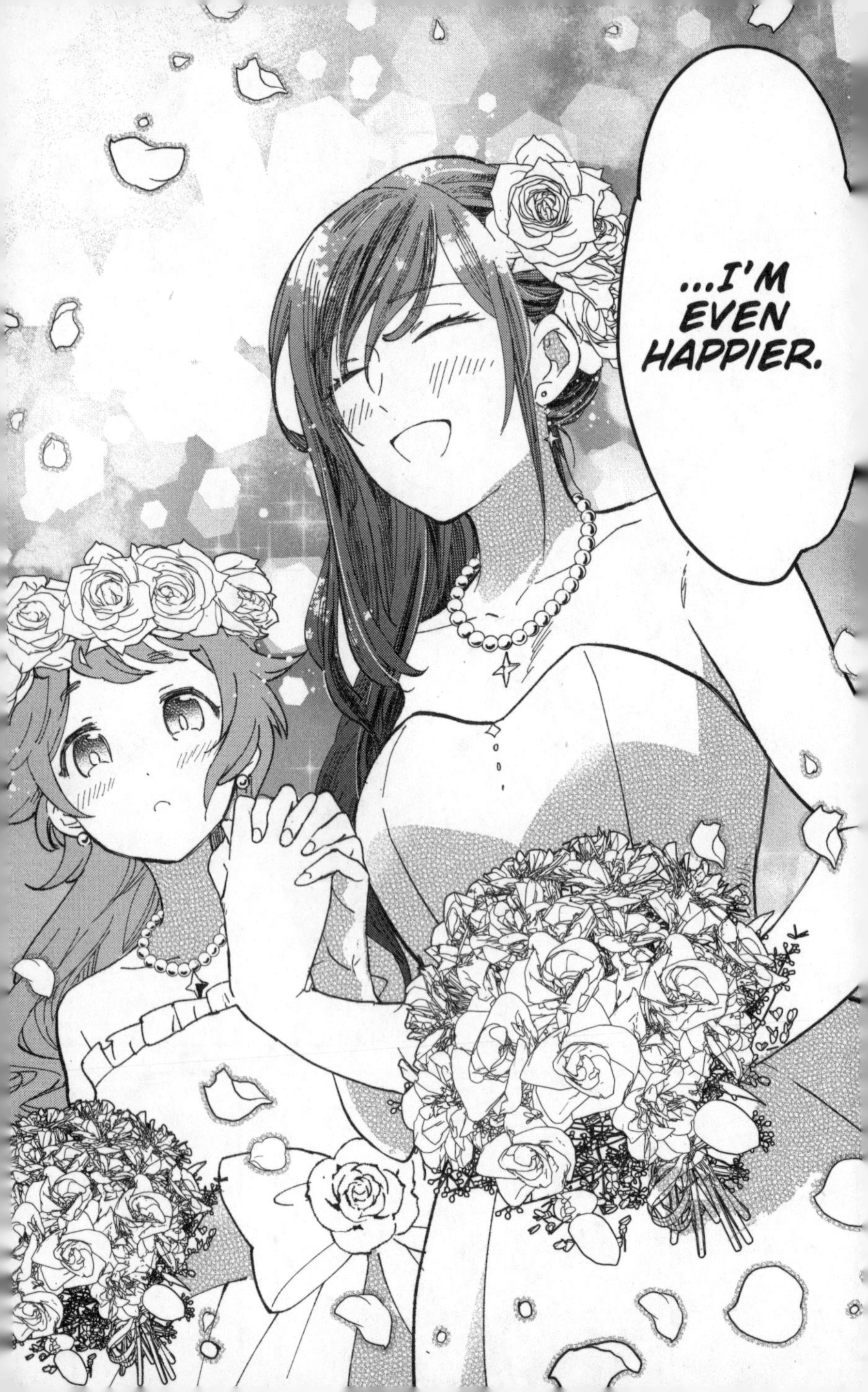
...I'M EVEN HAPPIER.

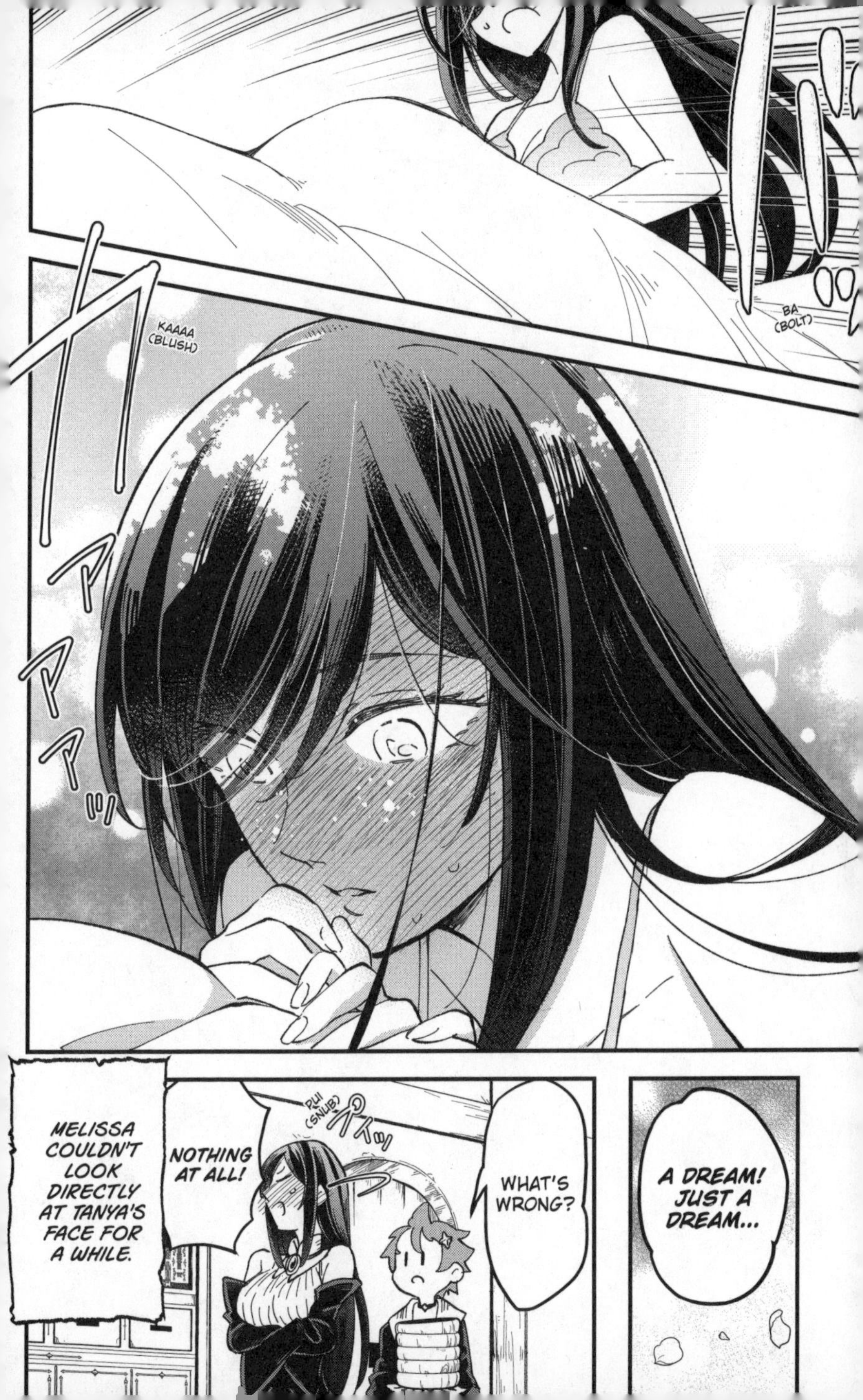
BA
(BOLT)
KAAAA
(BLUSH)
A DREAM! JUST A DREAM...
WHAT'S WRONG?
PUI
(SNUB)
NOTHING AT ALL!
MELISSA COULDN'T LOOK DIRECTLY AT TANYA'S FACE FOR A WHILE.

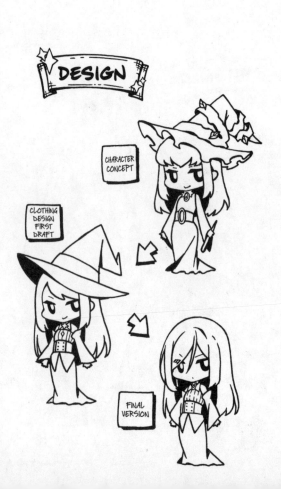

★ DESIGN

CHARACTER
CONCEPT

CLOTHING
DESIGN
FIRST
DRAFT

FINAL
VERSION

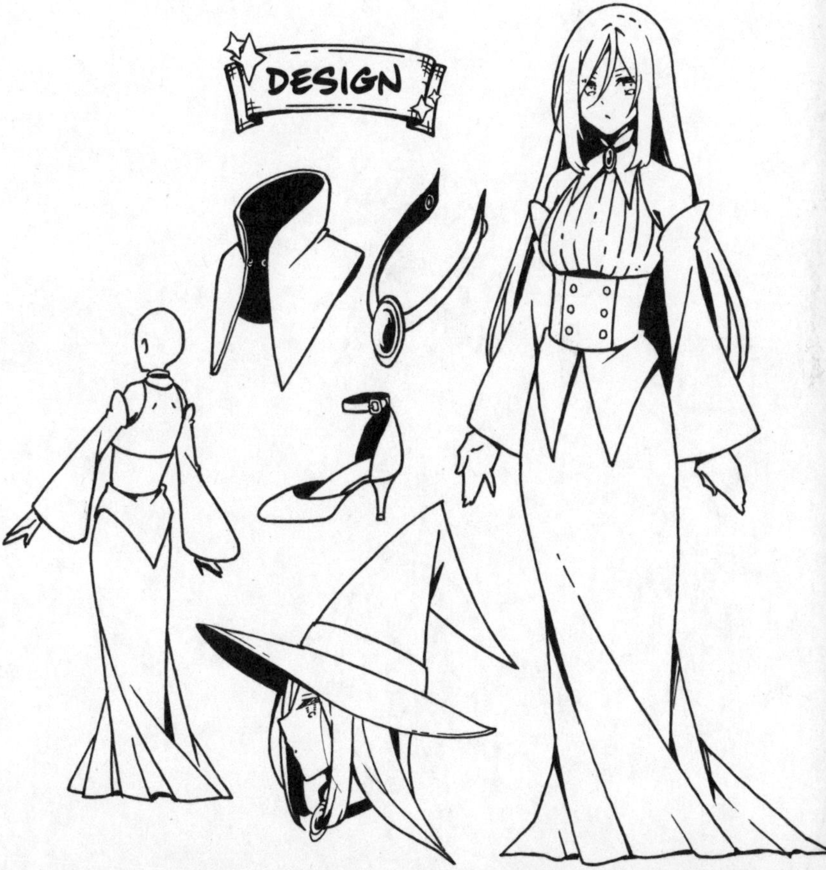
DESIGN

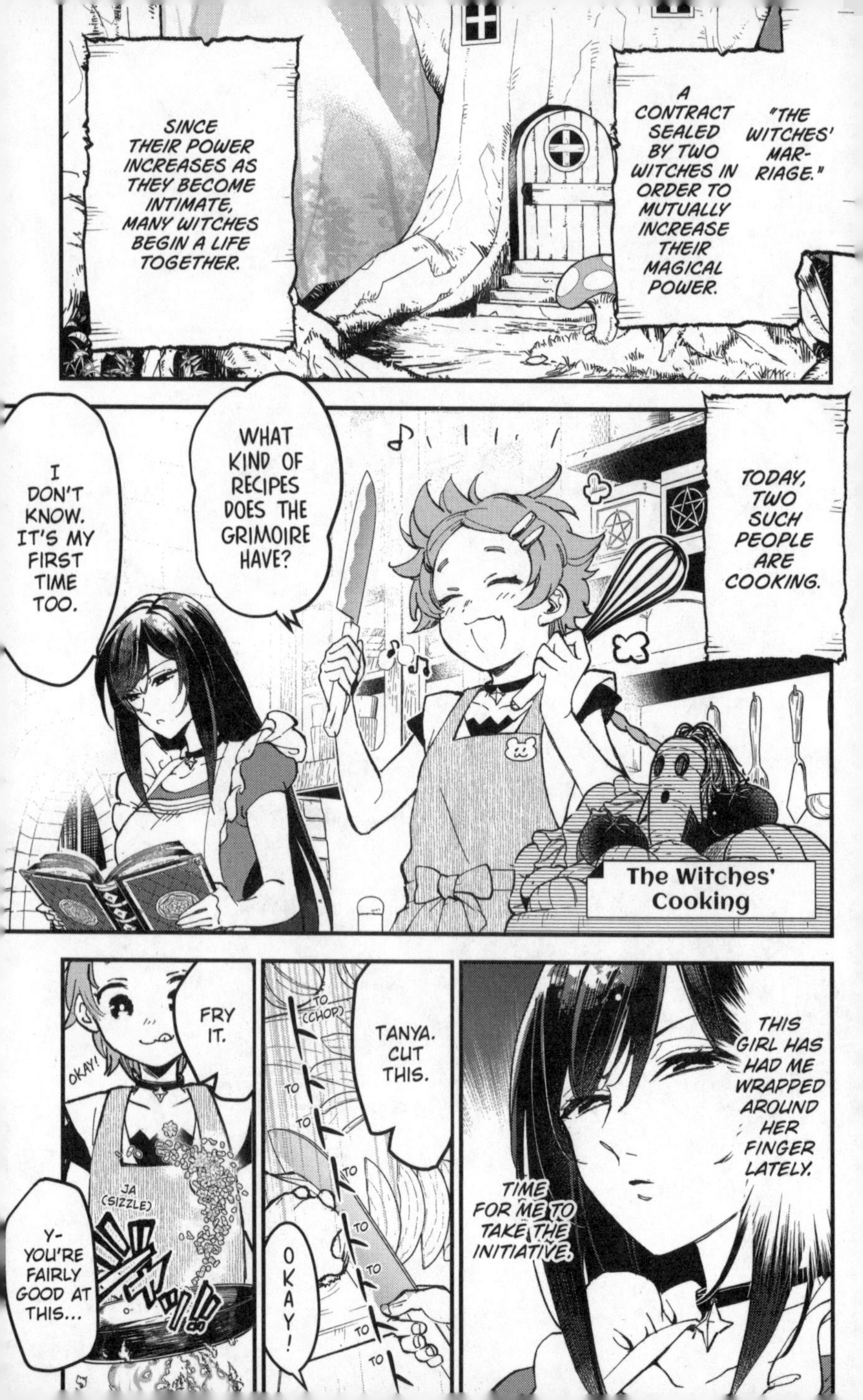
"THE WITCHES' MARRIAGE."
A CONTRACT SEALED BY TWO WITCHES IN ORDER TO MUTUALLY INCREASE THEIR MAGICAL POWER.
SINCE THEIR POWER INCREASES AS THEY BECOME INTIMATE, MANY WITCHES BEGIN A LIFE TOGETHER.
TODAY, TWO SUCH PEOPLE ARE COOKING.
WHAT KIND OF RECIPES DOES THE GRIMOIRE HAVE?
I DON'T KNOW. IT'S MY FIRST TIME TOO.
The Witches' Cooking
THIS GIRL HAS HAD ME WRAPPED AROUND HER FINGER LATELY.
TIME FOR ME TO TAKE THE INITIATIVE.
TANYA. CUT THIS.
TO (CHOP) TO TO TO TO TO TO TO
OKAY!
FRY IT.
OKAY!
JA (SIZZLE)
Y-YOU'RE FAIRLY GOOD AT THIS...

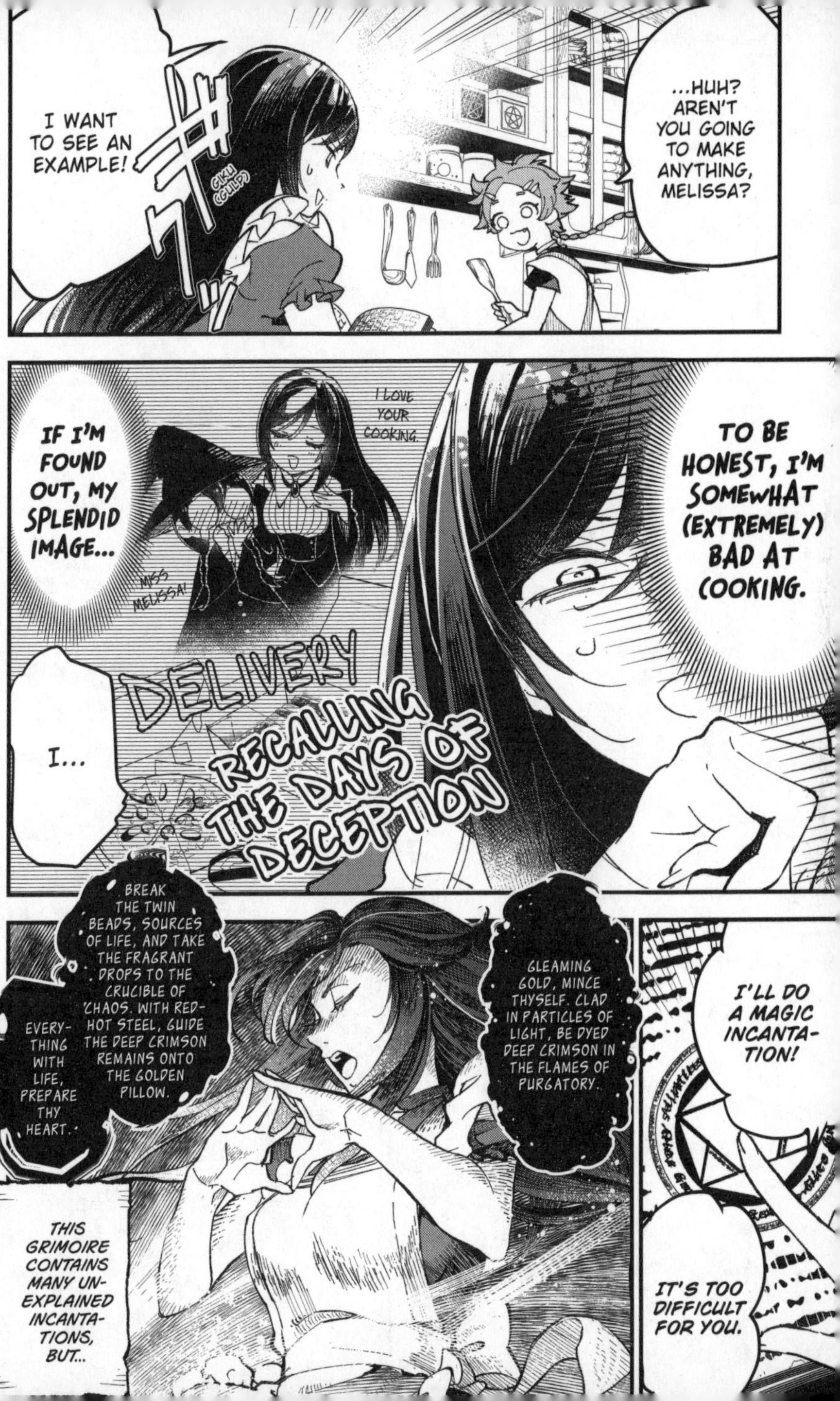
...HUH? AREN'T YOU GOING TO MAKE ANYTHING, MELISSA?
I WANT TO SEE AN EXAMPLE!
GIKU (GULP)
TO BE HONEST, I'M SOMEWHAT (EXTREMELY) BAD AT COOKING.
I LOVE YOUR COOKING.
IF I'M FOUND OUT, MY SPLENDID IMAGE...
MISS MELISSA!
DELIVERY
RECALLING THE DAYS OF DECEPTION
I...
I'LL DO A MAGIC INCANTATION!
IT'S TOO DIFFICULT FOR YOU.
GLEAMING GOLD, MINCE THYSELF. CLAD IN PARTICLES OF LIGHT, BE DYED DEEP CRIMSON IN THE FLAMES OF PURGATORY.
BREAK THE TWIN BEADS, SOURCES OF LIFE, AND TAKE THE FRAGRANT DROPS TO THE CRUCIBLE OF CHAOS. WITH RED-HOT STEEL, GUIDE THE DEEP CRIMSON REMAINS ONTO THE GOLDEN PILLOW.
EVERY-THING WITH LIFE, PREPARE THY HEART.
THIS GRIMOIRE CONTAINS MANY UN-EXPLAINED INCANTA-TIONS, BUT...

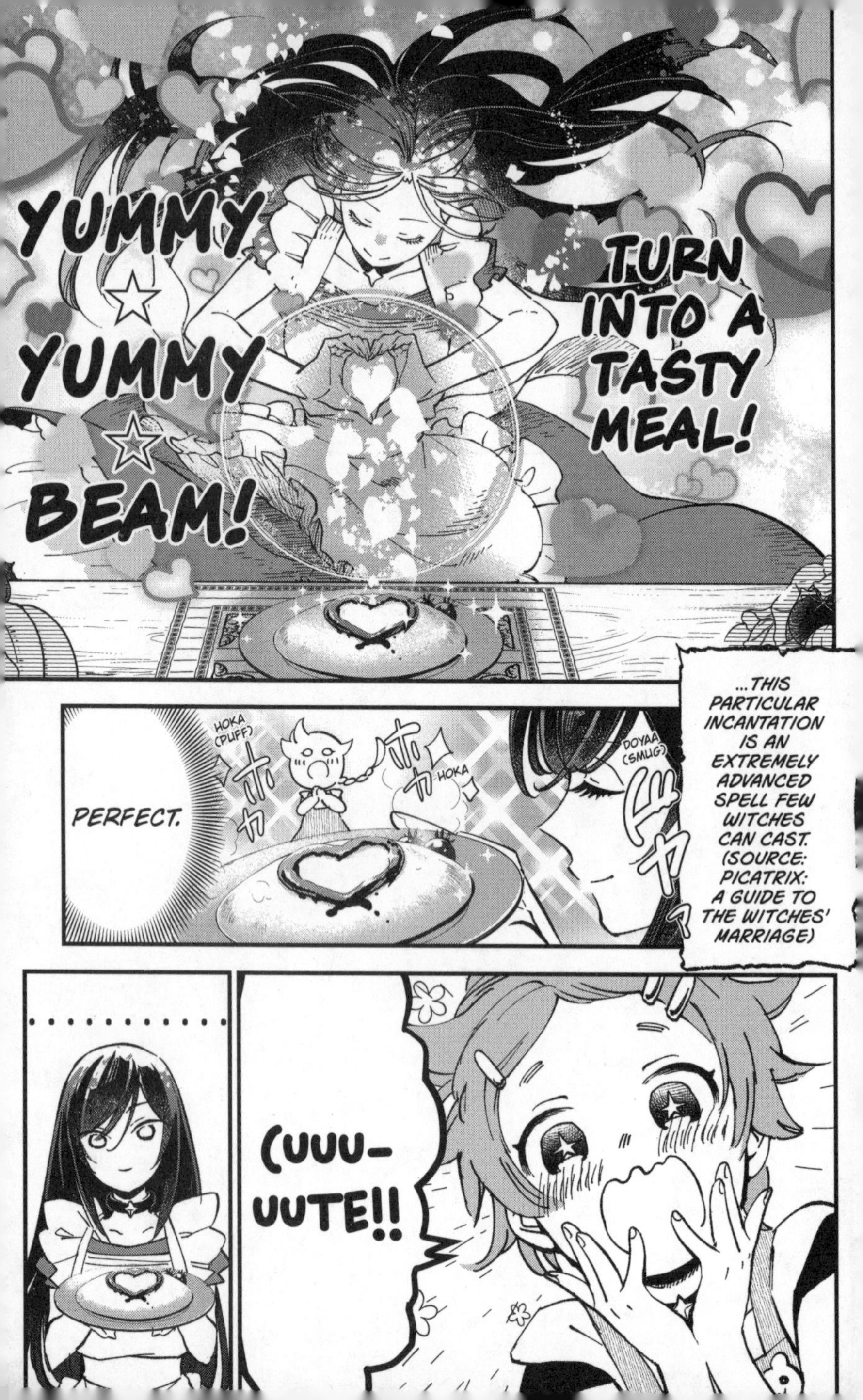
YUMMY ☆ YUMMY ☆ BEAM!
TURN INTO A TASTY MEAL!
...THIS PARTICULAR INCANTATION IS AN EXTREMELY ADVANCED SPELL FEW WITCHES CAN CAST. (SOURCE: PICATRIX: A GUIDE TO THE WITCHES' MARRIAGE)
DOYAA (SMUG)
HOKA
HOKA (PUFF)
PERFECT.
(UUUU-UUTE!!
....

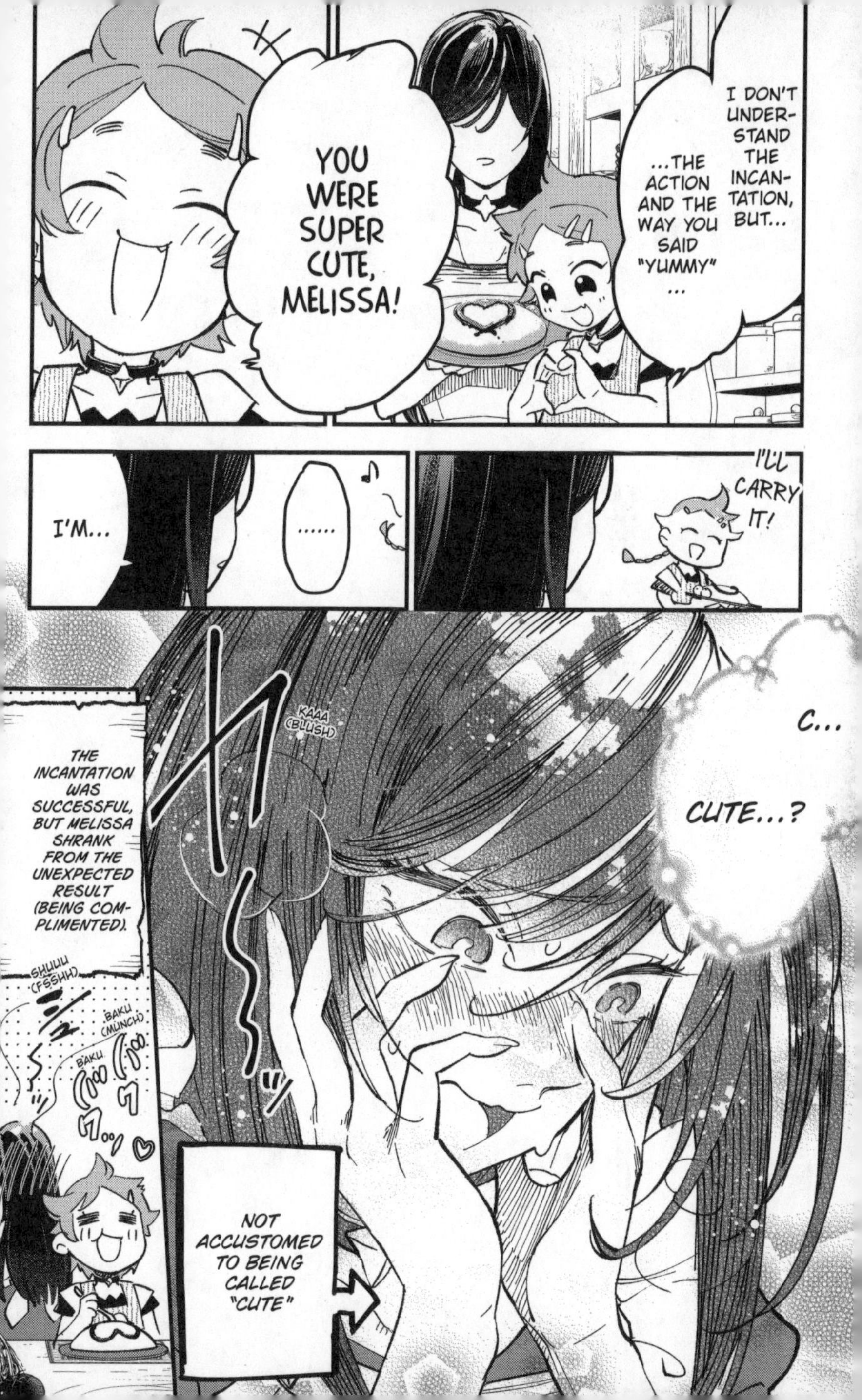
I DON'T UNDERSTAND THE INCANTATION, BUT...
...THE ACTION AND THE WAY YOU SAID "YUMMY" ...
YOU WERE SUPER CUTE, MELISSA!
I'LL CARRY IT!
......
I'M...
C...
CUTE...?
KAAA (BLUSH)
THE INCANTATION WAS SUCCESSFUL, BUT MELISSA SHRANK FROM THE UNEXPECTED RESULT (BEING COMPLIMENTED).
SHUUU (FSSHH)
BAKU (MUNCH)
BAKU
NOT ACCUSTOMED TO BEING CALLED "CUTE"

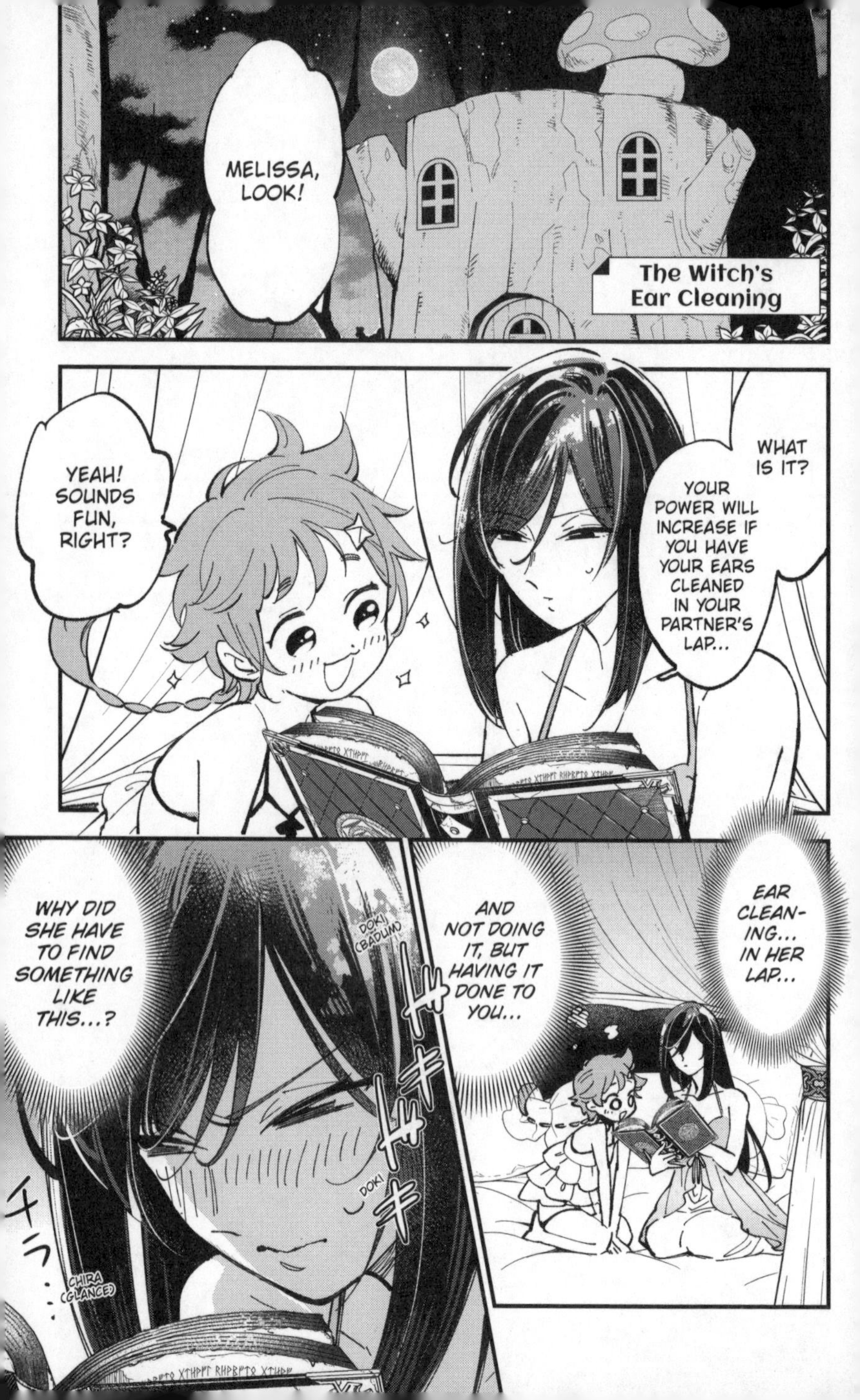
The Witch's Ear Cleaning
MELISSA, LOOK!
WHAT IS IT?
YOUR POWER WILL INCREASE IF YOU HAVE YOUR EARS CLEANED IN YOUR PARTNER'S LAP...
YEAH! SOUNDS FUN, RIGHT?
EAR CLEAN-ING... IN HER LAP...
AND NOT DOING IT, BUT HAVING IT DONE TO YOU...
DOKI (BADUM)
WHY DID SHE HAVE TO FIND SOMETHING LIKE THIS...?
DOKI
CHIRA (GLANCE)

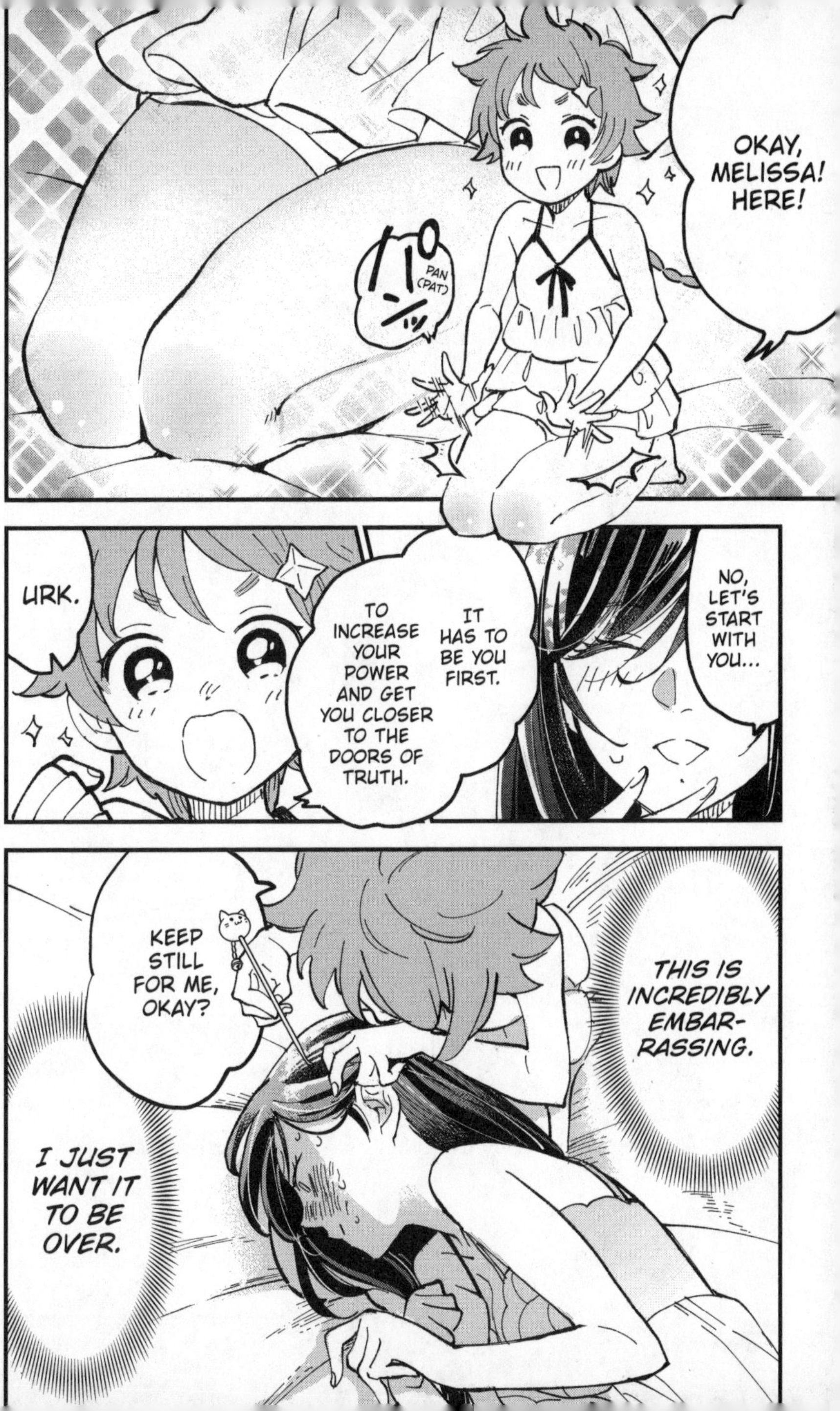
OKAY, MELISSA! HERE!
PAN (PAT)
NO, LET'S START WITH YOU...
IT HAS TO BE YOU FIRST.
TO INCREASE YOUR POWER AND GET YOU CLOSER TO THE DOORS OF TRUTH.
URK.
THIS IS INCREDIBLY EMBAR-RASSING.
KEEP STILL FOR ME, OKAY?
I JUST WANT IT TO BE OVER.

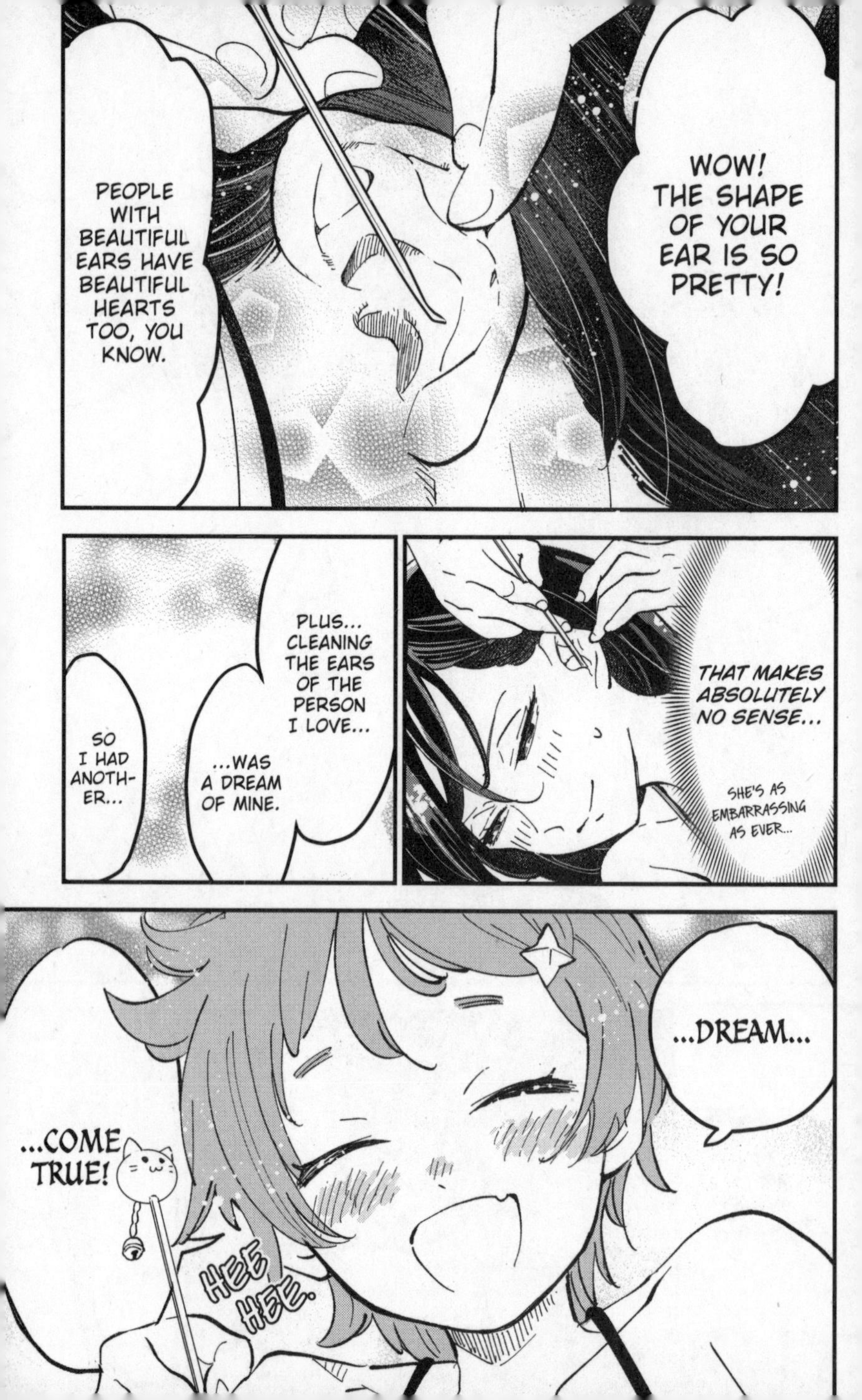
WOW! THE SHAPE OF YOUR EAR IS SO PRETTY!
PEOPLE WITH BEAUTIFUL EARS HAVE BEAUTIFUL HEARTS TOO, YOU KNOW.
THAT MAKES ABSOLUTELY NO SENSE...
SHE'S AS EMBARRASSING AS EVER...
PLUS... CLEANING THE EARS OF THE PERSON I LOVE...
...WAS A DREAM OF MINE.
SO I HAD ANOTHER...
...DREAM...
...COME TRUE!
HEE HEE.

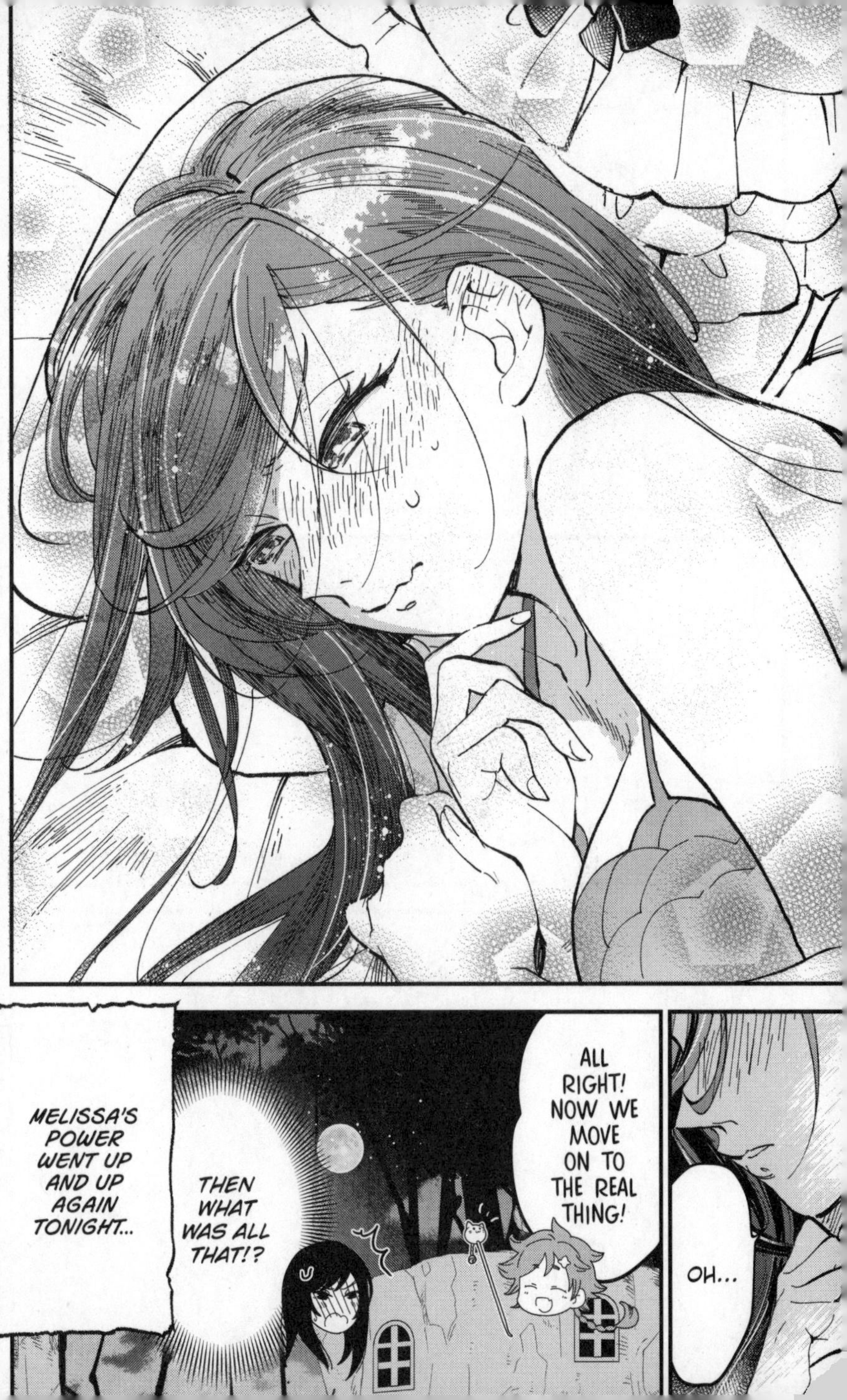
OH...
ALL RIGHT! NOW WE MOVE ON TO THE REAL THING!
THEN WHAT WAS ALL THAT!?
MELISSA'S POWER WENT UP AND UP AGAIN TONIGHT...

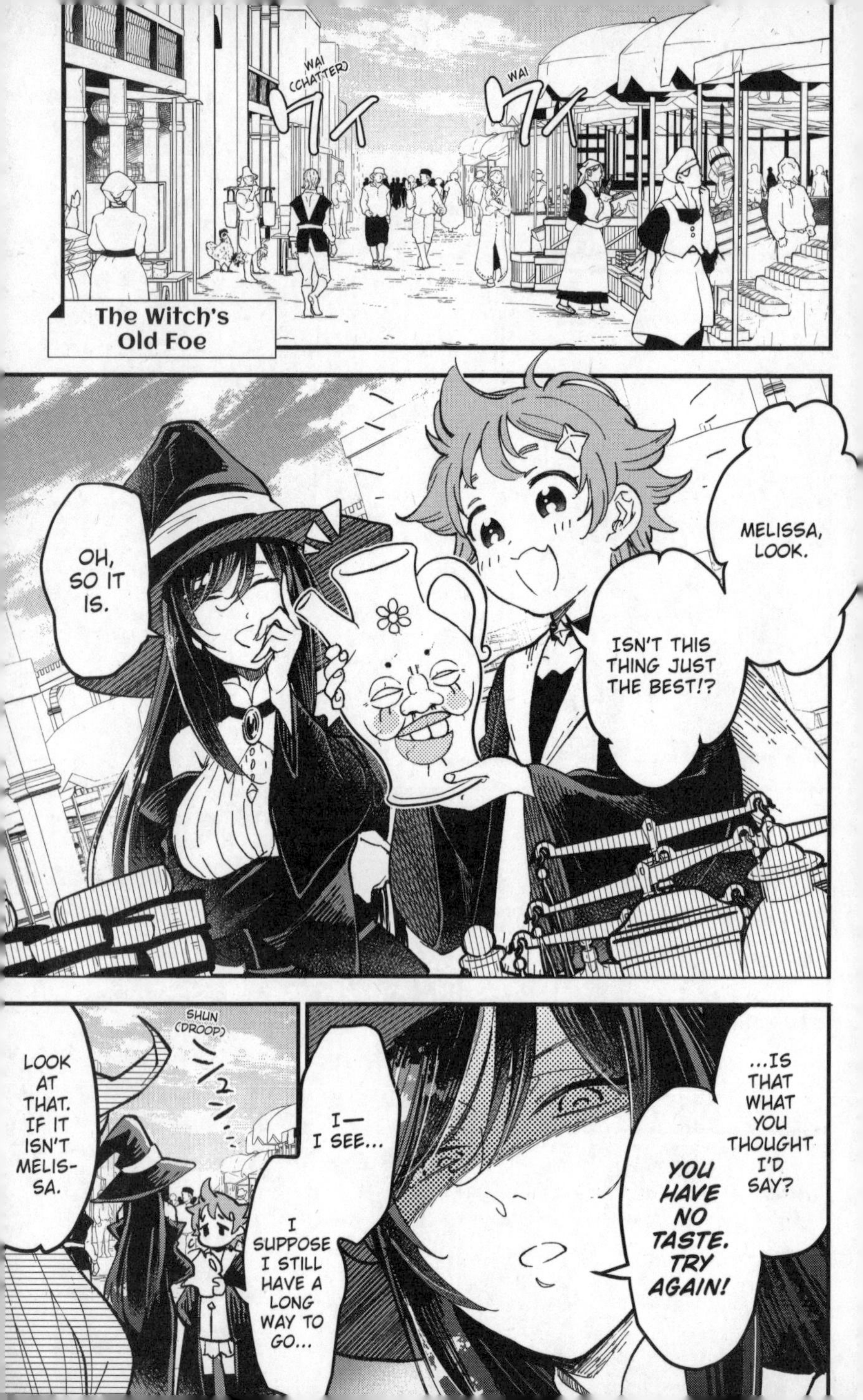
WAI
WAI (CHATTER)
The Witch's Old Foe
MELISSA, LOOK.
ISN'T THIS THING JUST THE BEST!?
OH, SO IT IS.
...IS THAT WHAT YOU THOUGHT I'D SAY?
YOU HAVE NO TASTE. TRY AGAIN!
I— I SEE...
I SUPPOSE I STILL HAVE A LONG WAY TO GO...
SHUN (DROOP)
LOOK AT THAT. IF IT ISN'T MELIS-SA.

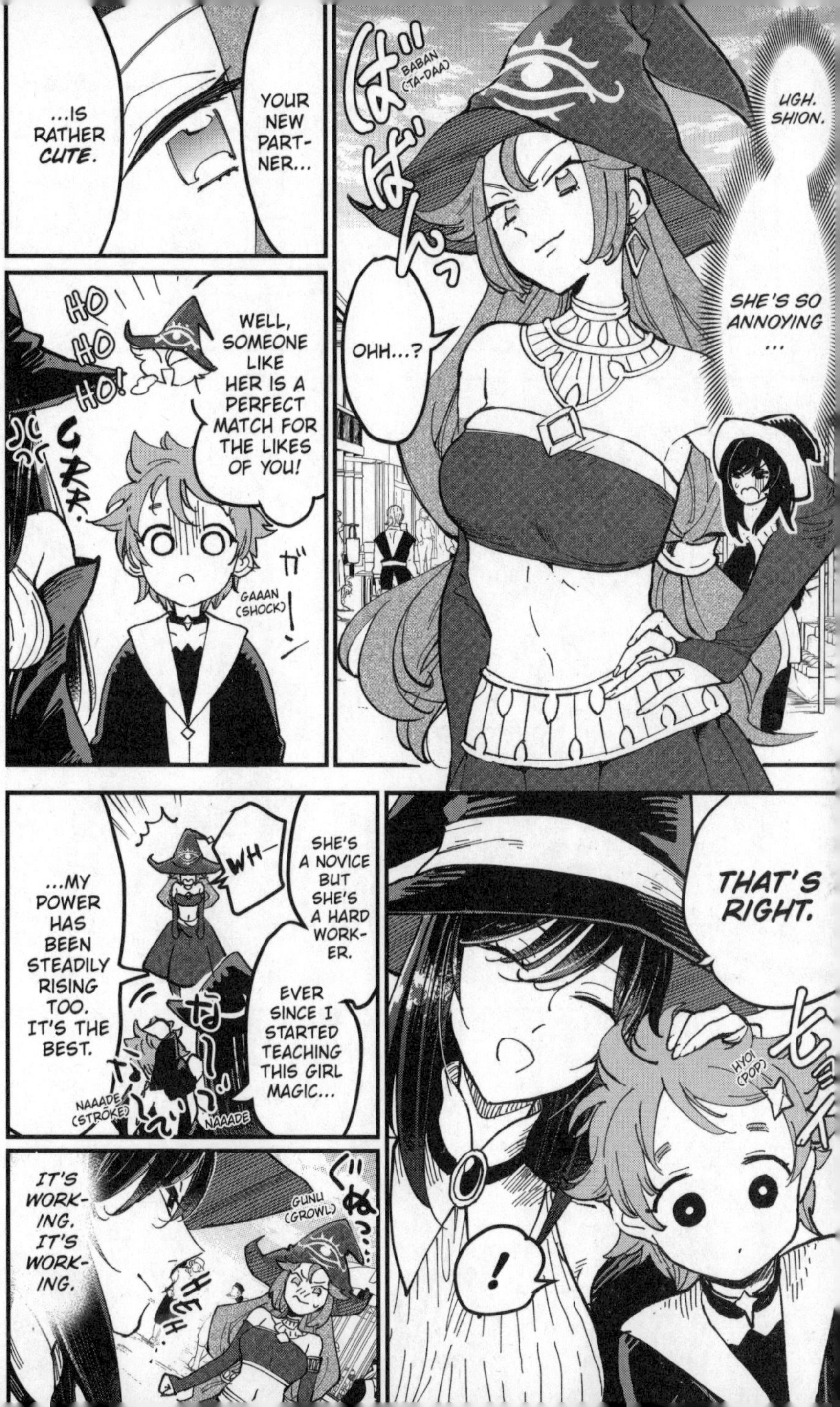
BABAN (TA-DAA)
UGH. SHION.
SHE'S SO ANNOYING ...
OHH...?
YOUR NEW PARTNER...
...IS RATHER CUTE.
WELL, SOMEONE LIKE HER IS A PERFECT MATCH FOR THE LIKES OF YOU!
HO HO HO!
GRR.
GAAAN (SHOCK)
THAT'S RIGHT.
HYOI (POP)
!
SHE'S A NOVICE BUT SHE'S A HARD WORKER.
EVER SINCE I STARTED TEACHING THIS GIRL MAGIC...
WH—
...MY POWER HAS BEEN STEADILY RISING TOO. IT'S THE BEST.
NAAADE (STROKE)
NAAADE
GUNU (GROWL)
HEH HEH
IT'S WORKING. IT'S WORKING.

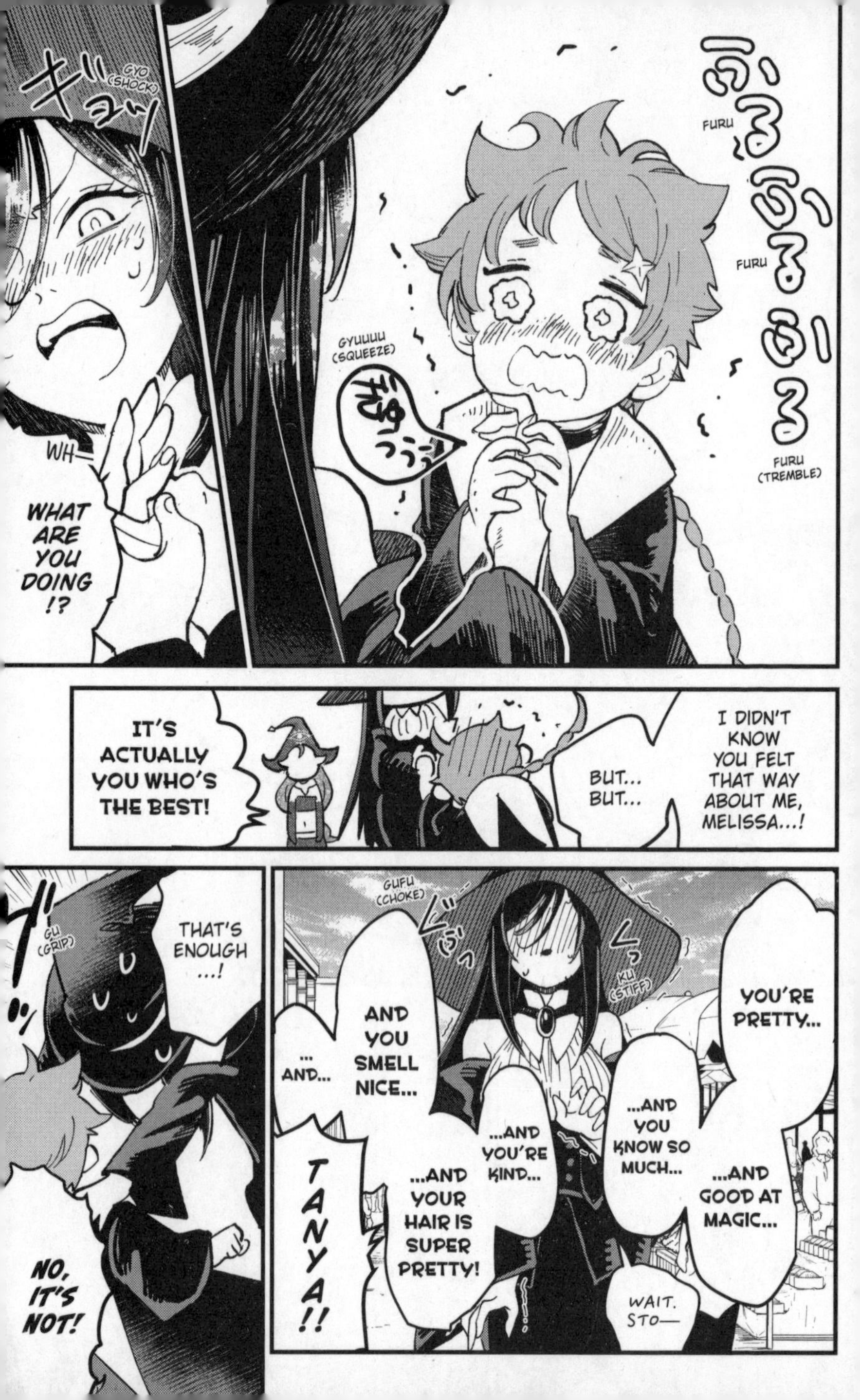

ふるふるふる
FURU
FURU
FURU (TREMBLE)
GYUUUU (SQUEEZE)
ぎゅううう
ギョッ
GYO (SHOCK)
WH—
WHAT ARE YOU DOING!?
I DIDN'T KNOW YOU FELT THAT WAY ABOUT ME, MELISSA...!
BUT... BUT...
IT'S ACTUALLY YOU WHO'S THE BEST!
YOU'RE PRETTY...
KU (STIFF)
GUFU (CHOKE)
...AND GOOD AT MAGIC...
...AND YOU KNOW SO MUCH...
...AND YOU'RE KIND...
AND YOU SMELL NICE...
... AND...
...AND YOUR HAIR IS SUPER PRETTY!
WAIT. STO—
TANYA!!
THAT'S ENOUGH...!
GU (GRIP)
NO, IT'S NOT!

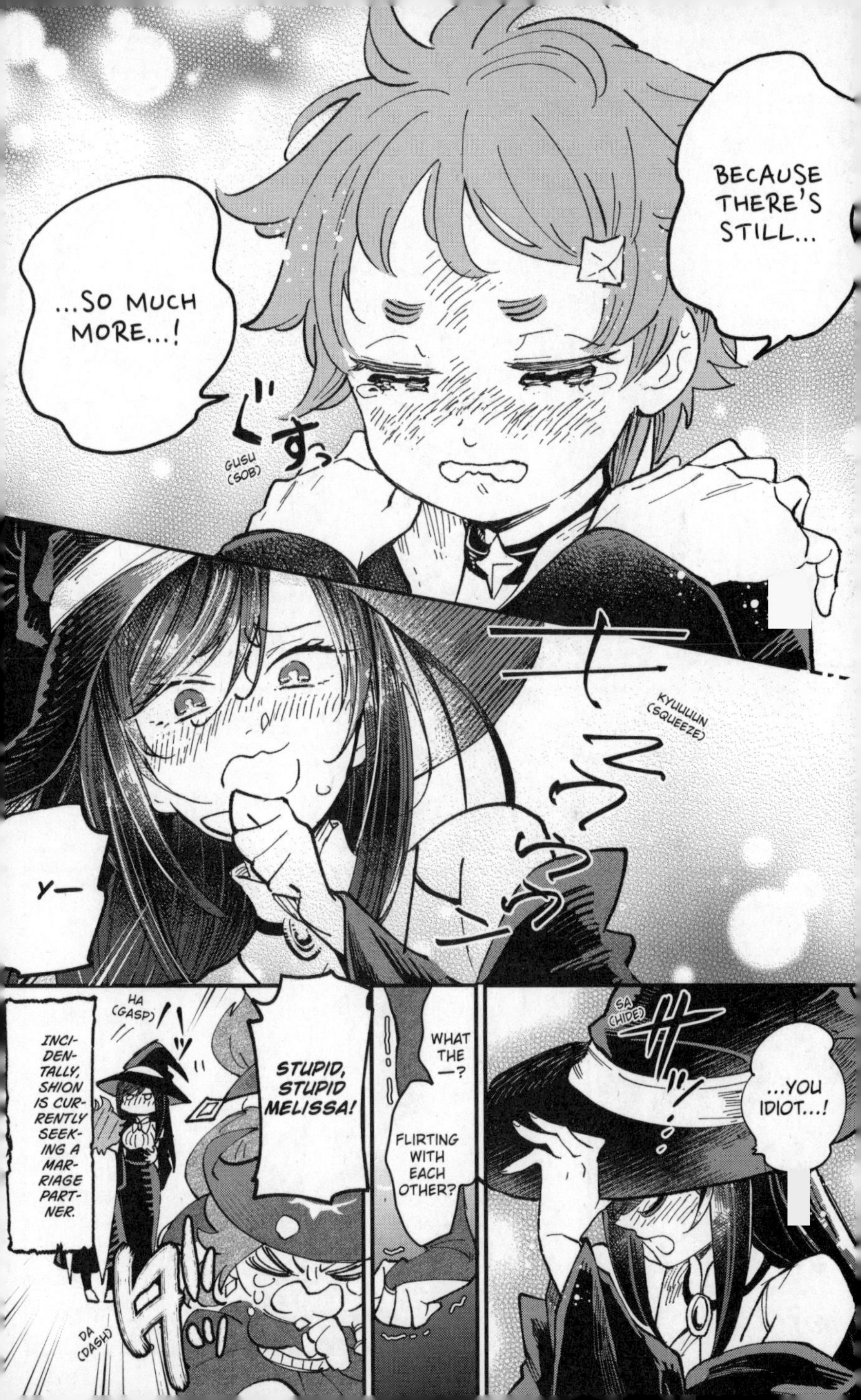
BECAUSE THERE'S STILL...
...SO MUCH MORE...!
GUSU (SOB)
KYUUUUN (SQUEEZE)
Y—
SA (HIDE)
...YOU IDIOT...!
WHAT THE—?
FLIRTING WITH EACH OTHER?
STUPID, STUPID MELISSA!
HA (GASP)
INCIDENTALLY, SHION IS CURRENTLY SEEKING A MARRIAGE PARTNER.
DA (DASH)

The Witch's Love Potion

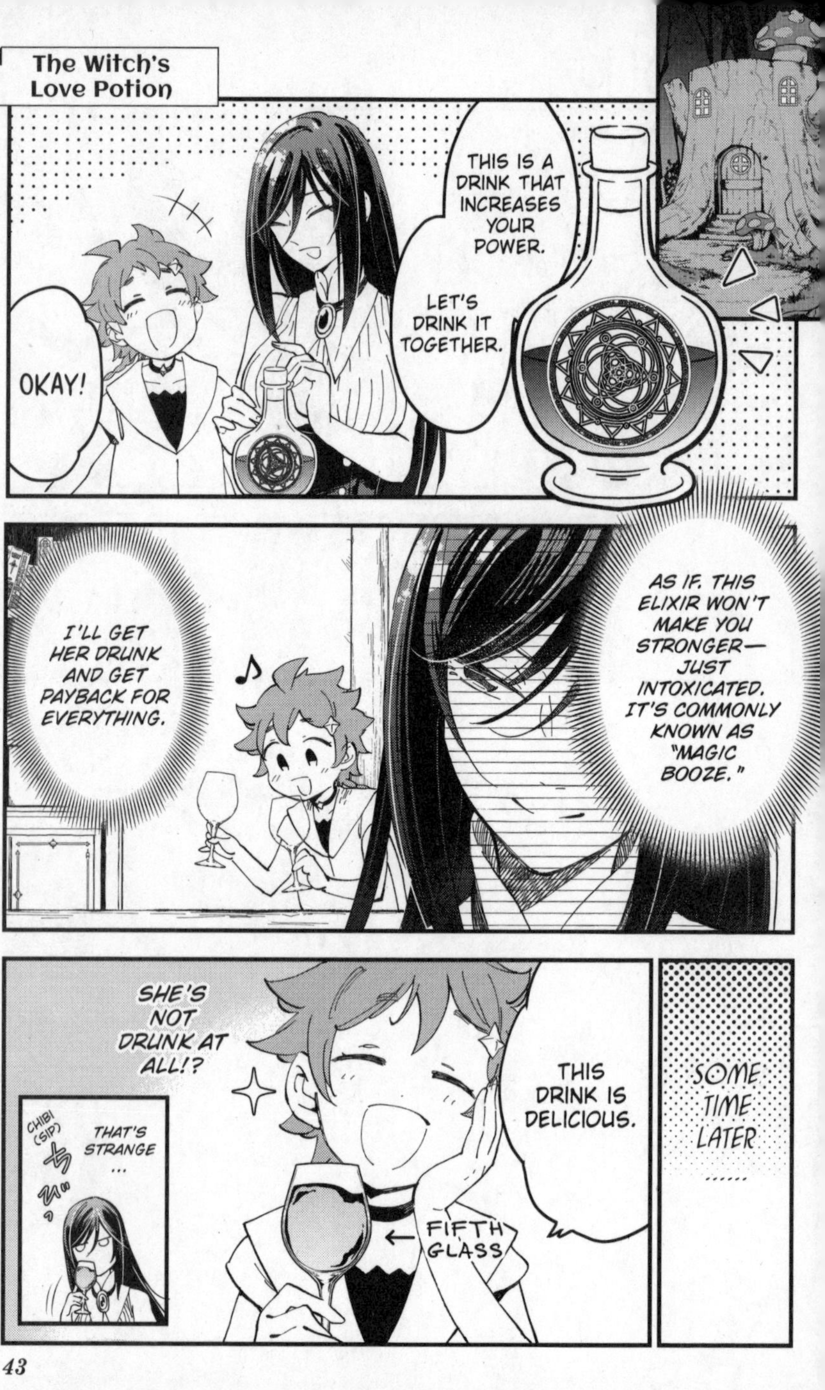
THIS IS A DRINK THAT INCREASES YOUR POWER.
LET'S DRINK IT TOGETHER.
OKAY!
AS IF. THIS ELIXIR WON'T MAKE YOU STRONGER—JUST INTOXICATED. IT'S COMMONLY KNOWN AS "MAGIC BOOZE."
I'LL GET HER DRUNK AND GET PAYBACK FOR EVERYTHING.
SOME TIME LATER......
THIS DRINK IS DELICIOUS.
FIFTH GLASS
SHE'S NOT DRUNK AT ALL!?
CHIBI (SIP)
THAT'S STRANGE ...

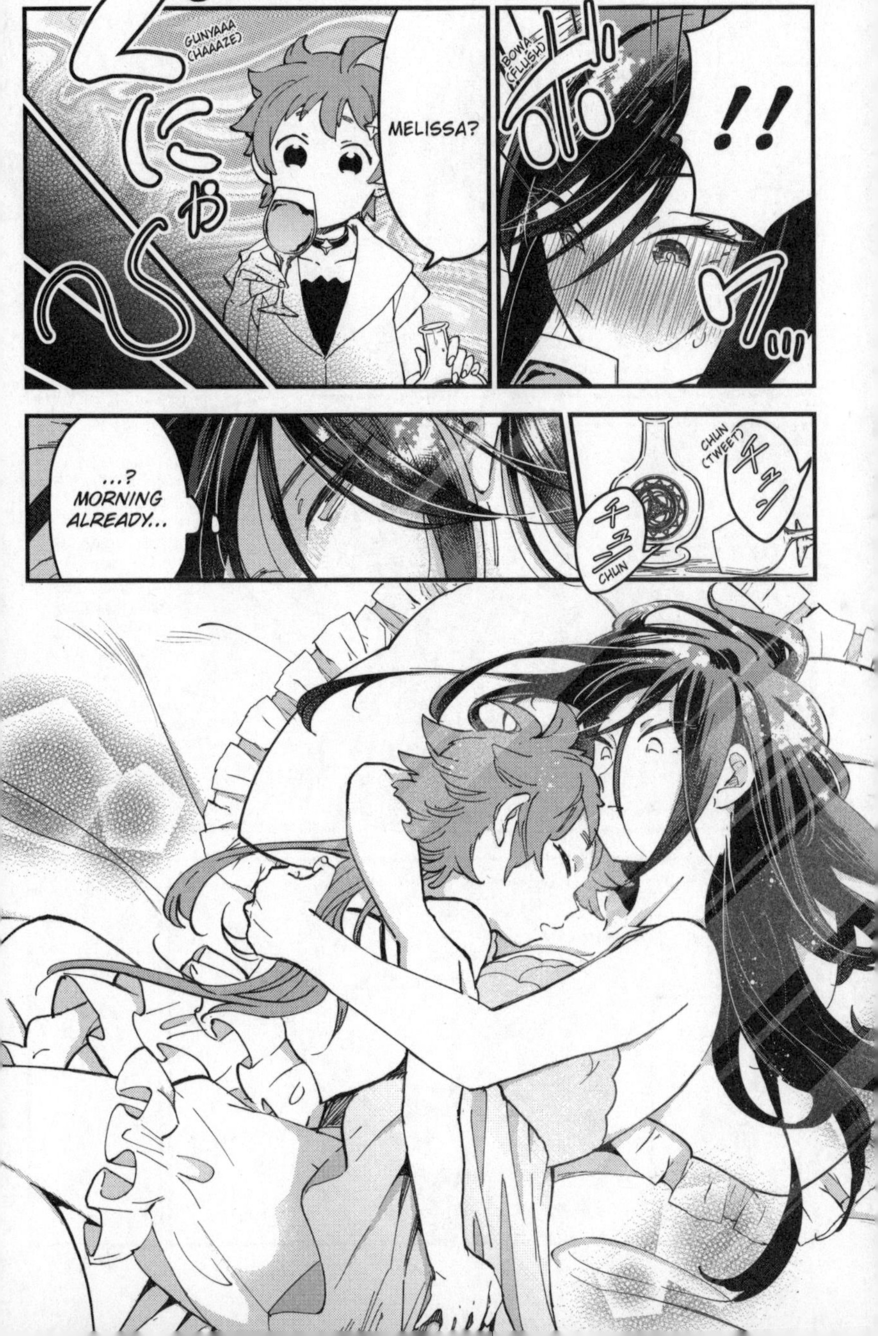
BOWA (FLUSH)
!!
GUNYAAA (HAAAZE)
MELISSA?
CHUN (TWEET)
CHUN
...? MORNING ALREADY...

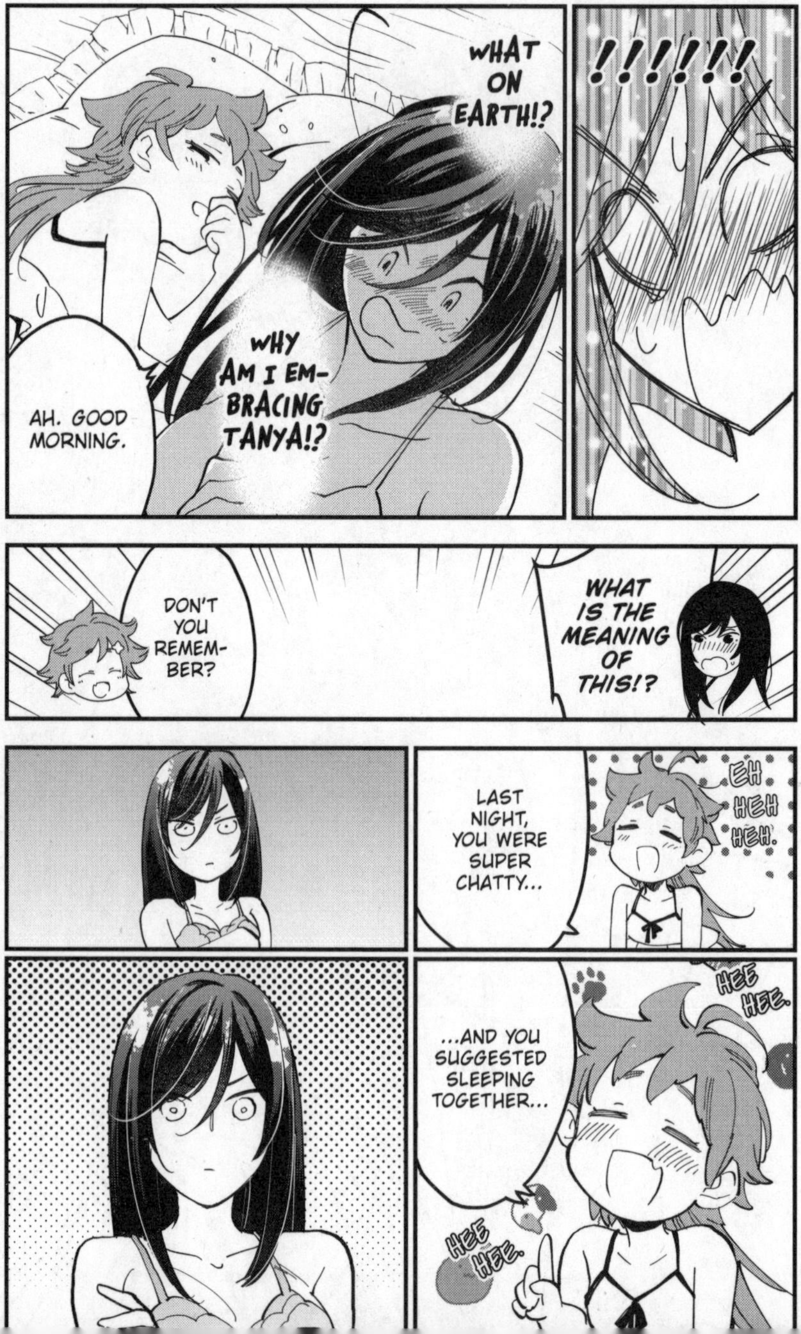
!!!!!!
WHAT ON EARTH!?
WHY AM I EMBRACING TANYA!?
AH. GOOD MORNING.
WHAT IS THE MEANING OF THIS!?
DON'T YOU REMEMBER?
EH HEH HEH.
LAST NIGHT, YOU WERE SUPER CHATTY...
HEE HEE.
...AND YOU SUGGESTED SLEEPING TOGETHER...
HEE HEE.

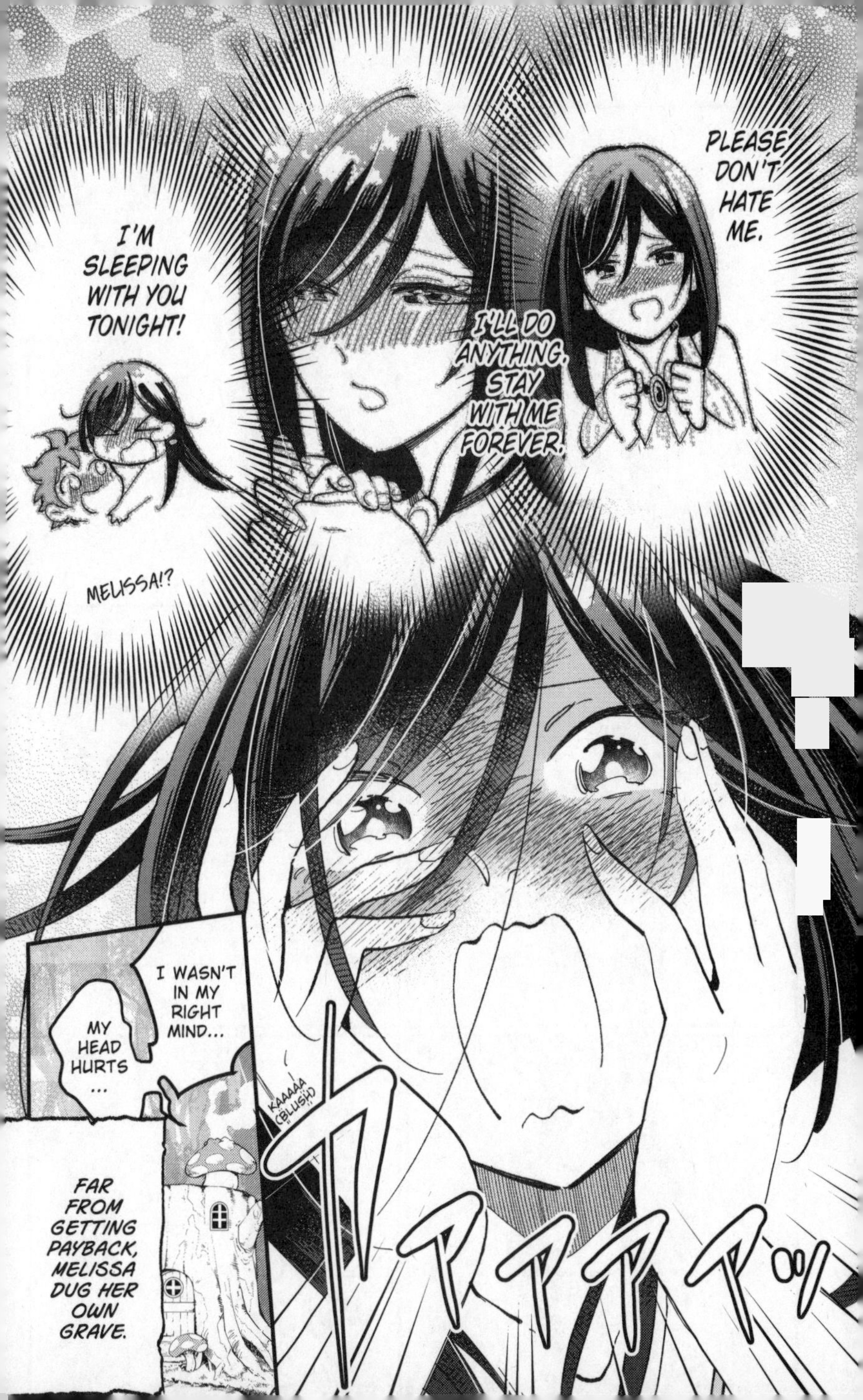
PLEASE DON'T HATE ME.
I'LL DO ANYTHING. STAY WITH ME FOREVER.
I'M SLEEPING WITH YOU TONIGHT!
MELISSA!?
KAAAAA (BLUSH)
I WASN'T IN MY RIGHT MIND...
MY HEAD HURTS...
FAR FROM GETTING PAYBACK, MELISSA DUG HER OWN GRAVE.

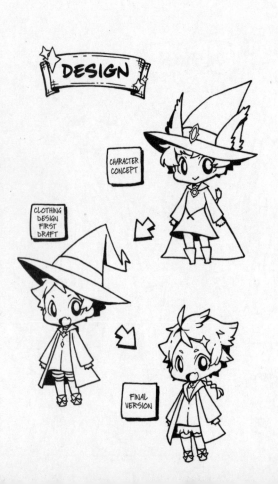

DESIGN

CHARACTER CONCEPT

CLOTHING DESIGN FIRST DRAFT

FINAL VERSION

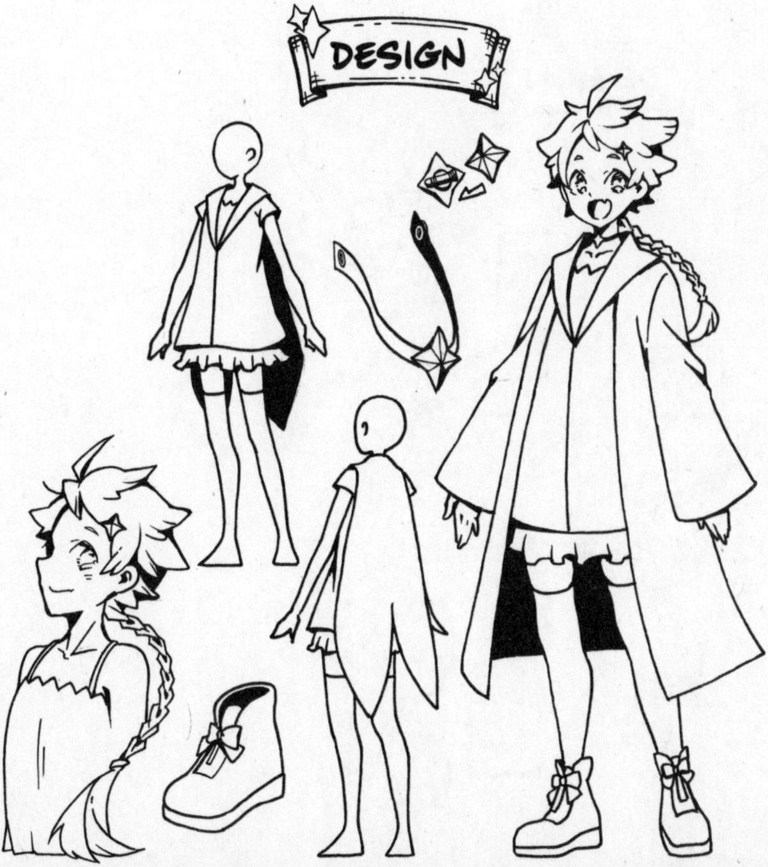
DESIGN

The Witches' Rain Shelter

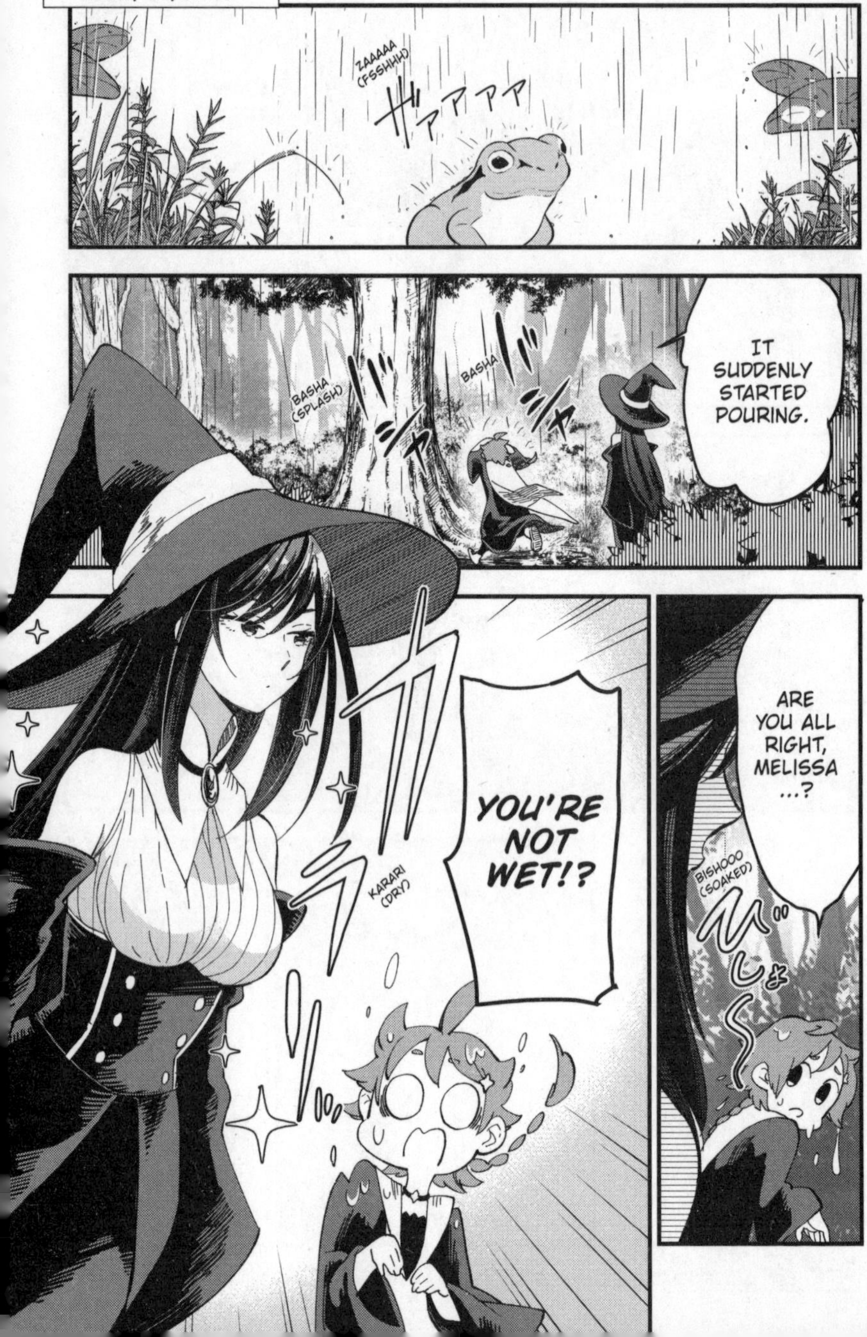
ZAAAAA (FSSHHH)
IT SUDDENLY STARTED POURING.
BASHA
BASHA (SPLASH)
ARE YOU ALL RIGHT, MELISSA ...?
BISHOOO (SOAKED)
YOU'RE NOT WET!?
KARARI (DRY)

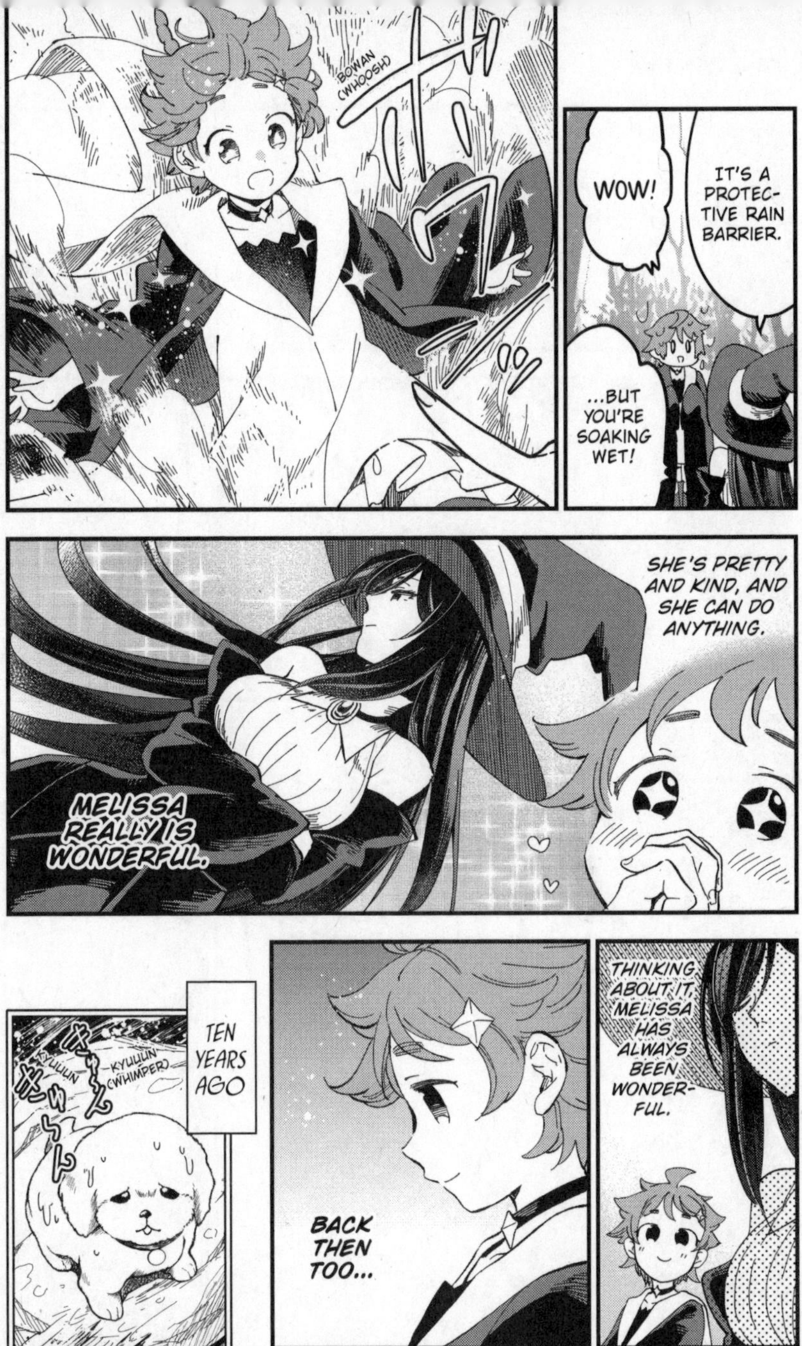
IT'S A PROTECTIVE RAIN BARRIER.
WOW!
...BUT YOU'RE SOAKING WET!
BOWAN (WHOOSH)
SHE'S PRETTY AND KIND, AND SHE CAN DO ANYTHING.
MELISSA REALLY IS WONDERFUL.
THINKING ABOUT IT, MELISSA HAS ALWAYS BEEN WONDERFUL.
BACK THEN TOO...
TEN YEARS AGO
KYUUUN (WHIMPER)
KYUUUN

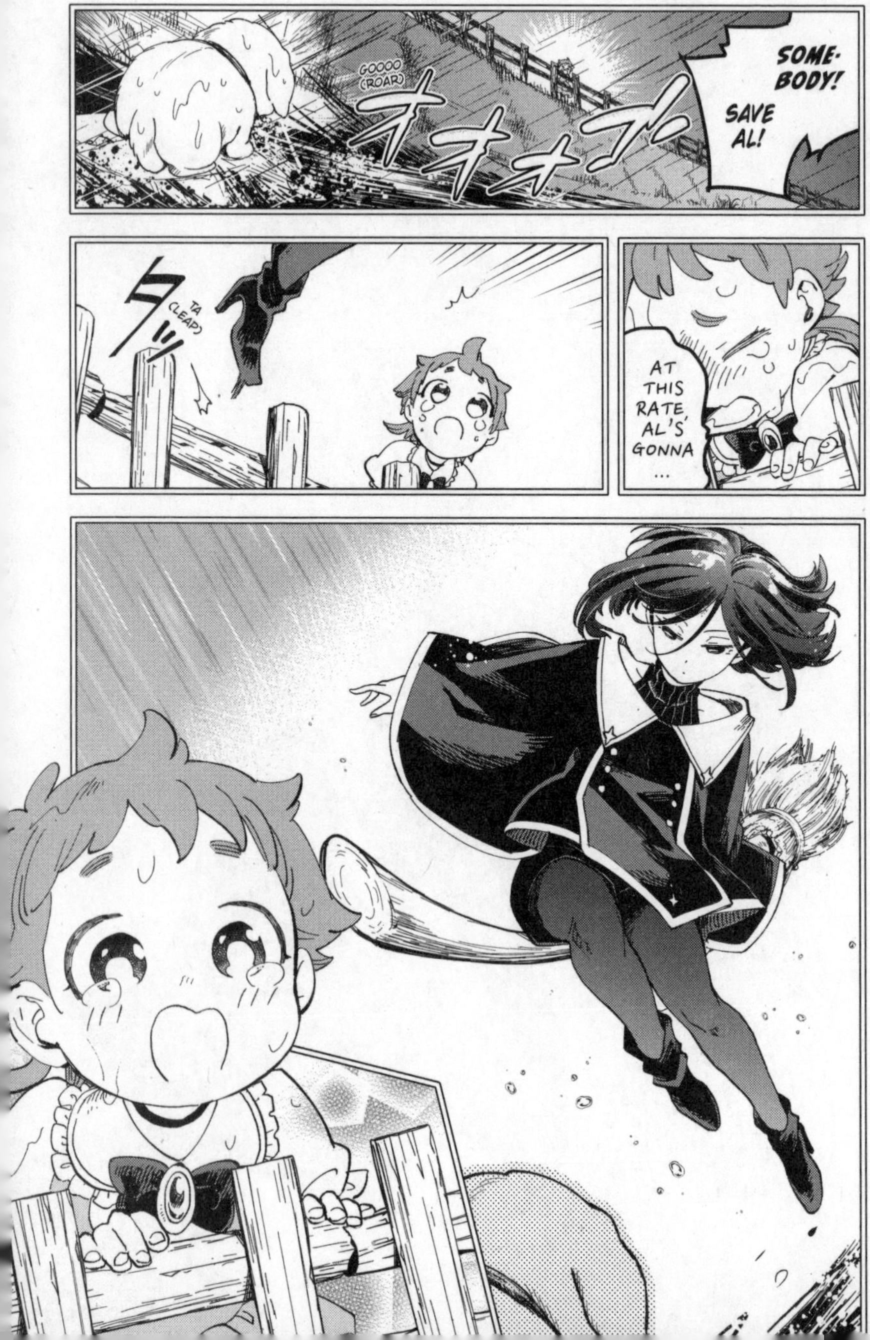
SOME-BODY!
SAVE AL!
GOOOO (ROAR)
AT THIS RATE, AL'S GONNA ...
TA (LEAP)

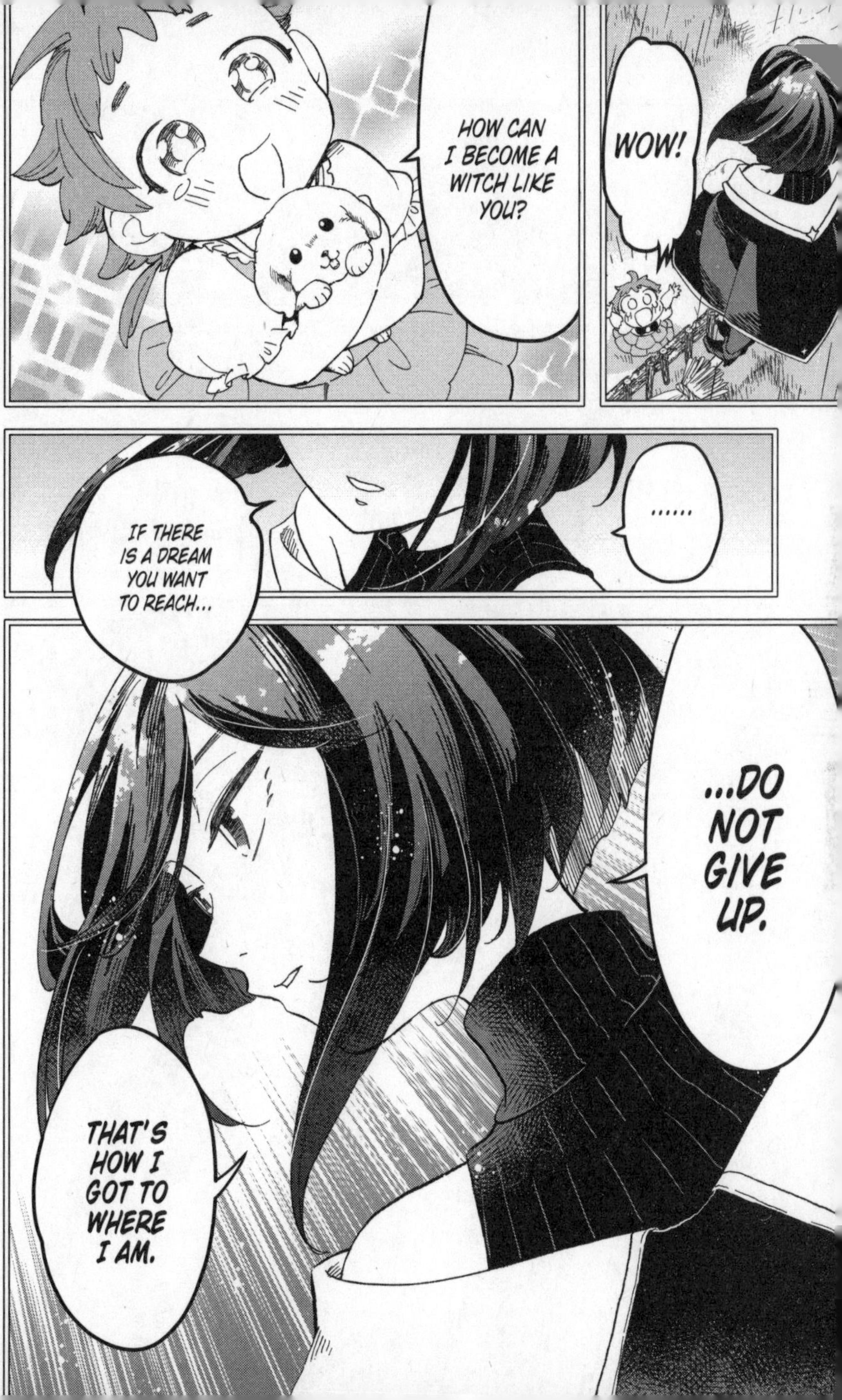
WOW!
HOW CAN I BECOME A WITCH LIKE YOU?
......
IF THERE IS A DREAM YOU WANT TO REACH...
...DO NOT GIVE UP.
THAT'S HOW I GOT TO WHERE I AM.

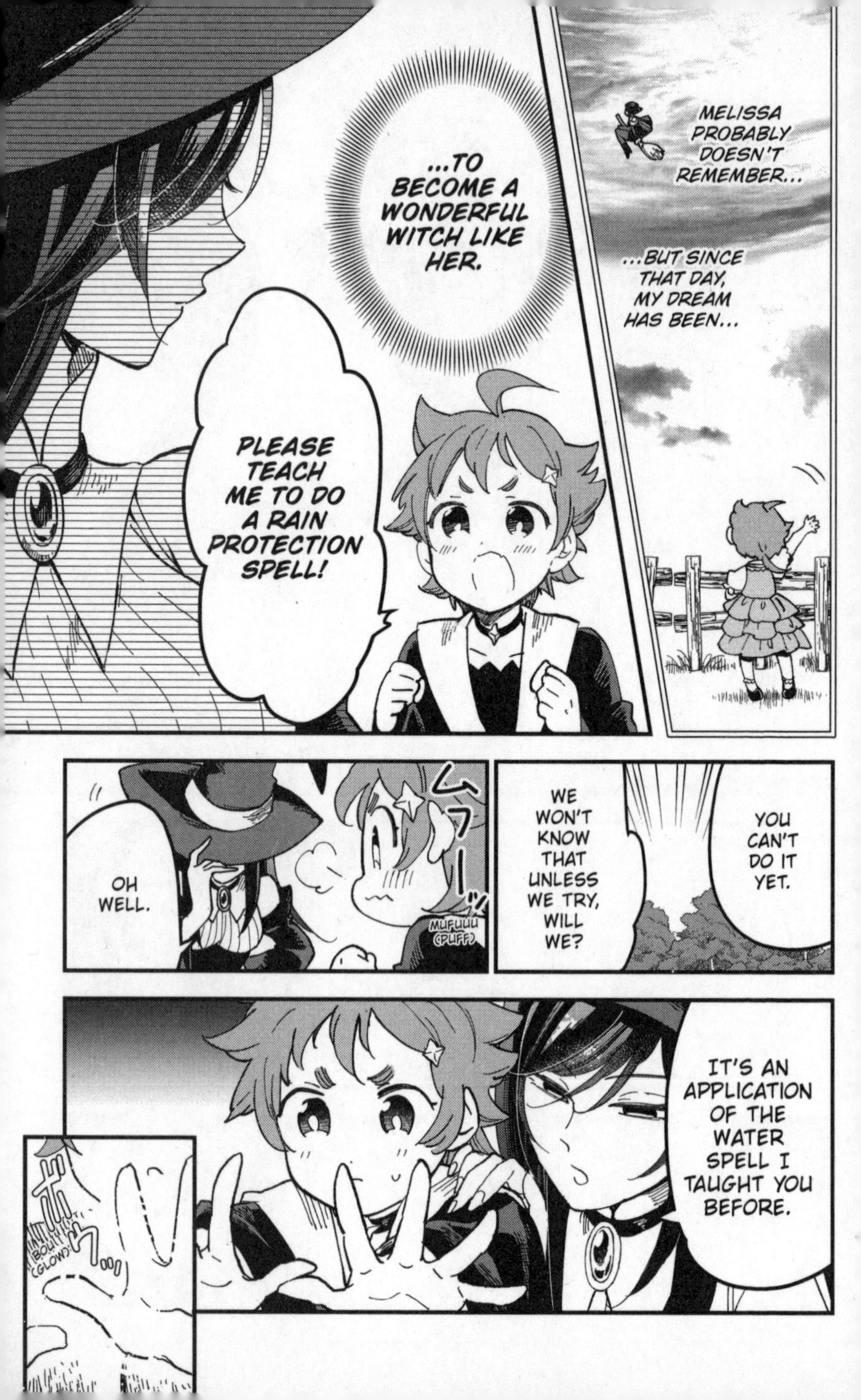
MELISSA PROBABLY DOESN'T REMEMBER...
...BUT SINCE THAT DAY, MY DREAM HAS BEEN...
...TO BECOME A WONDERFUL WITCH LIKE HER.
PLEASE TEACH ME TO DO A RAIN PROTECTION SPELL!
YOU CAN'T DO IT YET.
WE WON'T KNOW THAT UNLESS WE TRY, WILL WE?
MUFUUU (PUFF)
OH WELL.
IT'S AN APPLICATION OF THE WATER SPELL I TAUGHT YOU BEFORE.
BOU (GLOW)

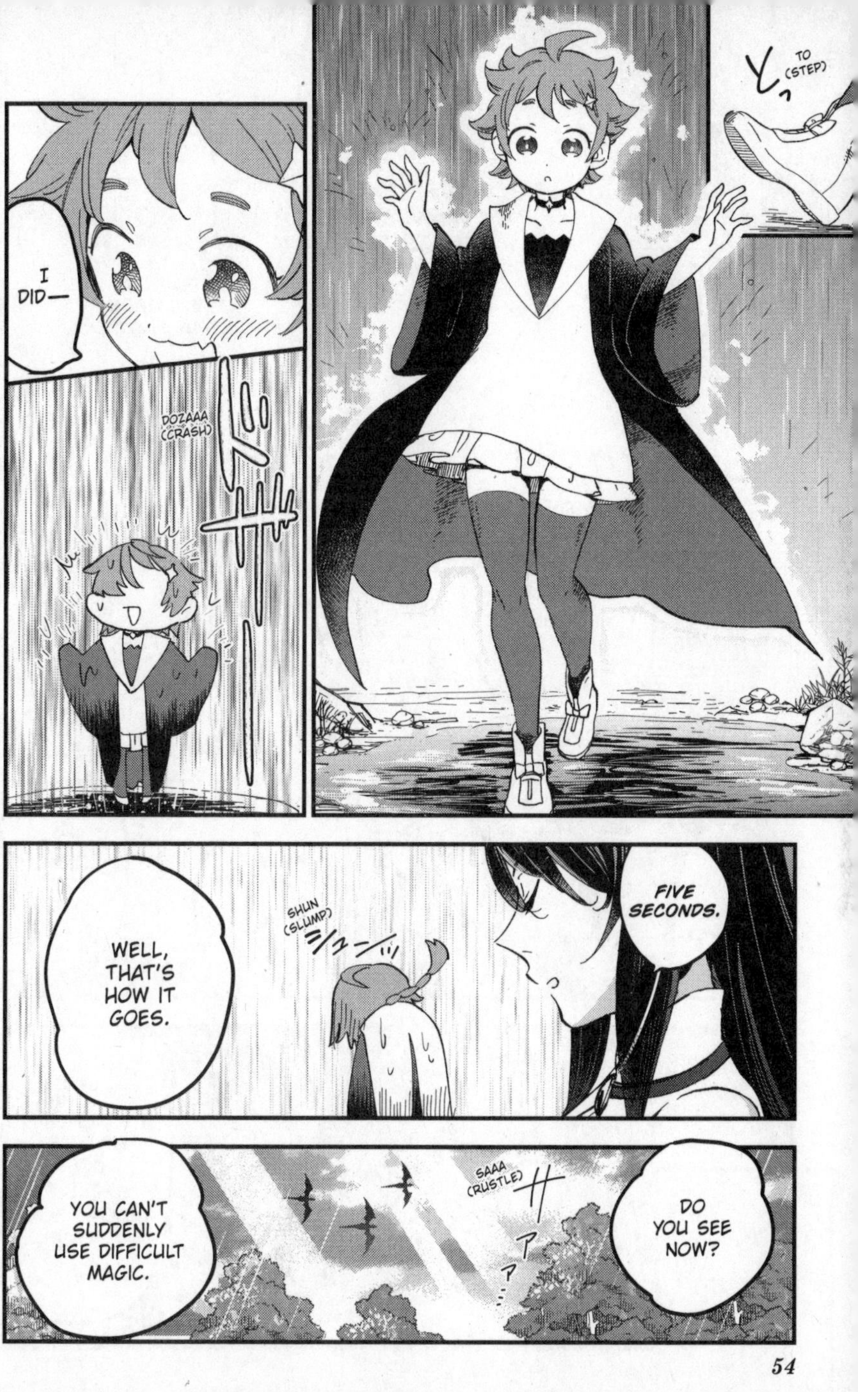
TO (STEP)
I DID—
DOZAAA (CRASH)
FIVE SECONDS.
SHUN (SLUMP)
WELL, THAT'S HOW IT GOES.
DO YOU SEE NOW?
SAAA (RUSTLE)
YOU CAN'T SUDDENLY USE DIFFICULT MAGIC.

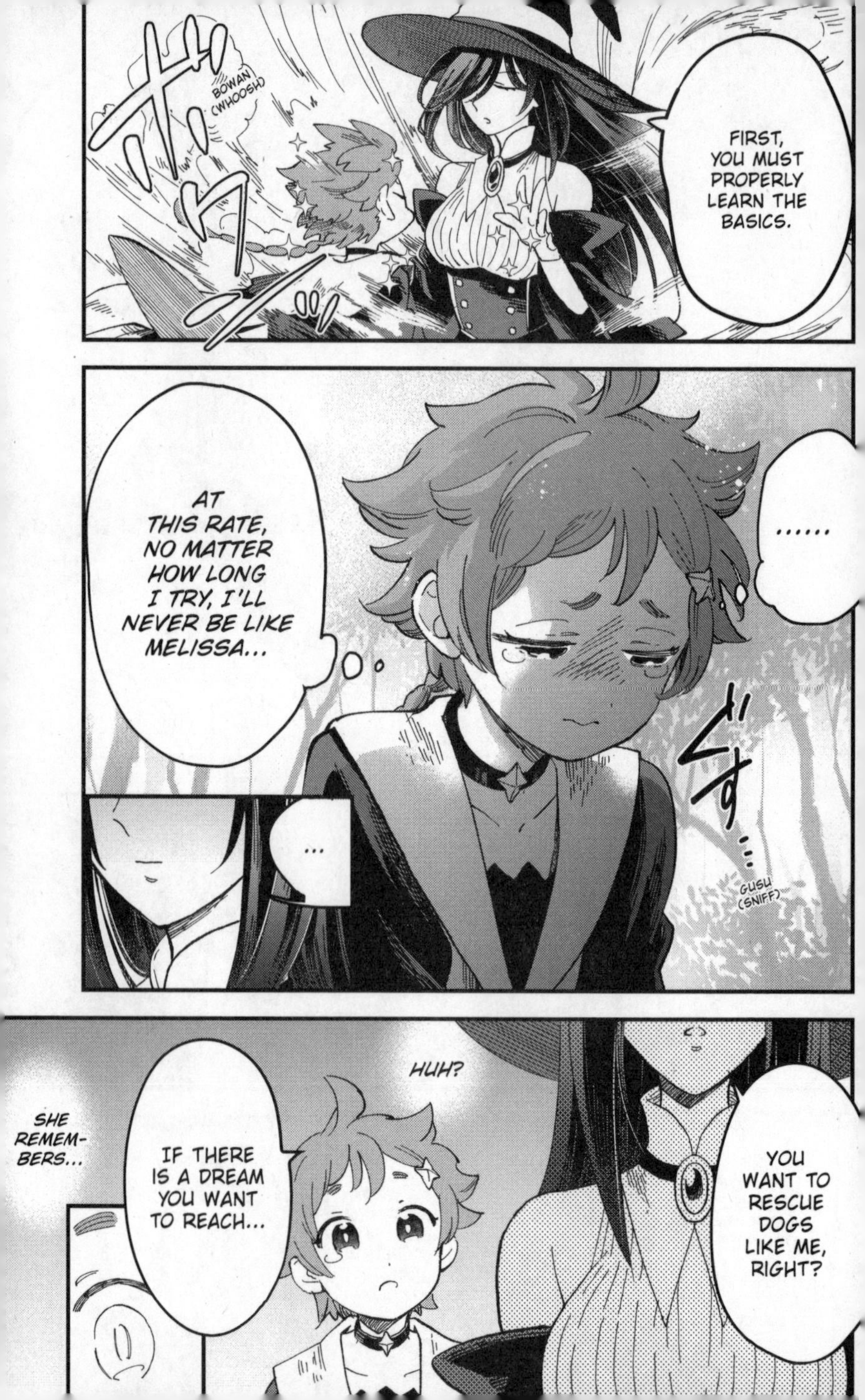
FIRST, YOU MUST PROPERLY LEARN THE BASICS.
BOWAN (WHOOSH)
......
AT THIS RATE, NO MATTER HOW LONG I TRY, I'LL NEVER BE LIKE MELISSA...
GUSU (SNIFF)
...
YOU WANT TO RESCUE DOGS LIKE ME, RIGHT?
HUH?
IF THERE IS A DREAM YOU WANT TO REACH...
SHE REMEM-BERS...

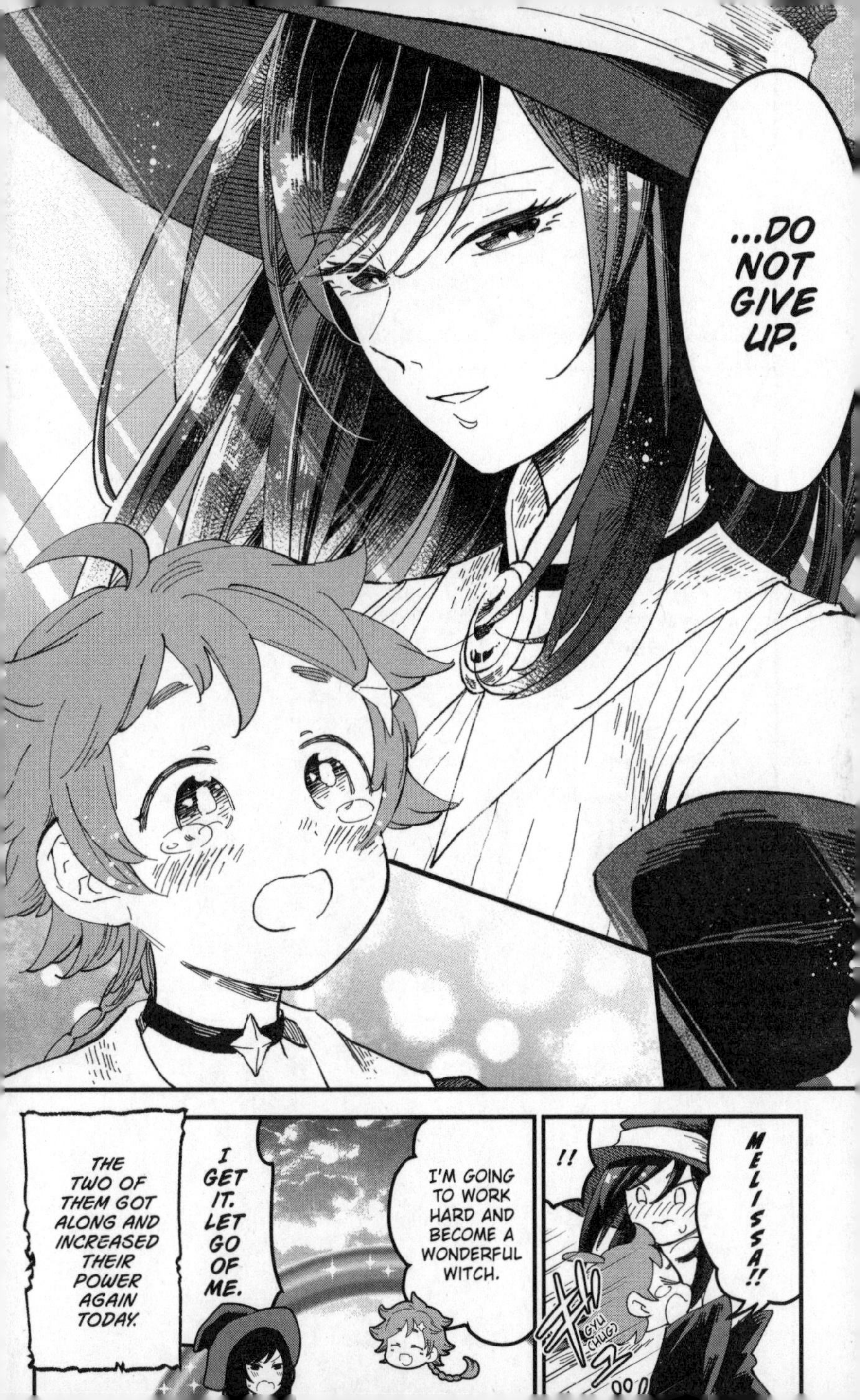
...DO NOT GIVE UP.
MELISSA!!
!!
GYU (HUG)
I'M GOING TO WORK HARD AND BECOME A WONDERFUL WITCH.
I GET IT. LET GO OF ME.
THE TWO OF THEM GOT ALONG AND INCREASED THEIR POWER AGAIN TODAY.

The Witch's Nursing ~Tanya Edition~

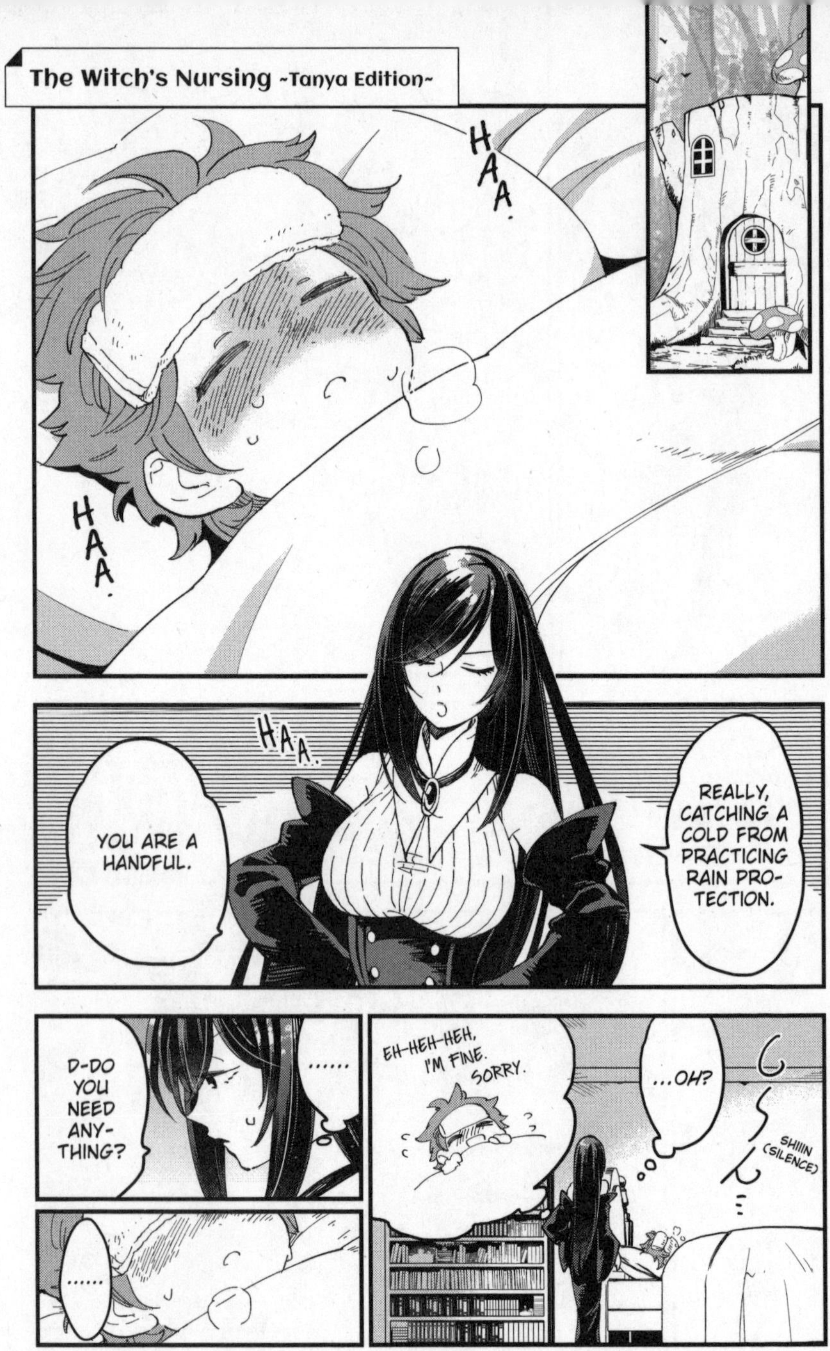
HAA.
HAA.
REALLY, CATCHING A COLD FROM PRACTICING RAIN PRO-TECTION.
HAA.
YOU ARE A HANDFUL.
...OH?
SHIIIN (SILENCE)
EH-HEH-HEH, I'M FINE. SORRY.
......
D-DO YOU NEED ANY-THING?
......

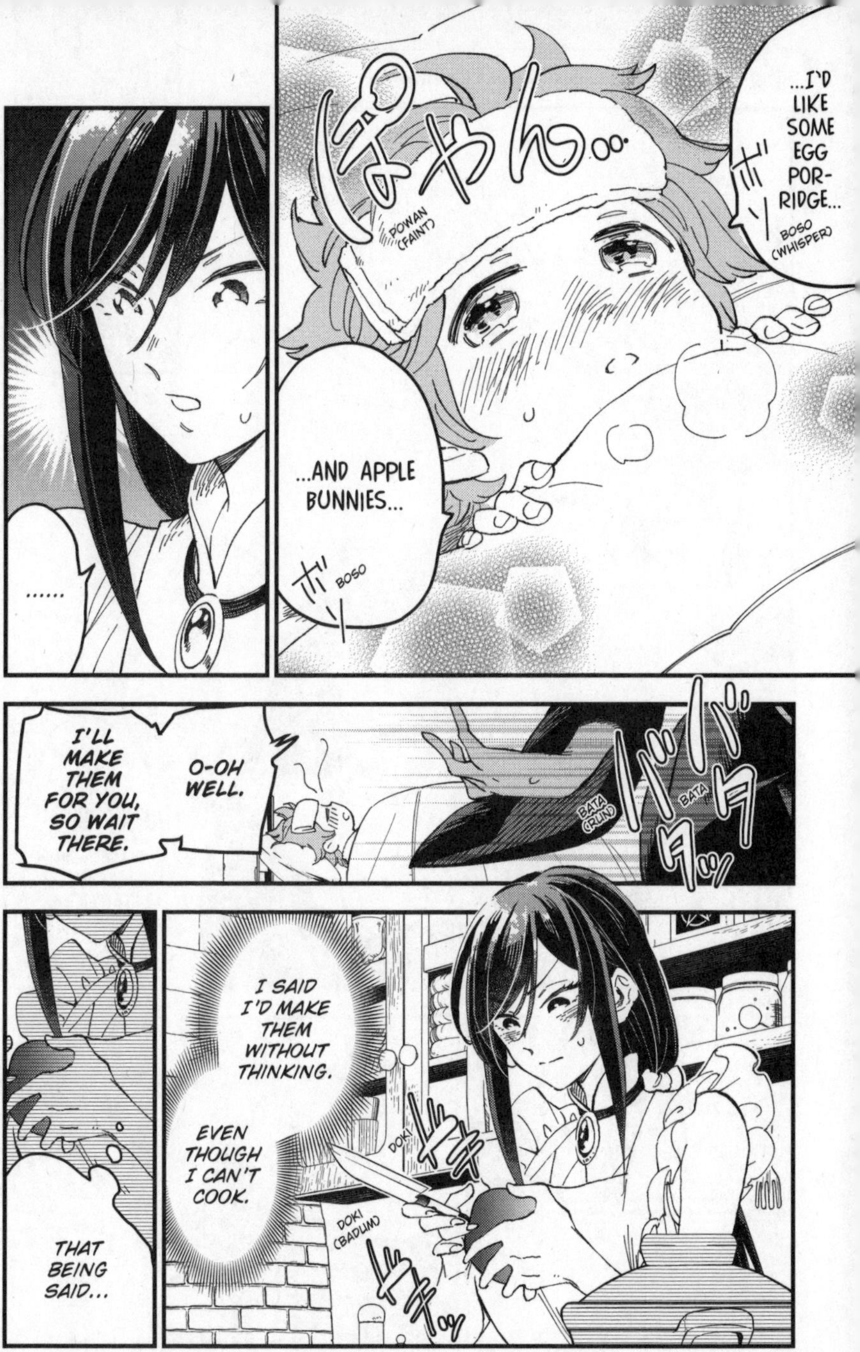
ぽやん。。
POWAN (FAINT)
...I'D LIKE SOME EGG POR-RIDGE...
ボソ
BOSO (WHISPER)
...AND APPLE BUNNIES...
ボソ
BOSO
......
バタ
BATA (RUN)
バタッ
BATA
O-OH WELL.
I'LL MAKE THEM FOR YOU, SO WAIT THERE.
I SAID I'D MAKE THEM WITHOUT THINKING.
EVEN THOUGH I CAN'T COOK.
ドキ
DOKI
ドキッ
DOKI (BADUM)
THAT BEING SAID...

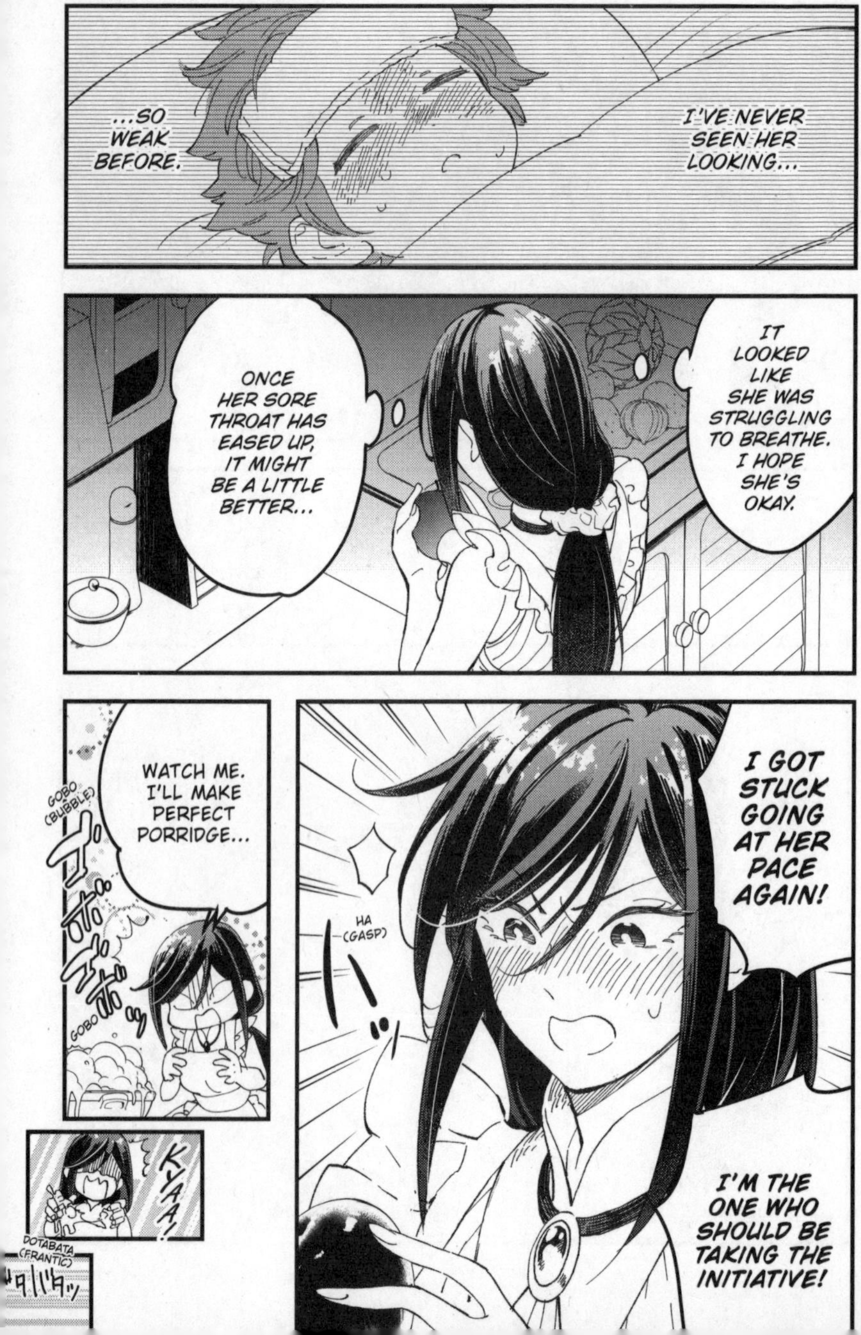
I'VE NEVER SEEN HER LOOKING...
...SO WEAK BEFORE.
IT LOOKED LIKE SHE WAS STRUGGLING TO BREATHE. I HOPE SHE'S OKAY.
ONCE HER SORE THROAT HAS EASED UP, IT MIGHT BE A LITTLE BETTER...
I GOT STUCK GOING AT HER PACE AGAIN!
HA (GASP)
I'M THE ONE WHO SHOULD BE TAKING THE INITIATIVE!
WATCH ME. I'LL MAKE PERFECT PORRIDGE...
GOBO (BUBBLE)
GOBO
KYAA!
DOTABATA (FRANTIC)

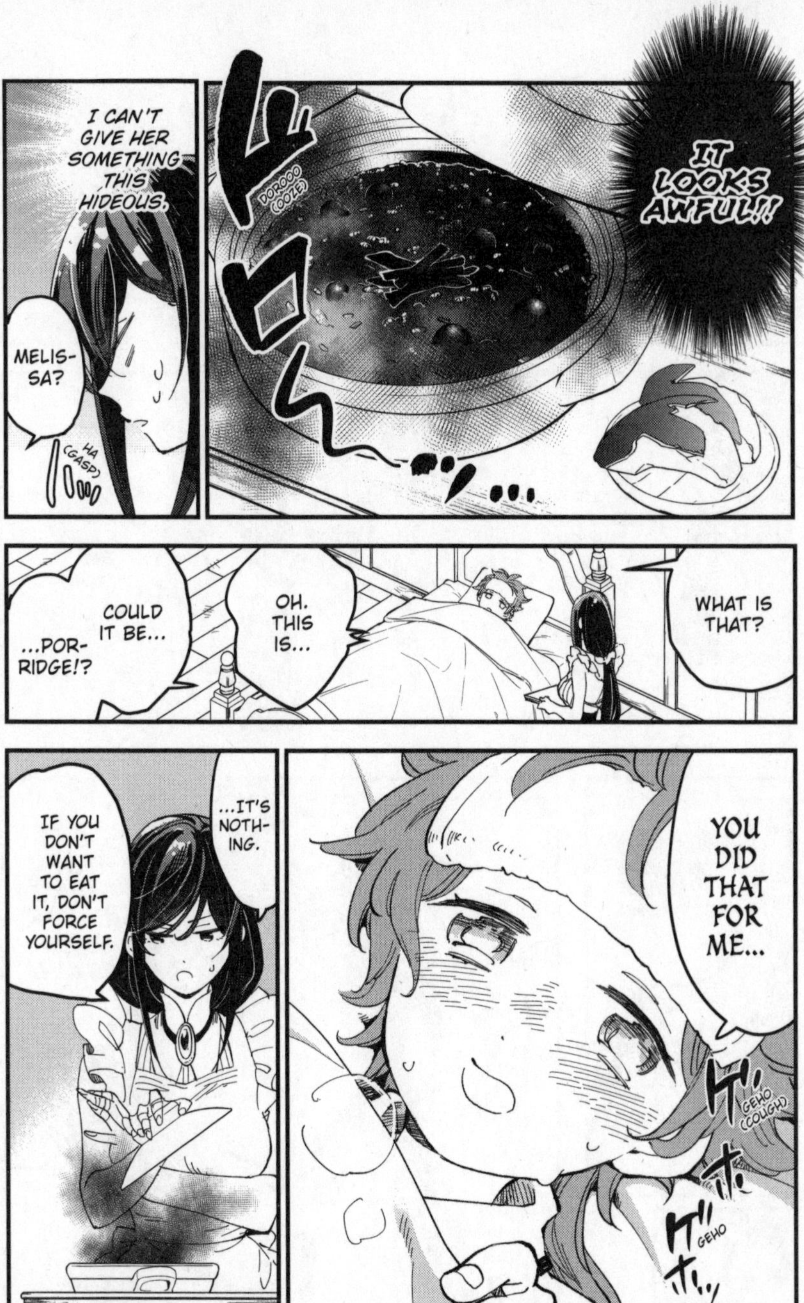
IT LOOKS AWFUL!!
DOROOO (OOZE)
I CAN'T GIVE HER SOMETHING THIS HIDEOUS.
MELIS-SA?
HA (GASP)
WHAT IS THAT?
OH. THIS IS...
COULD IT BE... ...POR-RIDGE!?
YOU DID THAT FOR ME...
GEHO (COUGH)
GEHO
...IT'S NOTH-ING.
IF YOU DON'T WANT TO EAT IT, DON'T FORCE YOURSELF.

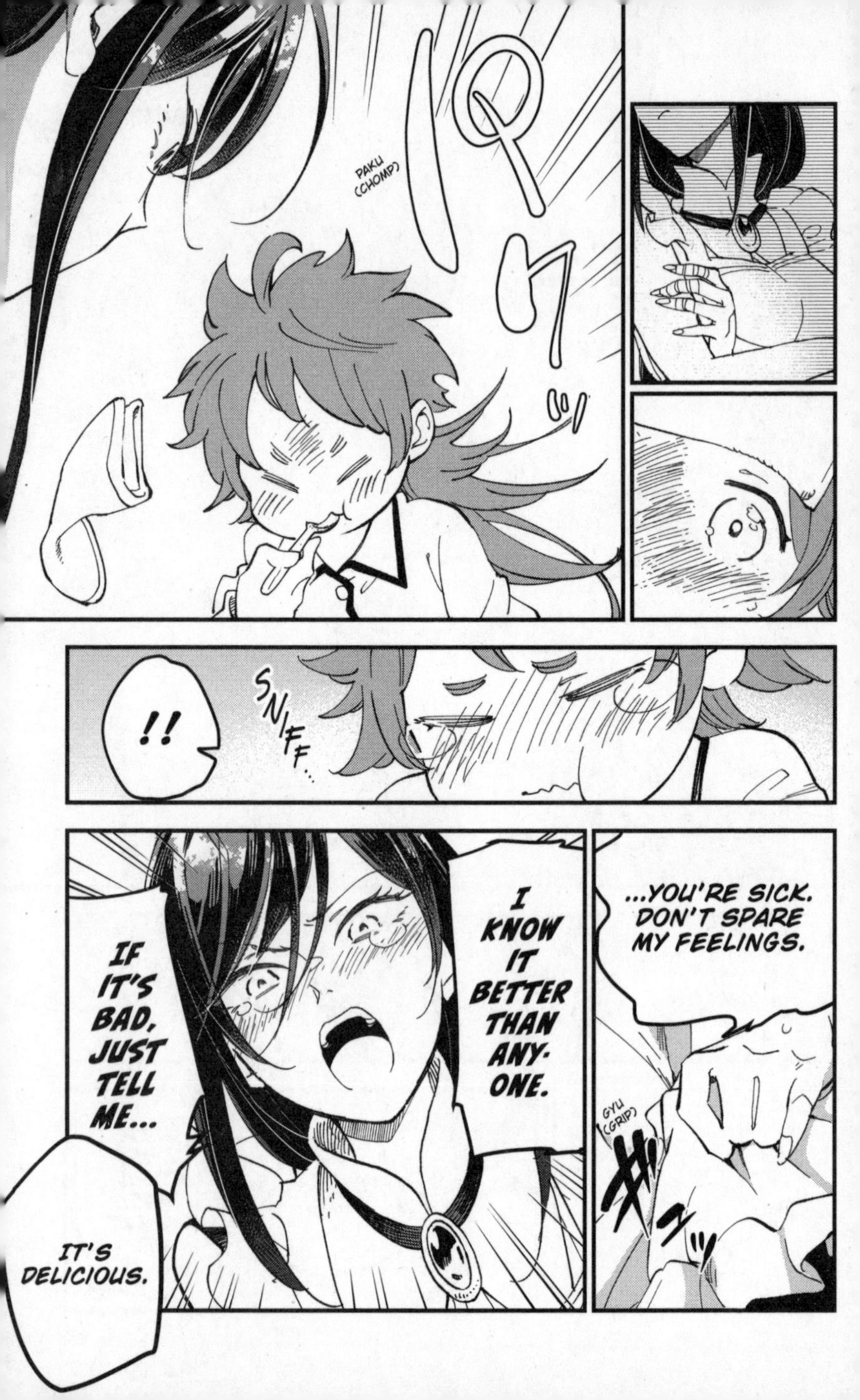
PAKU (CHOMP)
SNIFF...
!!
...YOU'RE SICK. DON'T SPARE MY FEELINGS.
GYU (GRIP)
I KNOW IT BETTER THAN ANY-ONE.
IF IT'S BAD, JUST TELL ME...
IT'S DELICIOUS.

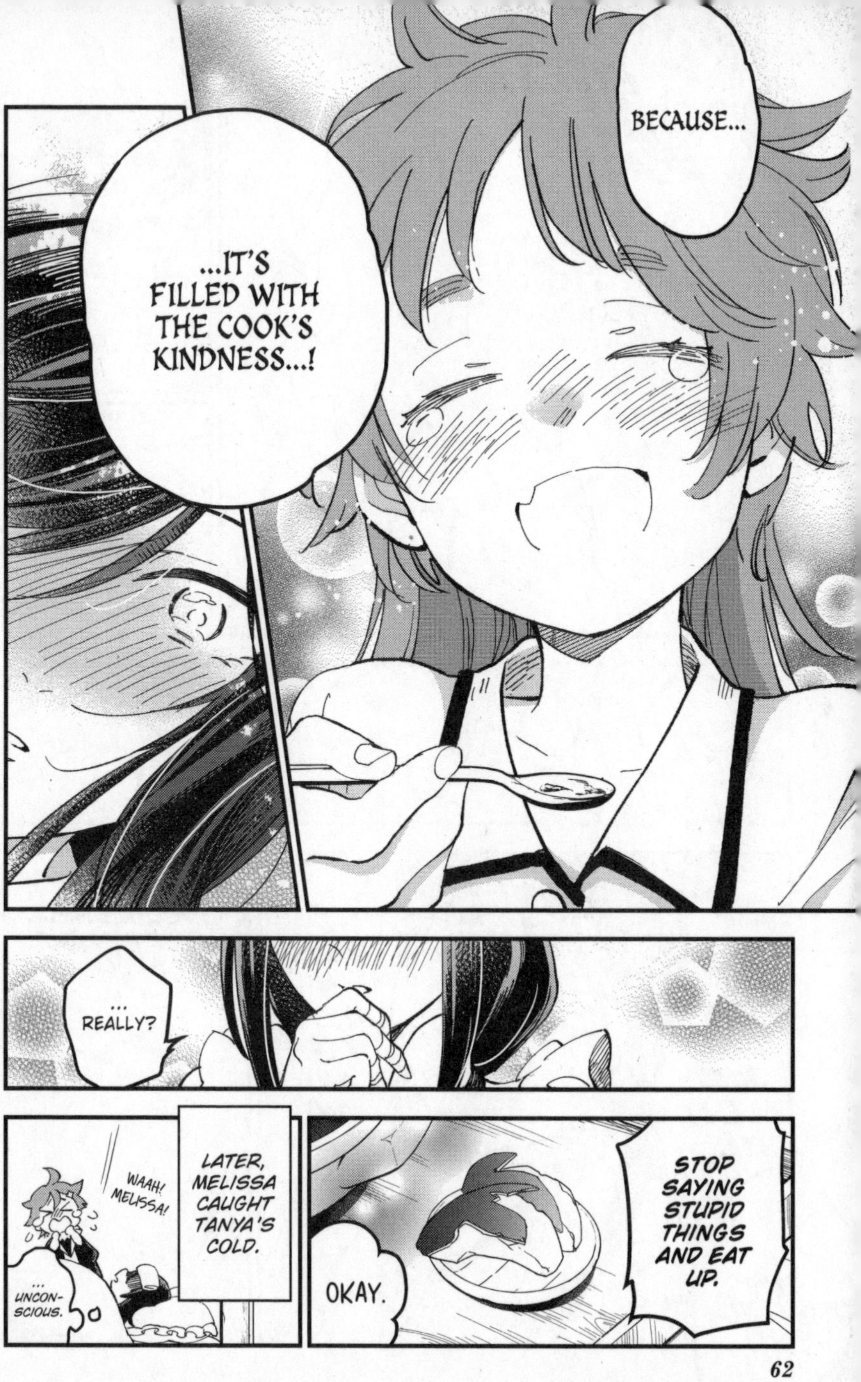
BECAUSE...
...IT'S FILLED WITH THE COOK'S KINDNESS...!
... REALLY?
STOP SAYING STUPID THINGS AND EAT UP.
OKAY.
LATER, MELISSA CAUGHT TANYA'S COLD.
WAAH! MELISSA!
... UNCON-SCIOUS.

The Witch's Nursing ~Melissa Edition~

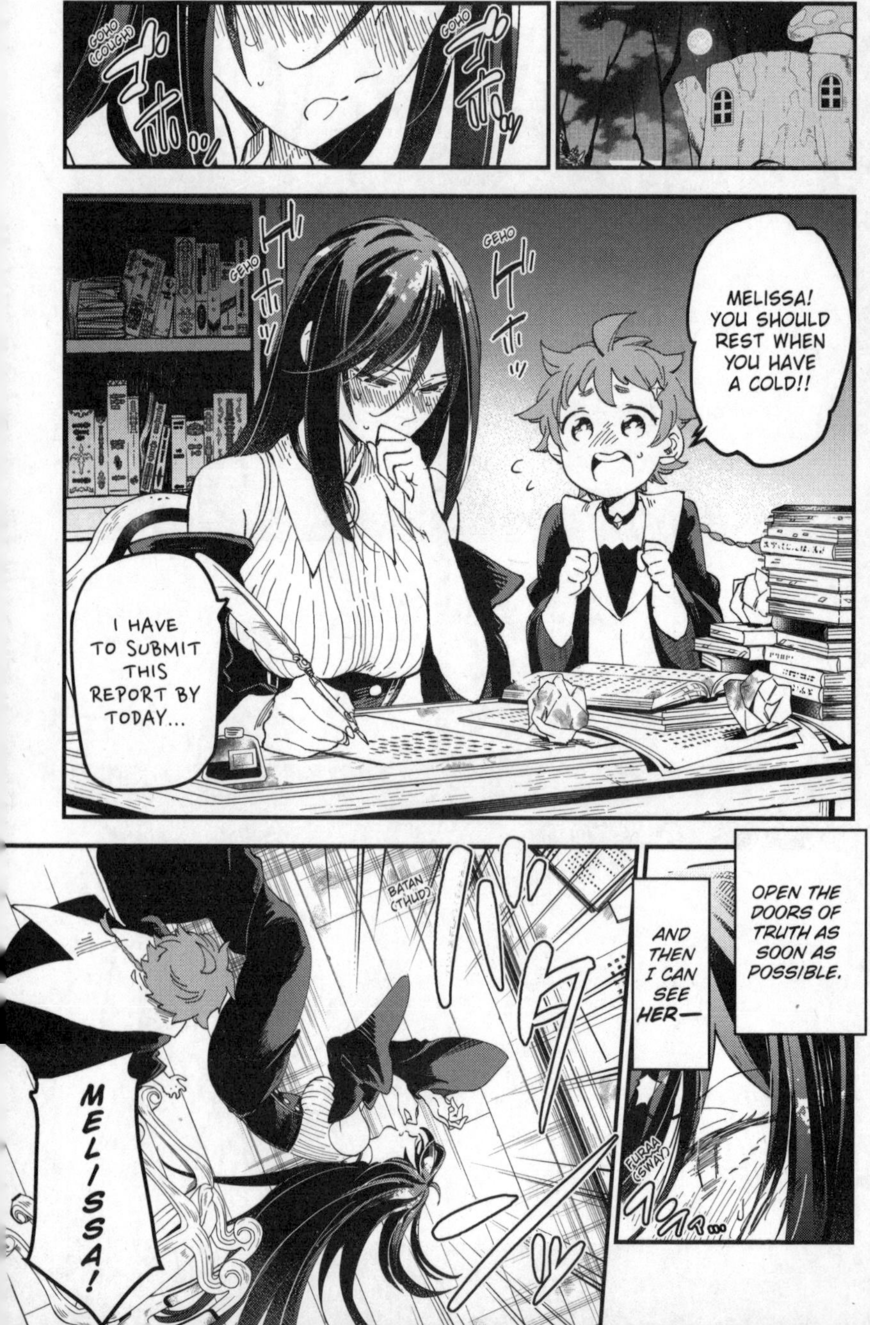
GOHO
GOHO (COUGH)
GEHO
GEHO
MELISSA! YOU SHOULD REST WHEN YOU HAVE A COLD!!
I HAVE TO SUBMIT THIS REPORT BY TODAY...
OPEN THE DOORS OF TRUTH AS SOONS AS POSSIBLE.
AND THEN I CAN SEE HER—
FURAA (SWAY)
BATAN (THUD)
MELISSA!

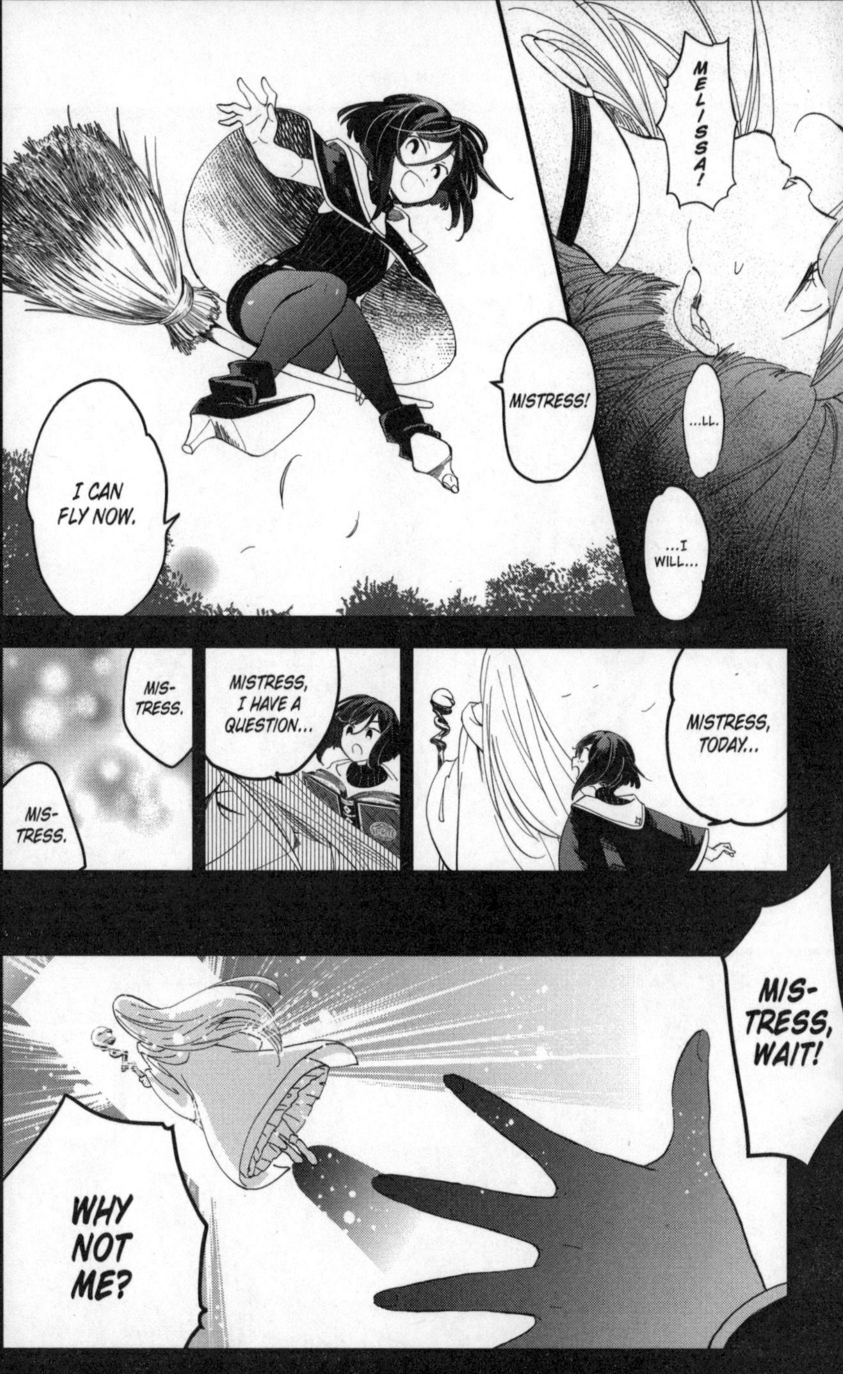
MELISSA!
...LL.
...I WILL...
MISTRESS!
I CAN FLY NOW.
MISTRESS, TODAY...
MISTRESS, I HAVE A QUESTION...
MIS-TRESS.
MIS-TRESS.
MIS-TRESS, WAIT!
WHY NOT ME?

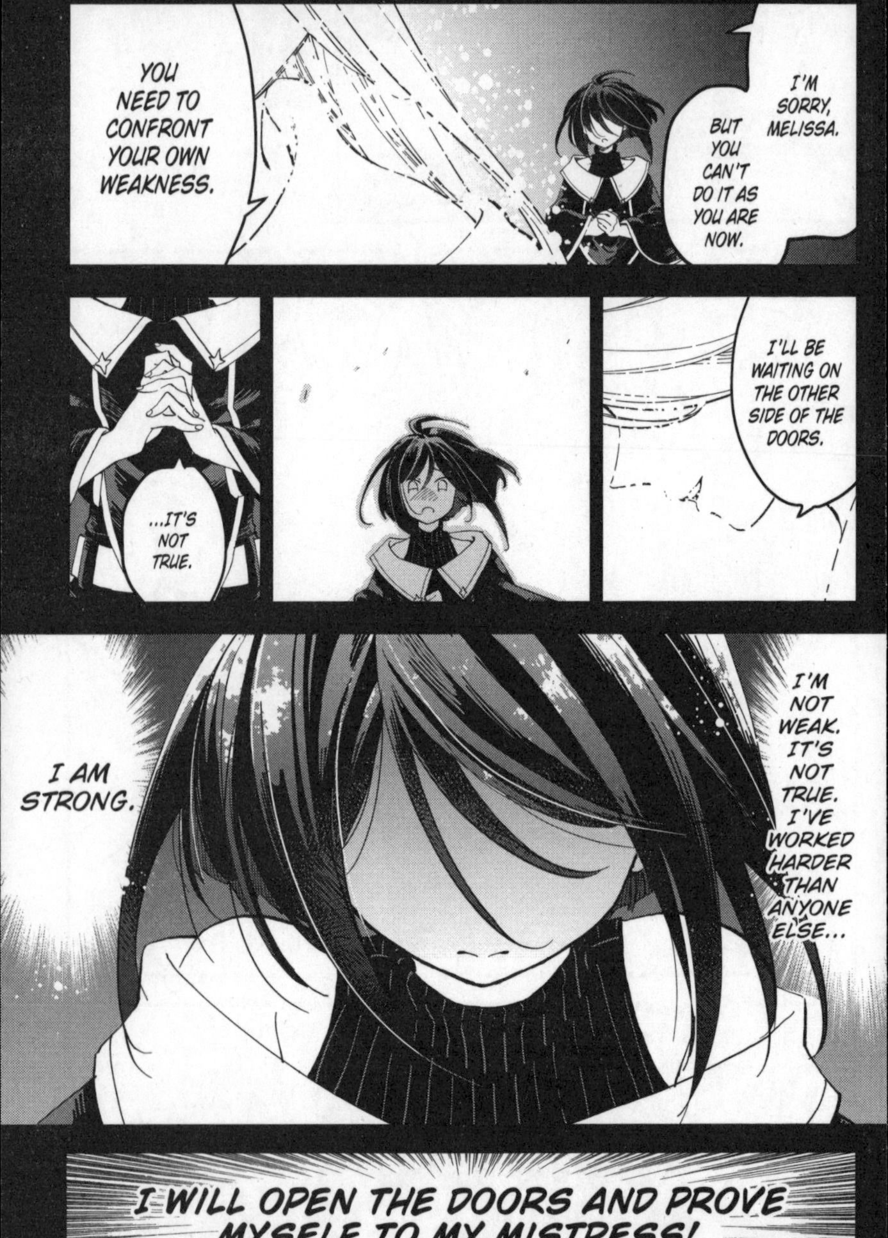
I'M SORRY, MELISSA.
BUT YOU CAN'T DO IT AS YOU ARE NOW.
YOU NEED TO CONFRONT YOUR OWN WEAKNESS.
I'LL BE WAITING ON THE OTHER SIDE OF THE DOORS.
...IT'S NOT TRUE.
I'M NOT WEAK. IT'S NOT TRUE. I'VE WORKED HARDER THAN ANYONE ELSE...
I AM STRONG.
I WILL OPEN THE DOORS AND PROVE MYSELF TO MY MISTRESS!

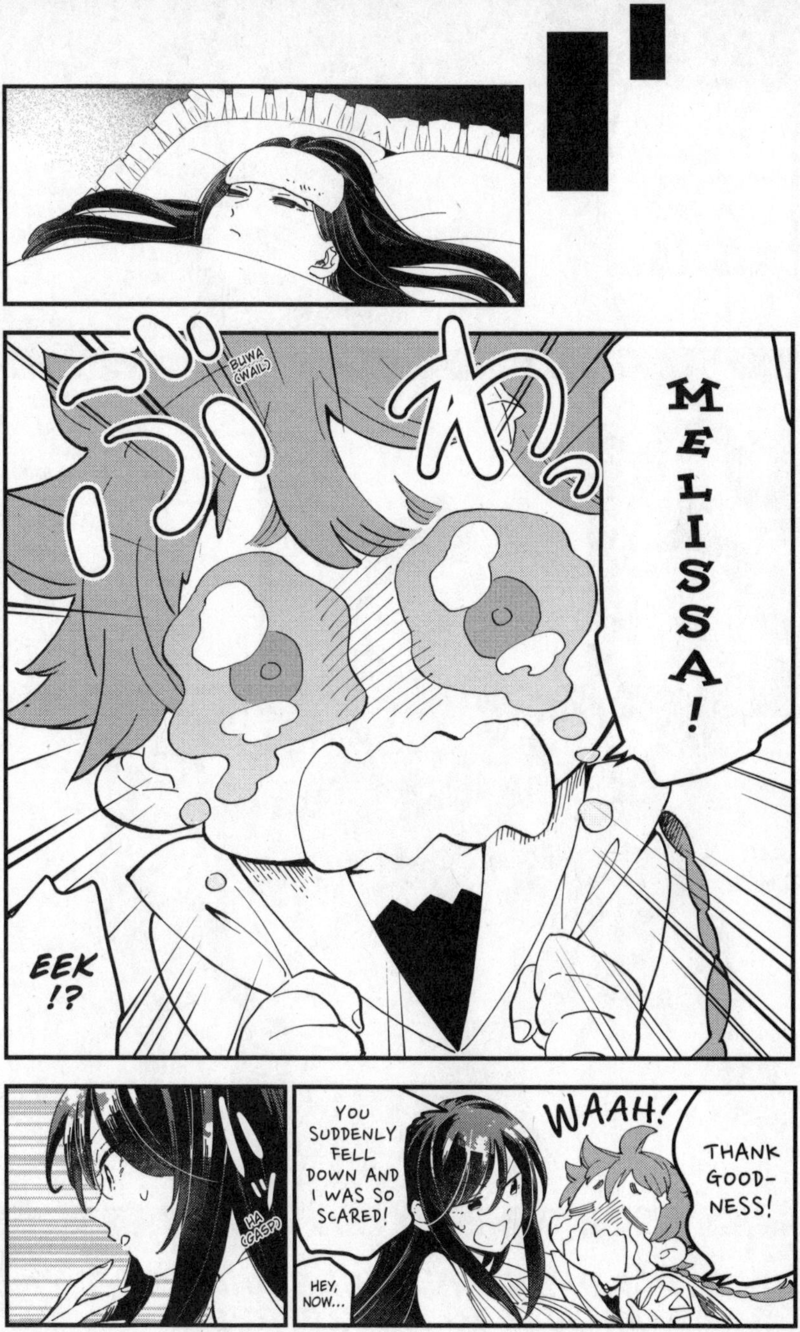
MELISSA!
BUWA (WAIL)
EEK !?
THANK GOOD-NESS!
WAAH!
YOU SUDDENLY FELL DOWN AND I WAS SO SCARED!
HEY, NOW...
HA (GASP)

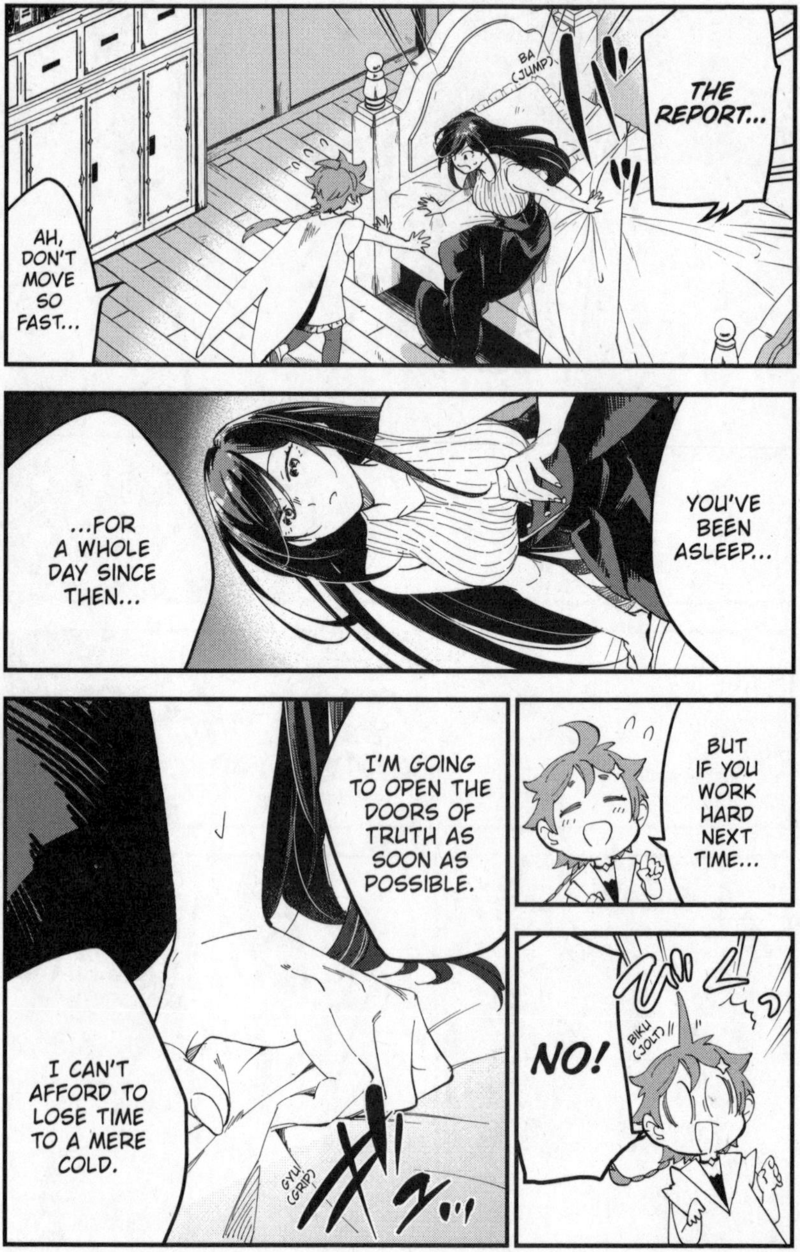
THE REPORT...
BA (JUMP)
AH, DON'T MOVE SO FAST...
YOU'VE BEEN ASLEEP...
...FOR A WHOLE DAY SINCE THEN...
BUT IF YOU WORK HARD NEXT TIME...
BIKU (JOLT)
NO!
I'M GOING TO OPEN THE DOORS OF TRUTH AS SOON AS POSSIBLE.
I CAN'T AFFORD TO LOSE TIME TO A MERE COLD.
GYU (GRIP)

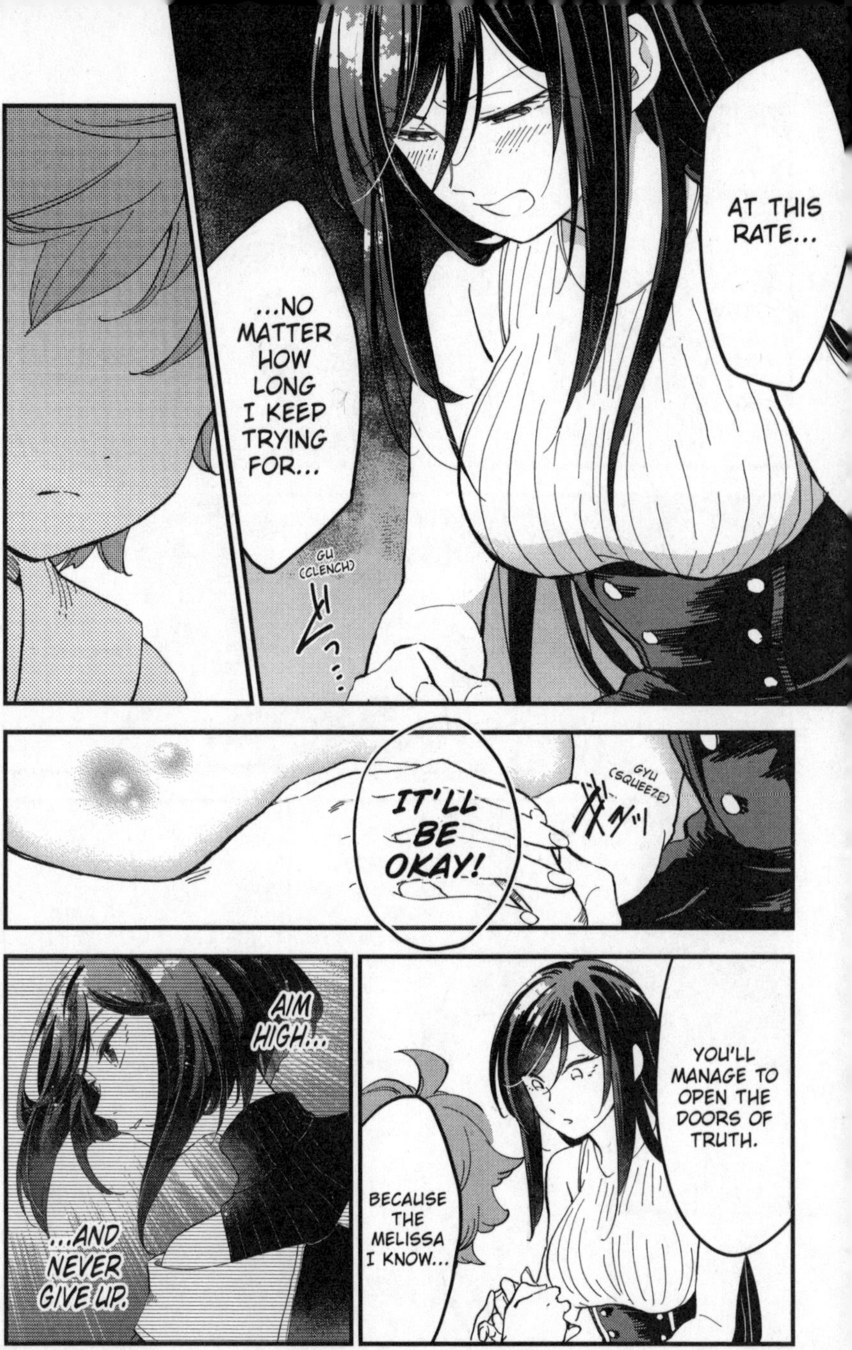
AT THIS RATE...
...NO MATTER HOW LONG I KEEP TRYING FOR...
GU (CLENCH)
GYU (SQUEEZE)
IT'LL BE OKAY!
YOU'LL MANAGE TO OPEN THE DOORS OF TRUTH.
BECAUSE THE MELISSA I KNOW...
AIM HIGH...
...AND NEVER GIVE UP.

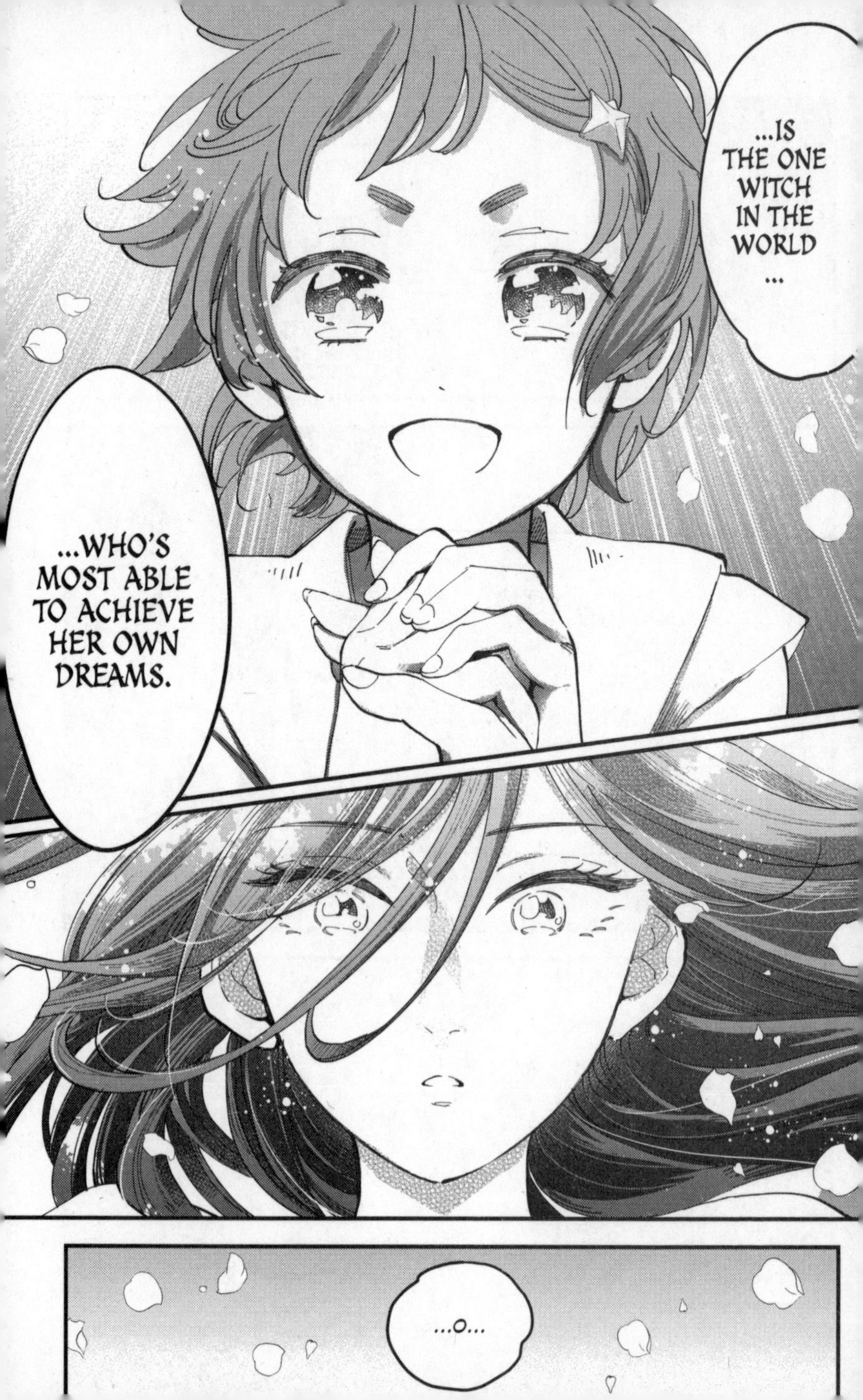
...IS THE ONE WITCH IN THE WORLD ...
...WHO'S MOST ABLE TO ACHIEVE HER OWN DREAMS.
...O...

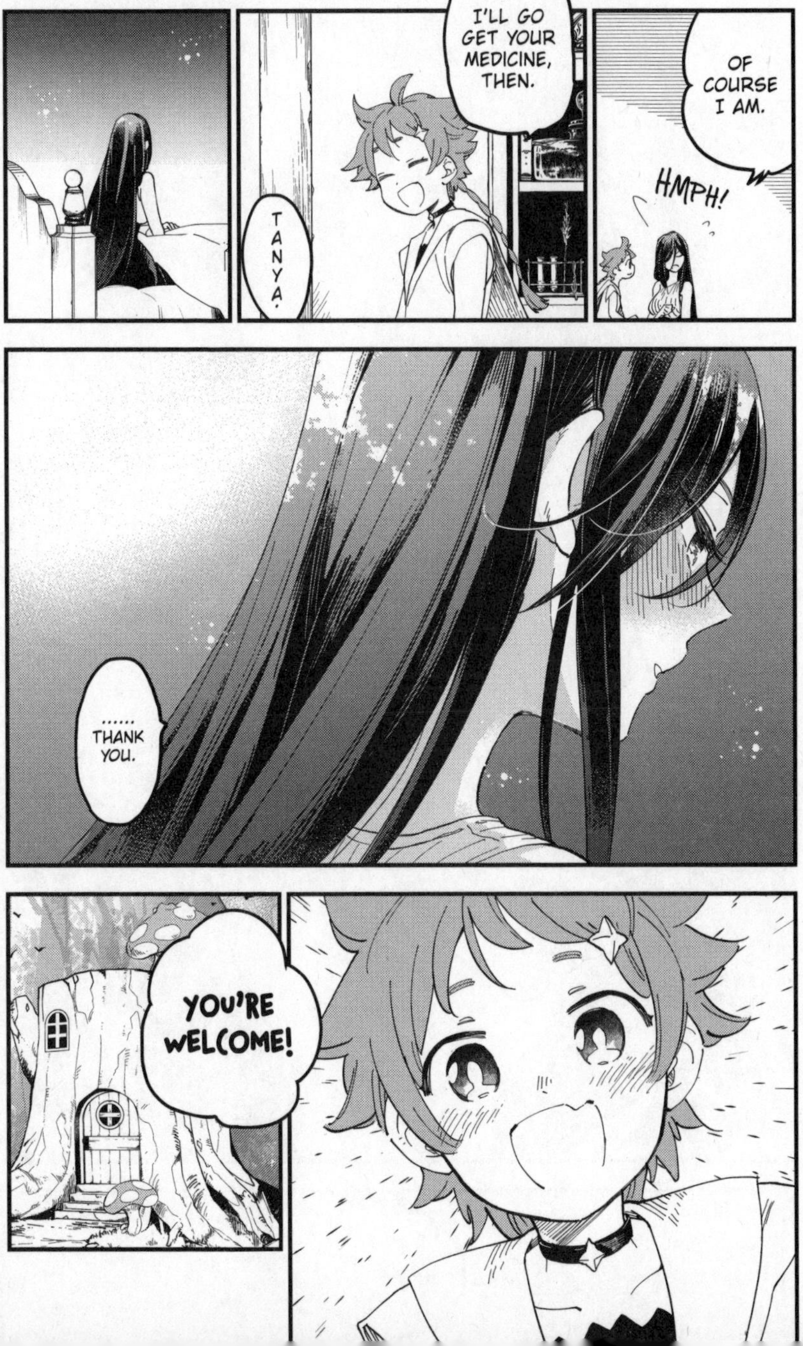
OF COURSE I AM.
HMPH!
I'LL GO GET YOUR MEDICINE, THEN.
TANYA.
...... THANK YOU.
YOU'RE WELCOME!

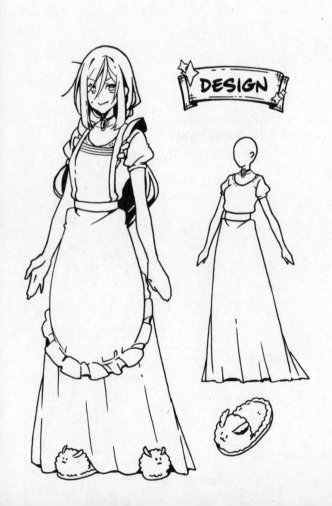

DESIGN

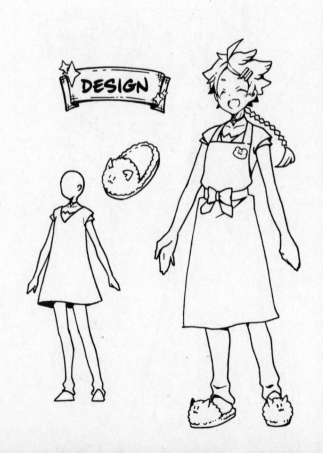

DESIGN

The Witch's True Character

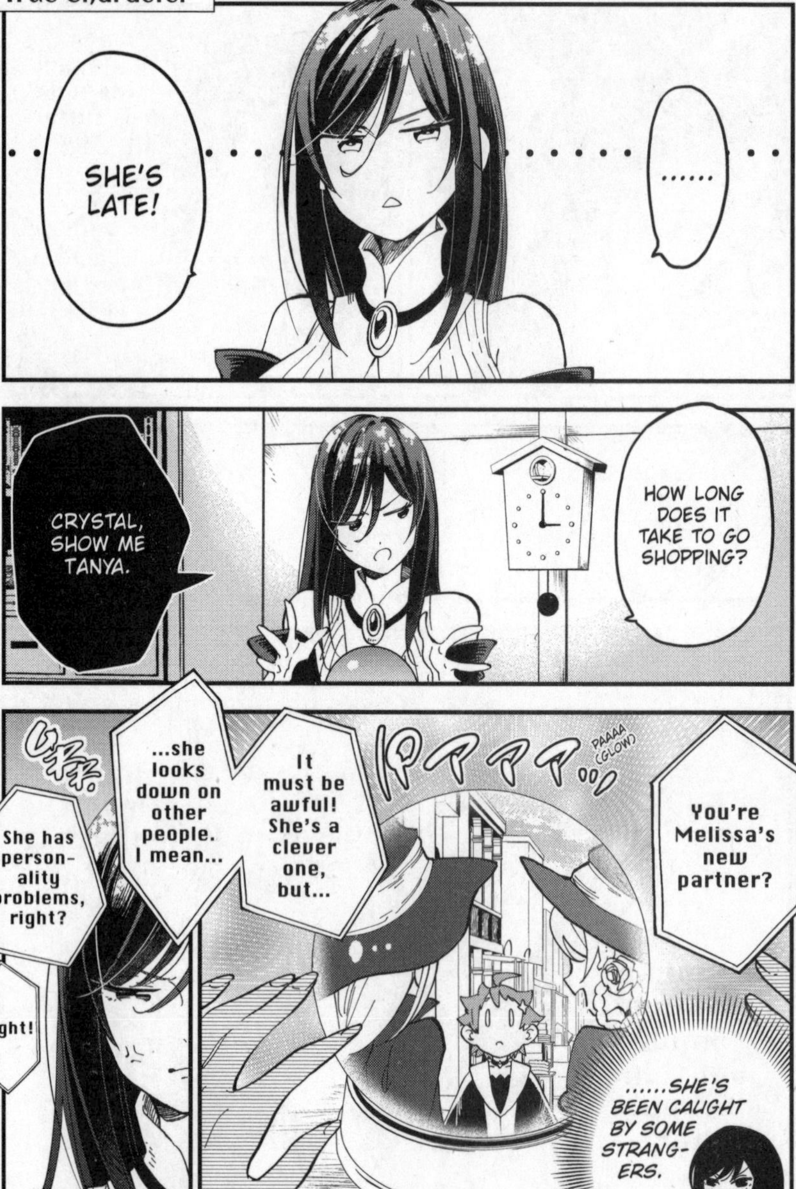
......
SHE'S LATE!
HOW LONG DOES IT TAKE TO GO SHOPPING?
CRYSTAL, SHOW ME TANYA.
PAAAA (GLOW)
You're Melissa's new partner?
It must be awful! She's a clever one, but...
...she looks down on other people. I mean...
......SHE'S BEEN CAUGHT BY SOME STRANGERS.
She has personality problems, right?
Right!

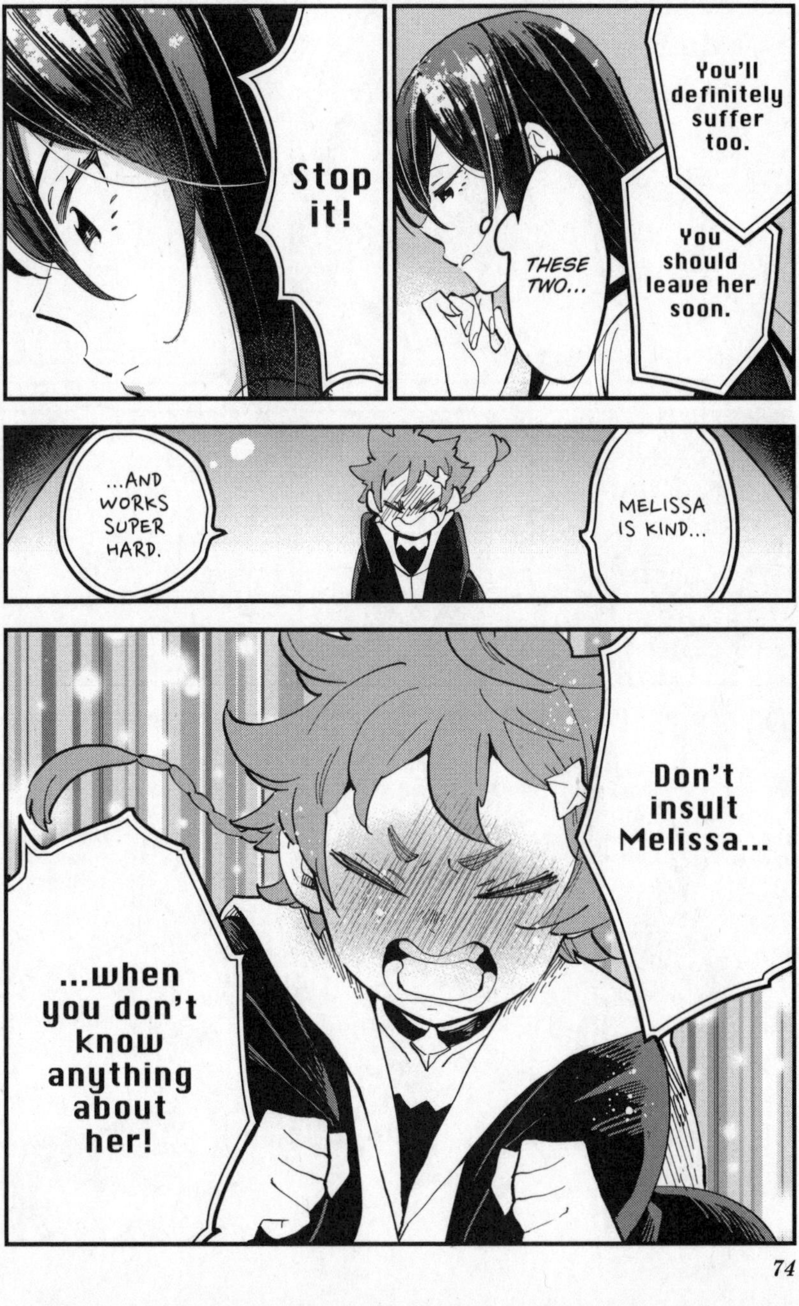

You'll definitely suffer too.
You should leave her soon.
THESE TWO...
Stop it!
MELISSA IS KIND...
...AND WORKS SUPER HARD.
Don't insult Melissa...
...when you don't know anything about her!

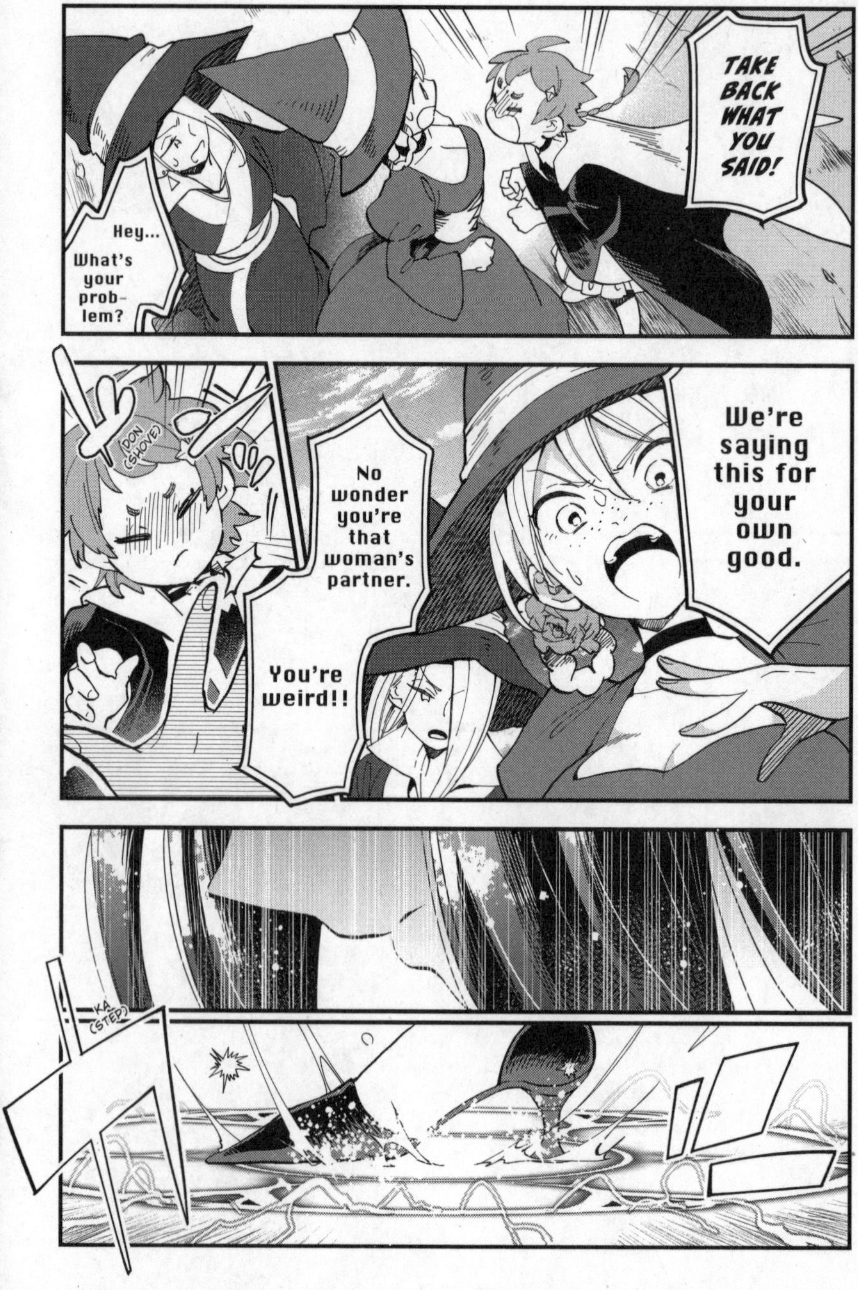
TAKE BACK WHAT YOU SAID!
Hey... What's your prob-lem?
We're saying this for your own good.
No wonder you're that woman's partner.
You're weird!!
DON (SHOVE)
KA (STEP)

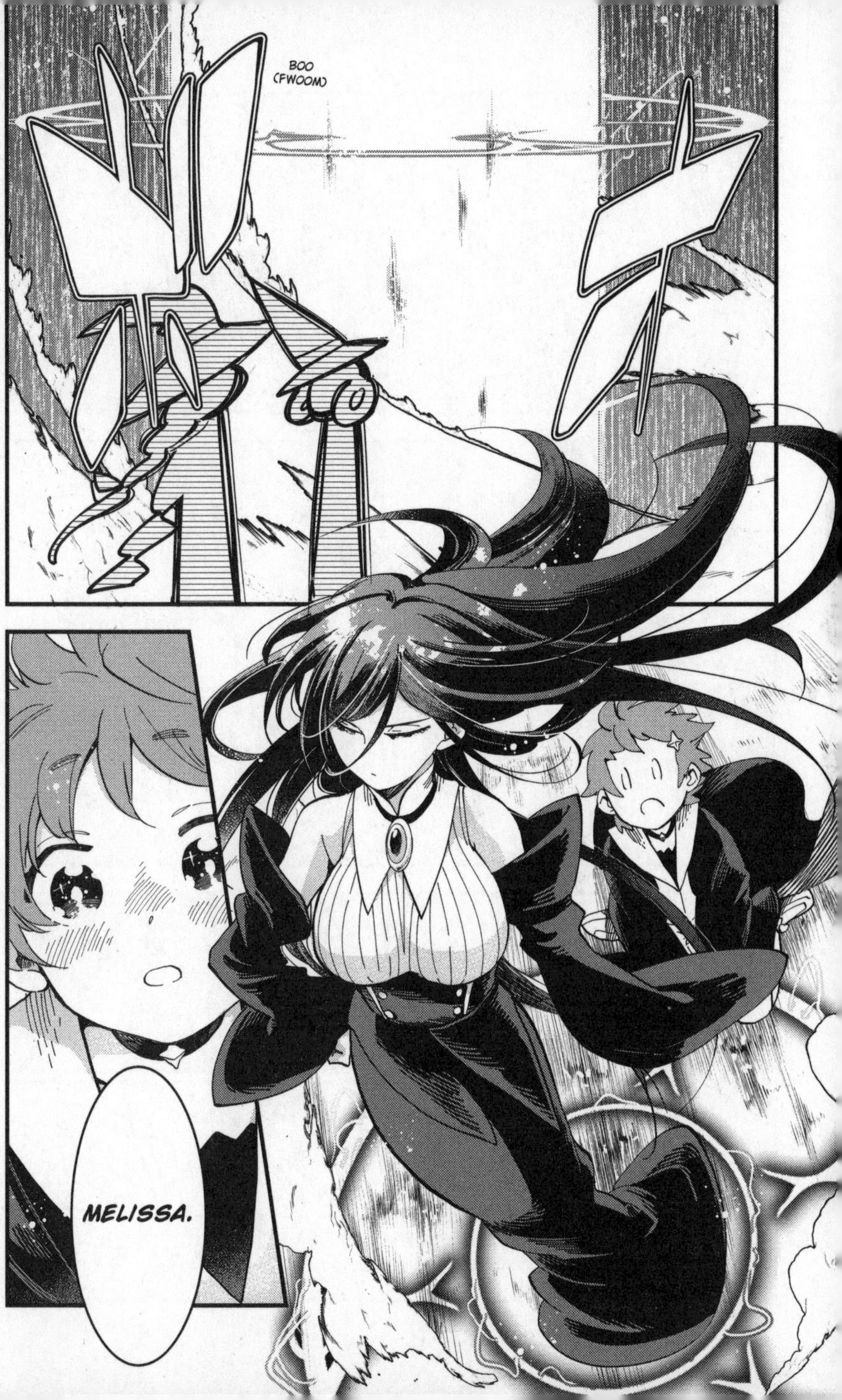
BOO
(FWOOM)
MELISSA.

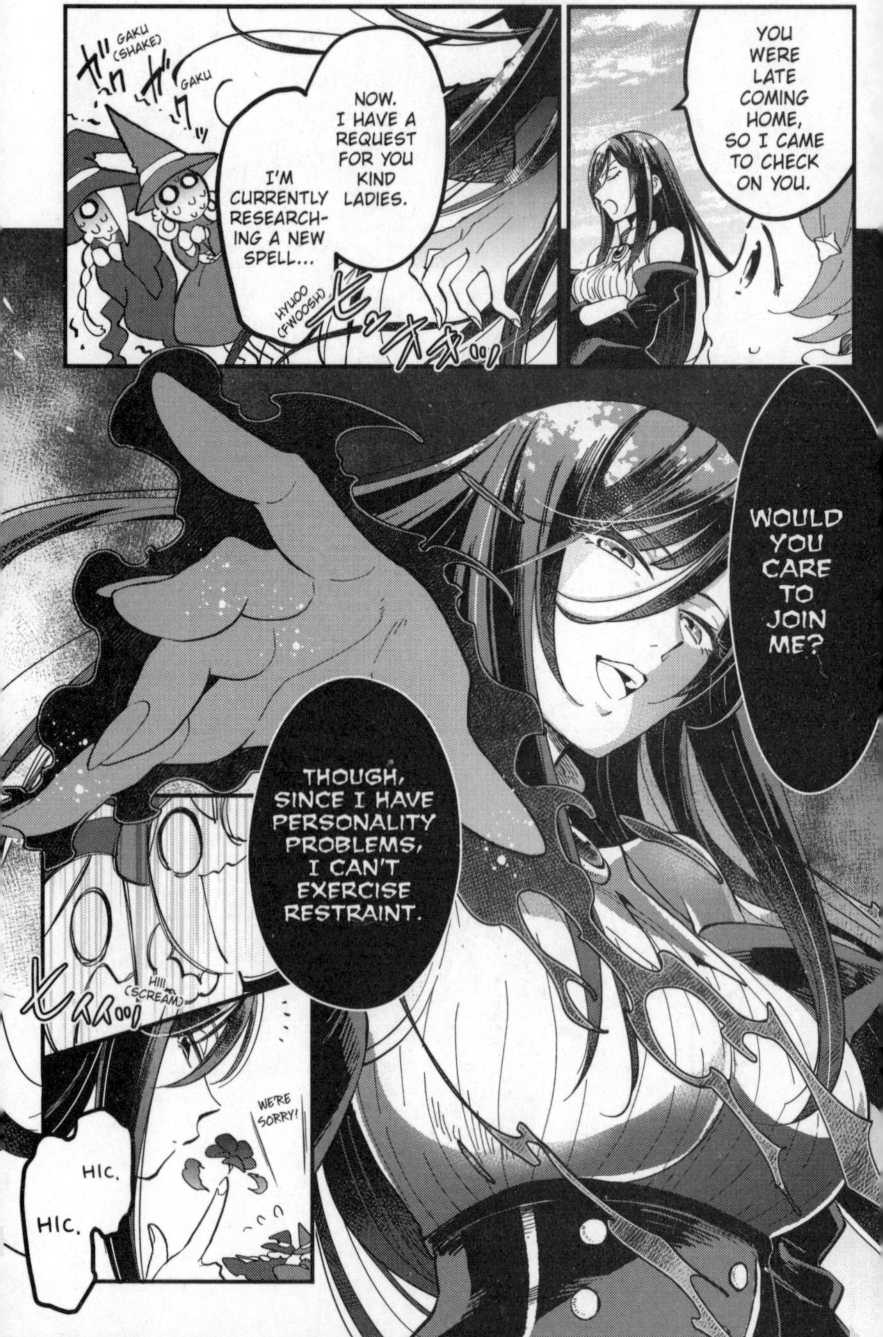

YOU WERE LATE COMING HOME, SO I CAME TO CHECK ON YOU.
GAKU (SHAKE)
GAKU
NOW. I HAVE A REQUEST FOR YOU KIND LADIES.
I'M CURRENTLY RESEARCHING A NEW SPELL...
HYUOO (FWOOSH)
WOULD YOU CARE TO JOIN ME?
THOUGH, SINCE I HAVE PERSONALITY PROBLEMS, I CAN'T EXERCISE RESTRAINT.
HIII (SCREAM)
WE'RE SORRY!
HIC.
HIC.

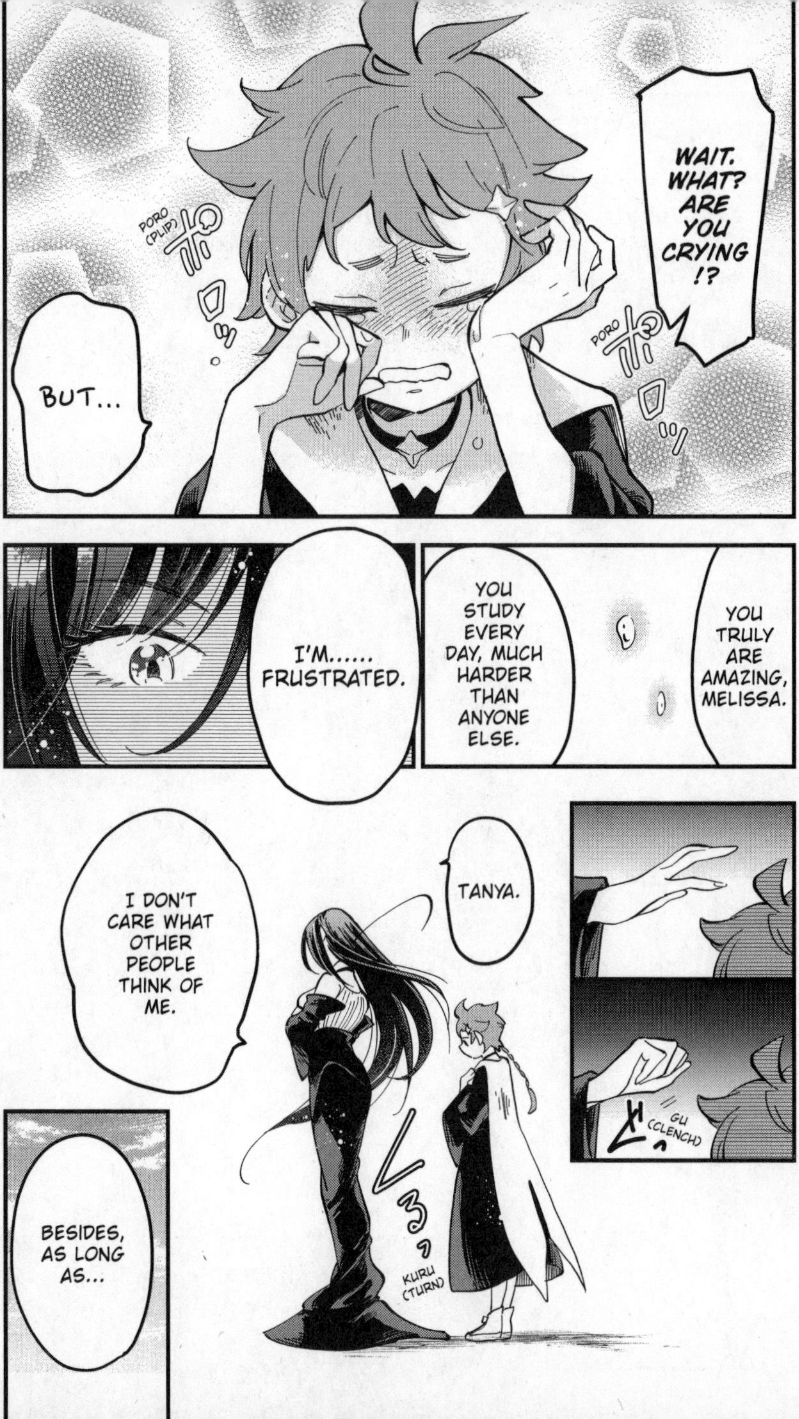
WAIT. WHAT? ARE YOU CRYING !?
PORO
PORO (PLIP)
BUT...
YOU TRULY ARE AMAZING, MELISSA.
YOU STUDY EVERY DAY, MUCH HARDER THAN ANYONE ELSE.
I'M...... FRUSTRATED.
GU (CLENCH)
TANYA.
I DON'T CARE WHAT OTHER PEOPLE THINK OF ME.
KURU (TURN)
BESIDES, AS LONG AS...

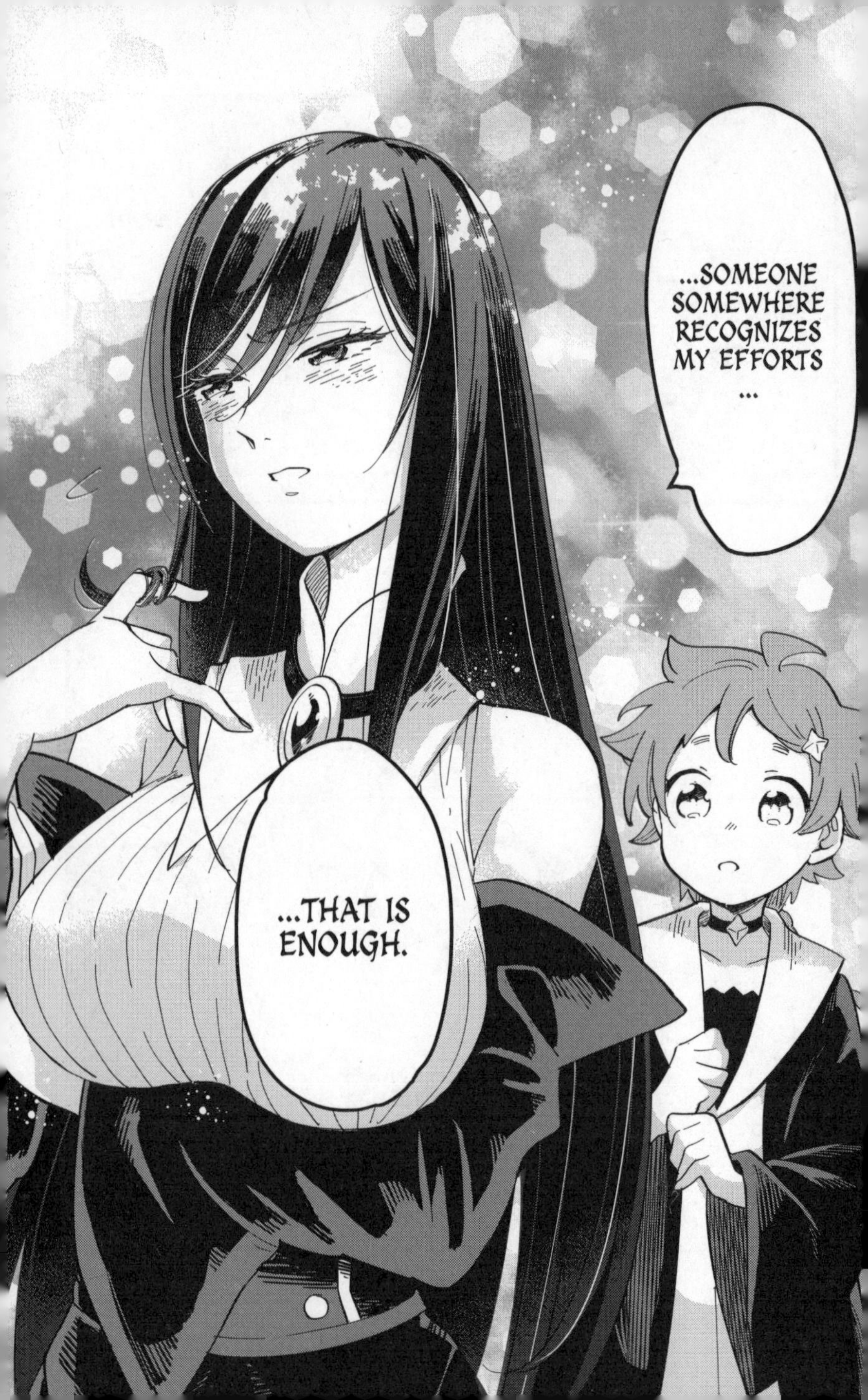
...SOMEONE SOMEWHERE RECOGNIZES MY EFFORTS ...
...THAT IS ENOUGH.

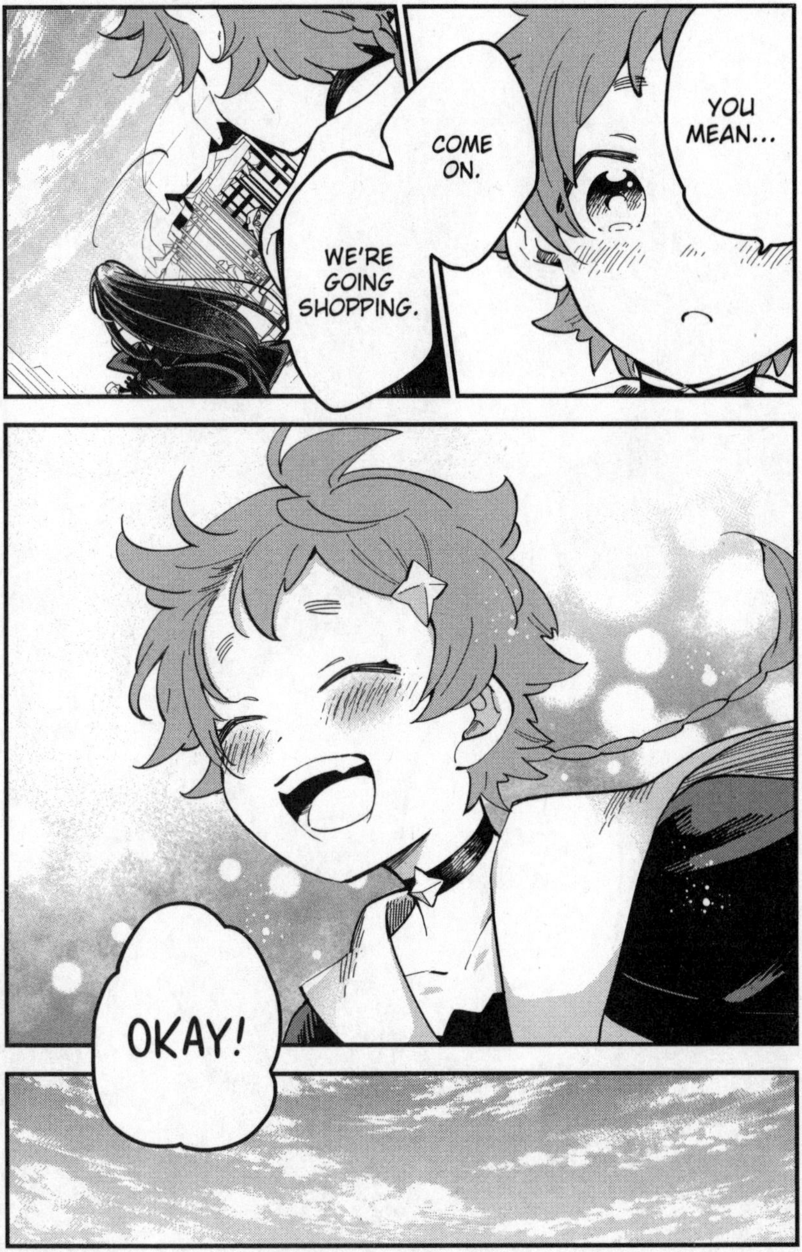
YOU MEAN...
COME ON.
WE'RE GOING SHOPPING.
OKAY!

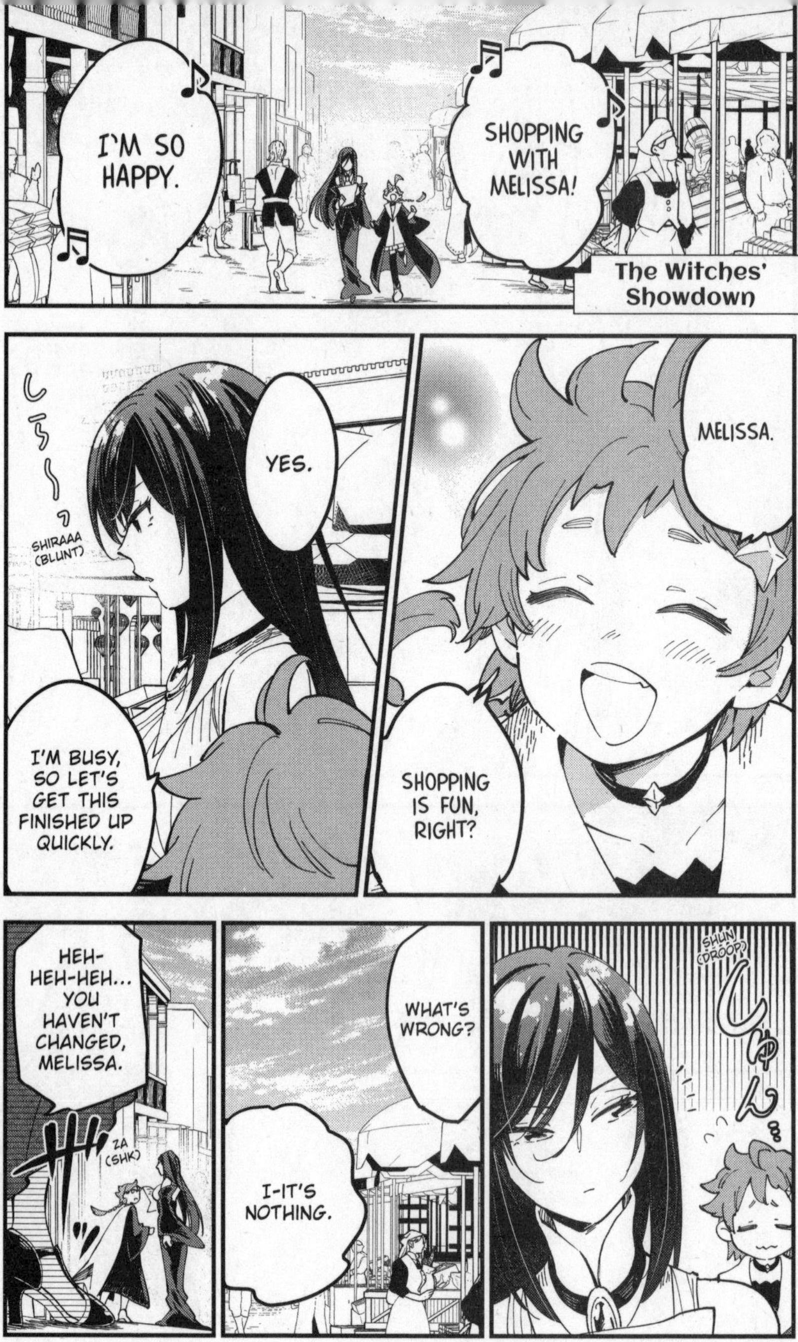
The Witches' Showdown
SHOPPING WITH MELISSA!
I'M SO HAPPY.
MELISSA.
SHOPPING IS FUN, RIGHT?
YES.
SHIRAAA (BLUNT)
I'M BUSY, SO LET'S GET THIS FINISHED UP QUICKLY.
SHUN (DROOP)
WHAT'S WRONG?
I-IT'S NOTHING.
HEH-HEH-HEH... YOU HAVEN'T CHANGED, MELISSA.
ZA (SHK)

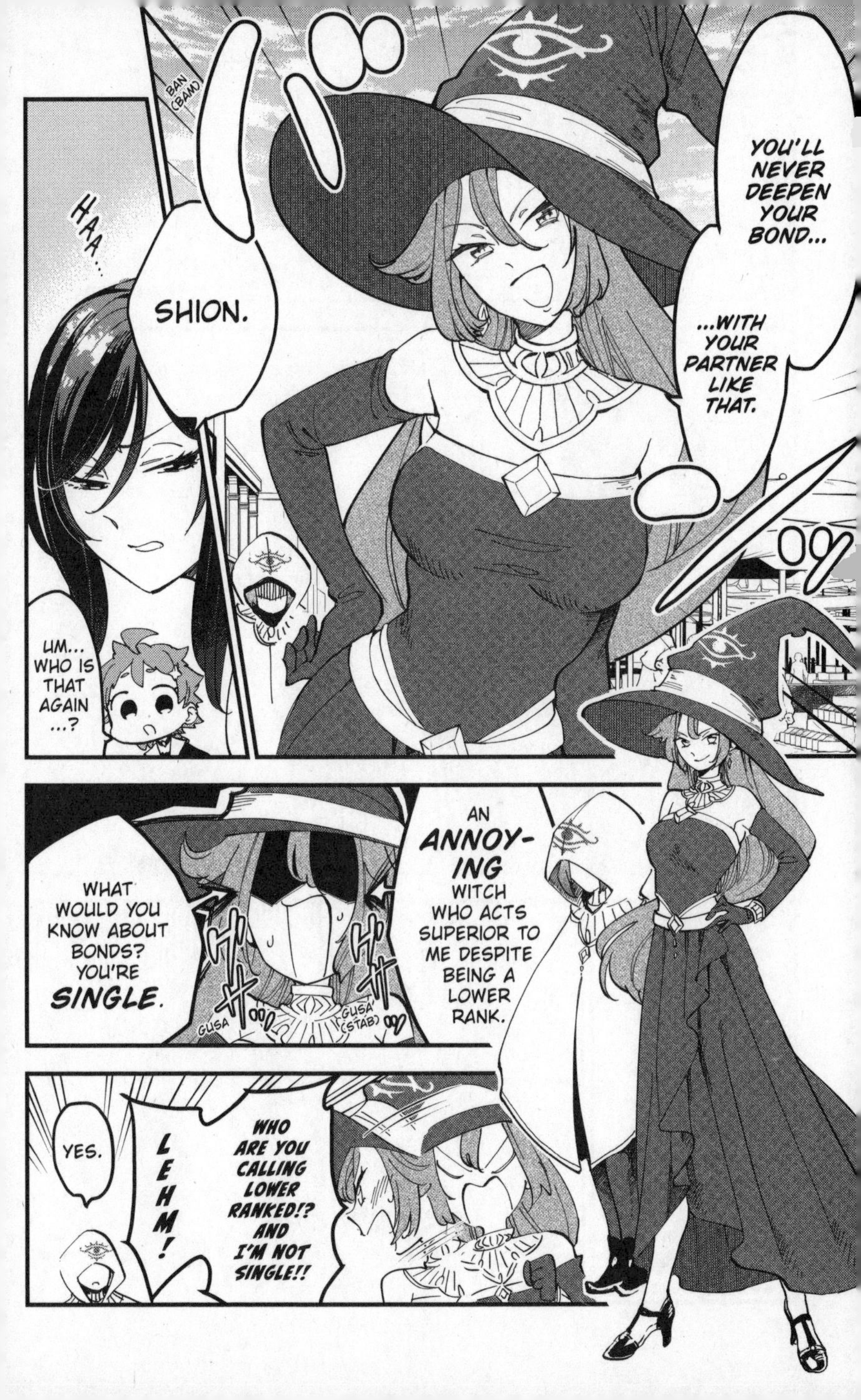
YOU'LL NEVER DEEPEN YOUR BOND...
...WITH YOUR PARTNER LIKE THAT.
BAN (BAM)
SHION.
HAA...
UM... WHO IS THAT AGAIN ...?
AN ANNOYING WITCH WHO ACTS SUPERIOR TO ME DESPITE BEING A LOWER RANK.
WHAT WOULD YOU KNOW ABOUT BONDS? YOU'RE SINGLE.
GUSA (STAB)
GUSA
LEHM!
WHO ARE YOU CALLING LOWER RANKED!? AND I'M NOT SINGLE!!
YES.

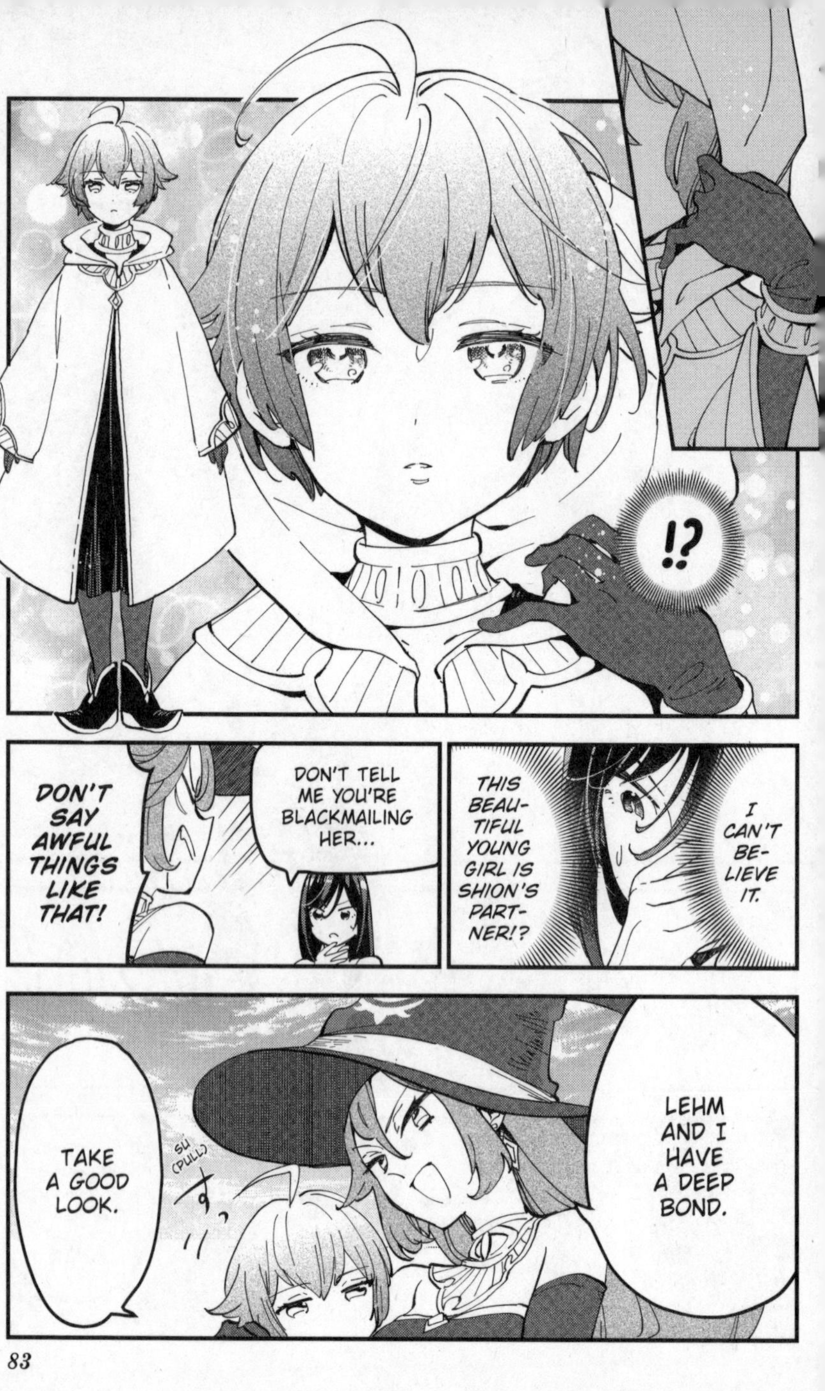
!?
I CAN'T BE-LIEVE IT.
THIS BEAU-TIFUL YOUNG GIRL IS SHION'S PART-NER!?
DON'T TELL ME YOU'RE BLACKMAILING HER...
DON'T SAY AWFUL THINGS LIKE THAT!
LEHM AND I HAVE A DEEP BOND.
SU (PULL)
TAKE A GOOD LOOK.

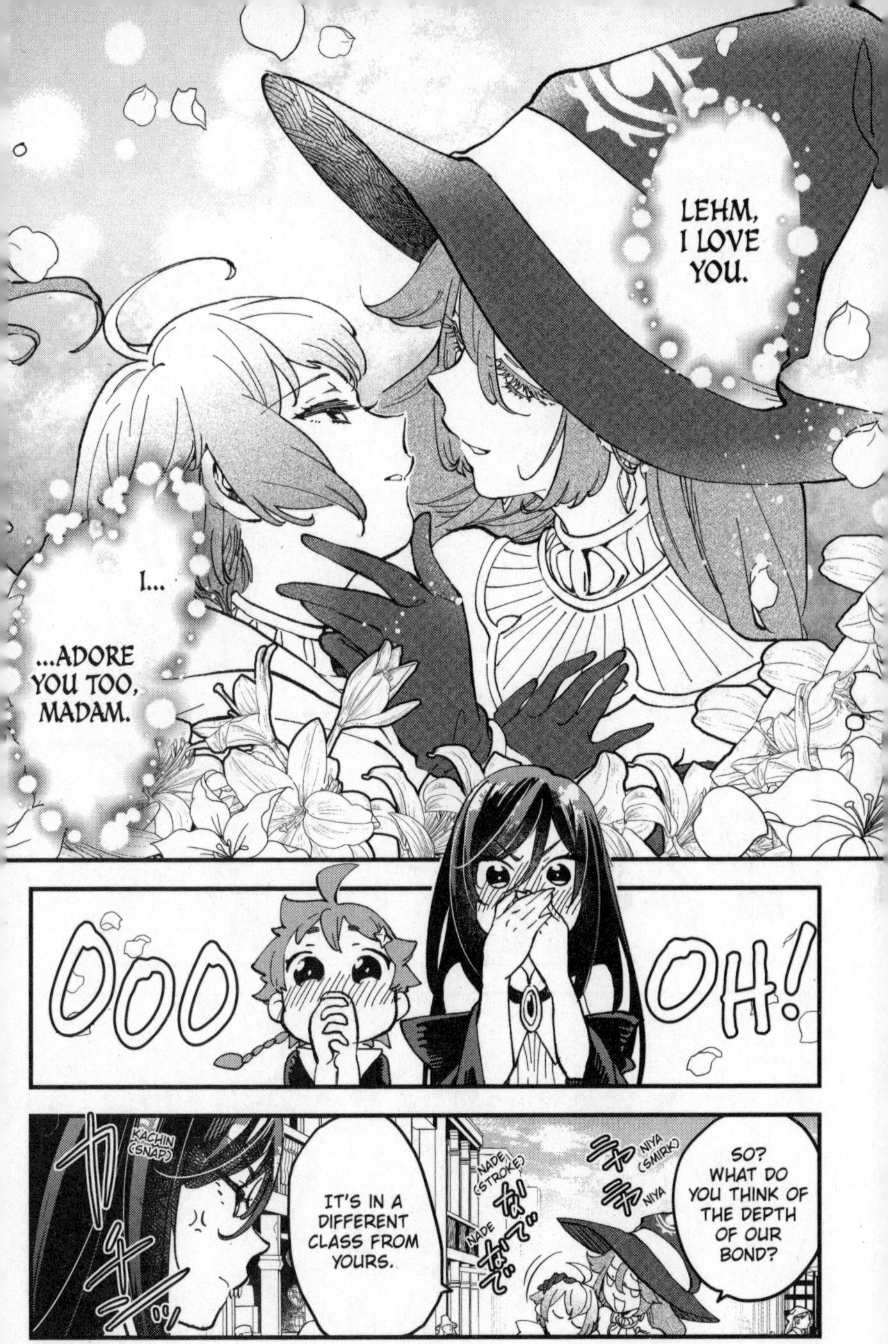
LEHM, I LOVE YOU.
I...
...ADORE YOU TOO, MADAM.
OOOOH!
SO? WHAT DO YOU THINK OF THE DEPTH OF OUR BOND?
NIYA (SMIRK)
NIYA
NADE (STROKE)
NADE
IT'S IN A DIFFERENT CLASS FROM YOURS.
KACHIN (SNAP)

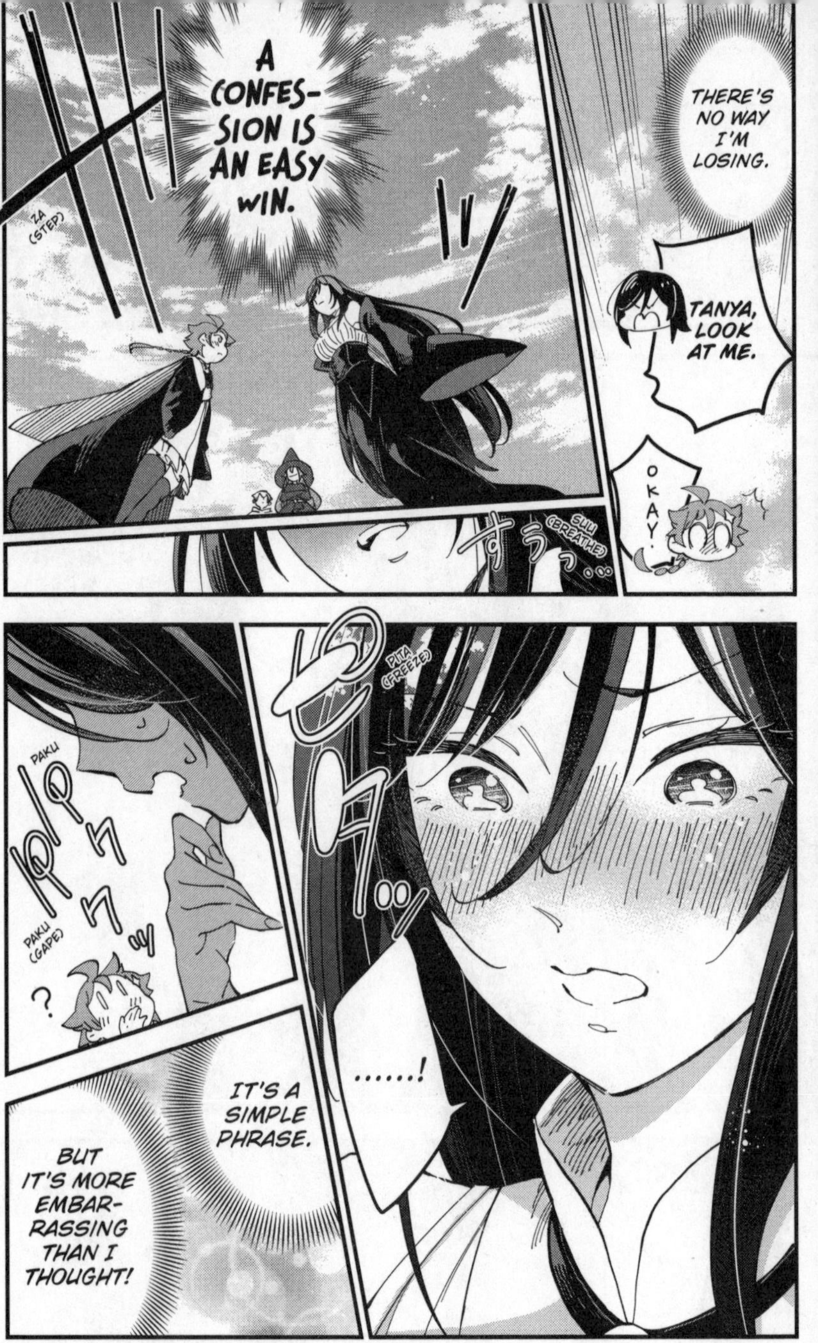

THERE'S NO WAY I'M LOSING.
TANYA, LOOK AT ME.
OKAY.
A CONFESSION IS AN EASY WIN.
ZA (STEP)
SUU (BREATHE)
PITA (FREEZE)
......!
PAKU
PAKU (GAPE)
?
IT'S A SIMPLE PHRASE.
BUT IT'S MORE EMBARRASSING THAN I THOUGHT!

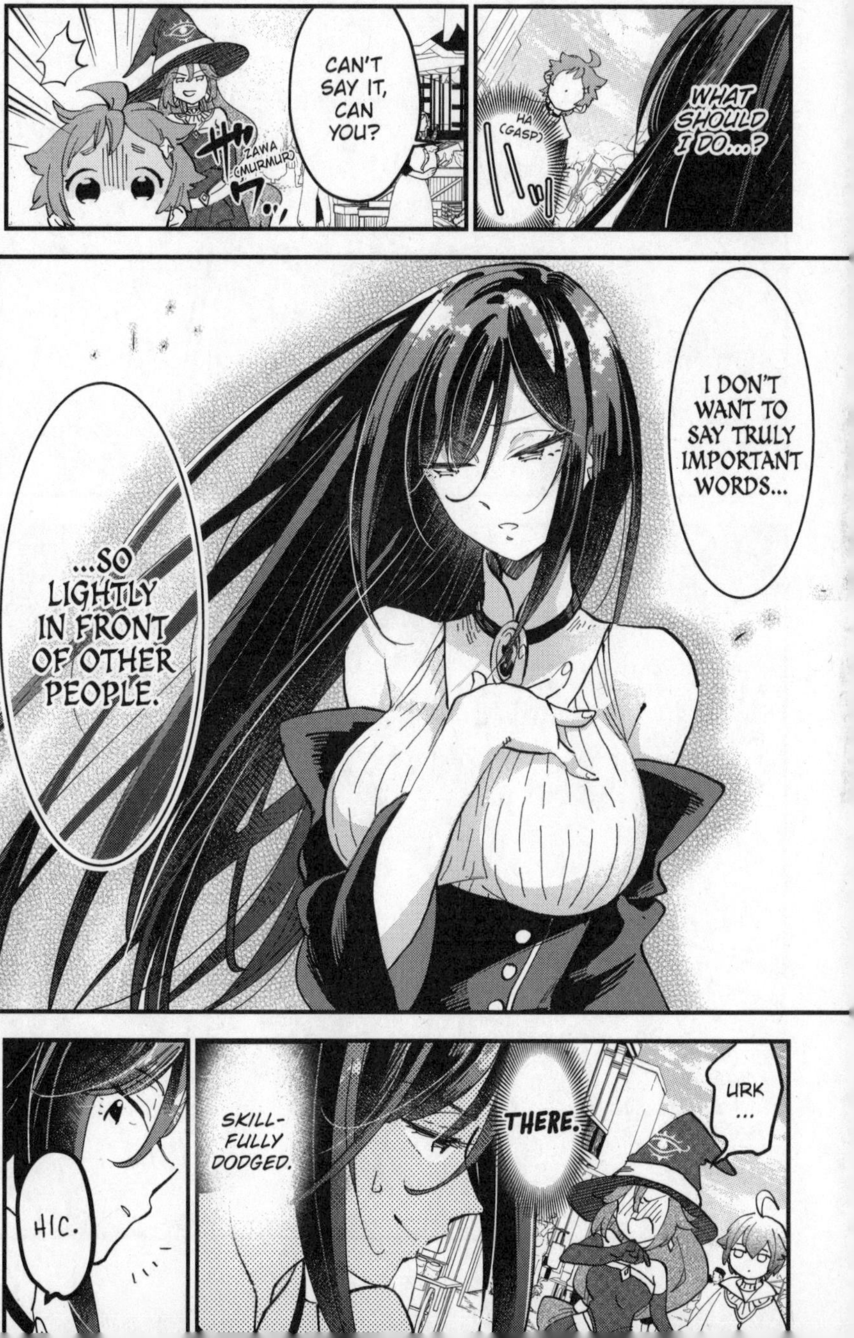
WHAT SHOULD I DO...?
HA (GASP)
CAN'T SAY IT, CAN YOU?
ZAWA (MURMUR)
I DON'T WANT TO SAY TRULY IMPORTANT WORDS...
...SO LIGHTLY IN FRONT OF OTHER PEOPLE.
URK ...
THERE.
SKILL-FULLY DODGED.
HIC.

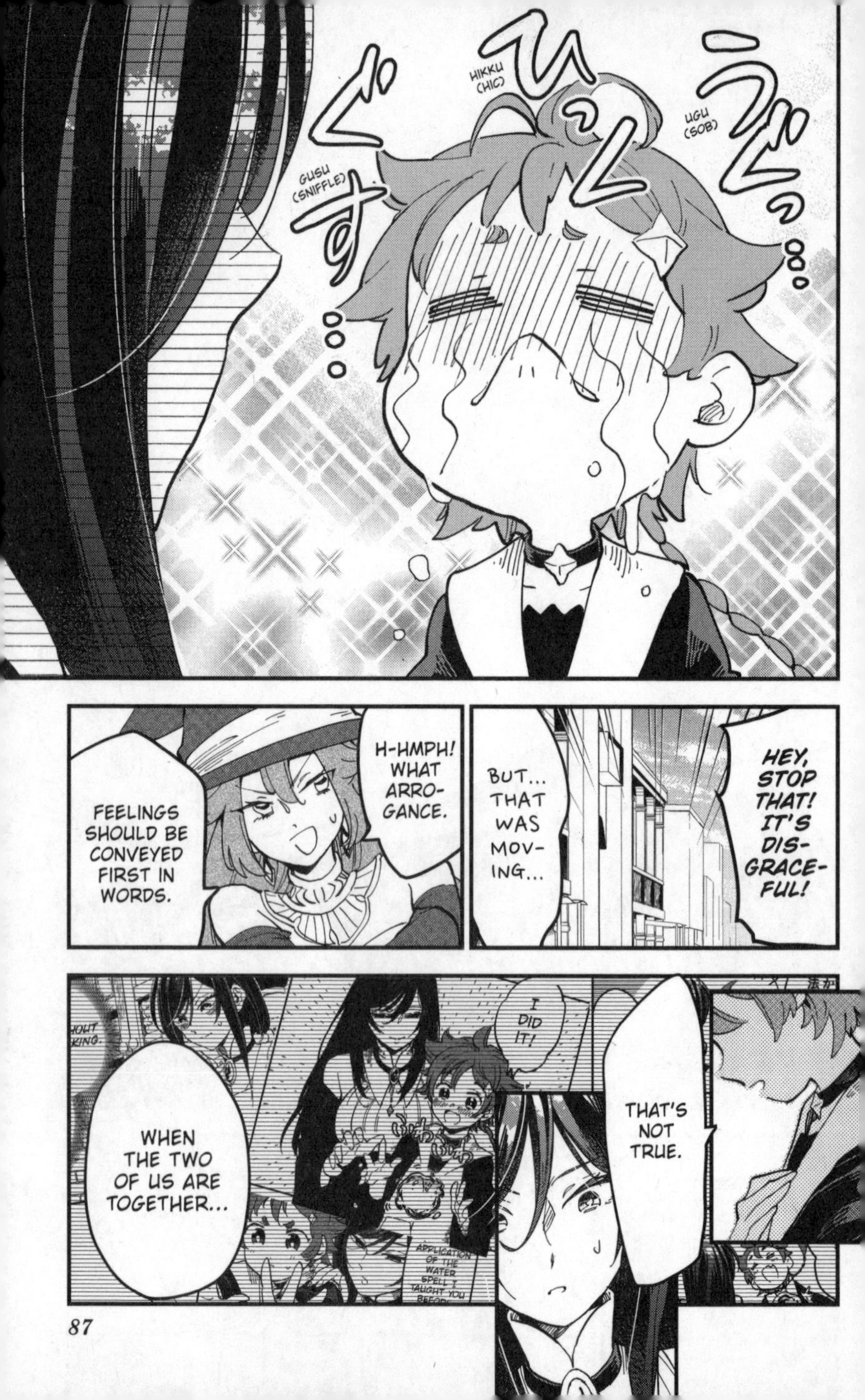
UGU (SOB)
HIKKU (HIC)
GUSU (SNIFFLE)
HEY, STOP THAT! IT'S DIS-GRACE-FUL!
BUT... THAT WAS MOV-ING...
H-HMPH! WHAT ARRO-GANCE.
FEELINGS SHOULD BE CONVEYED FIRST IN WORDS.
THAT'S NOT TRUE.
I DID IT!
WHEN THE TWO OF US ARE TOGETHER...
APPLICATION OF THE WATER SPELL I TAUGHT YOU

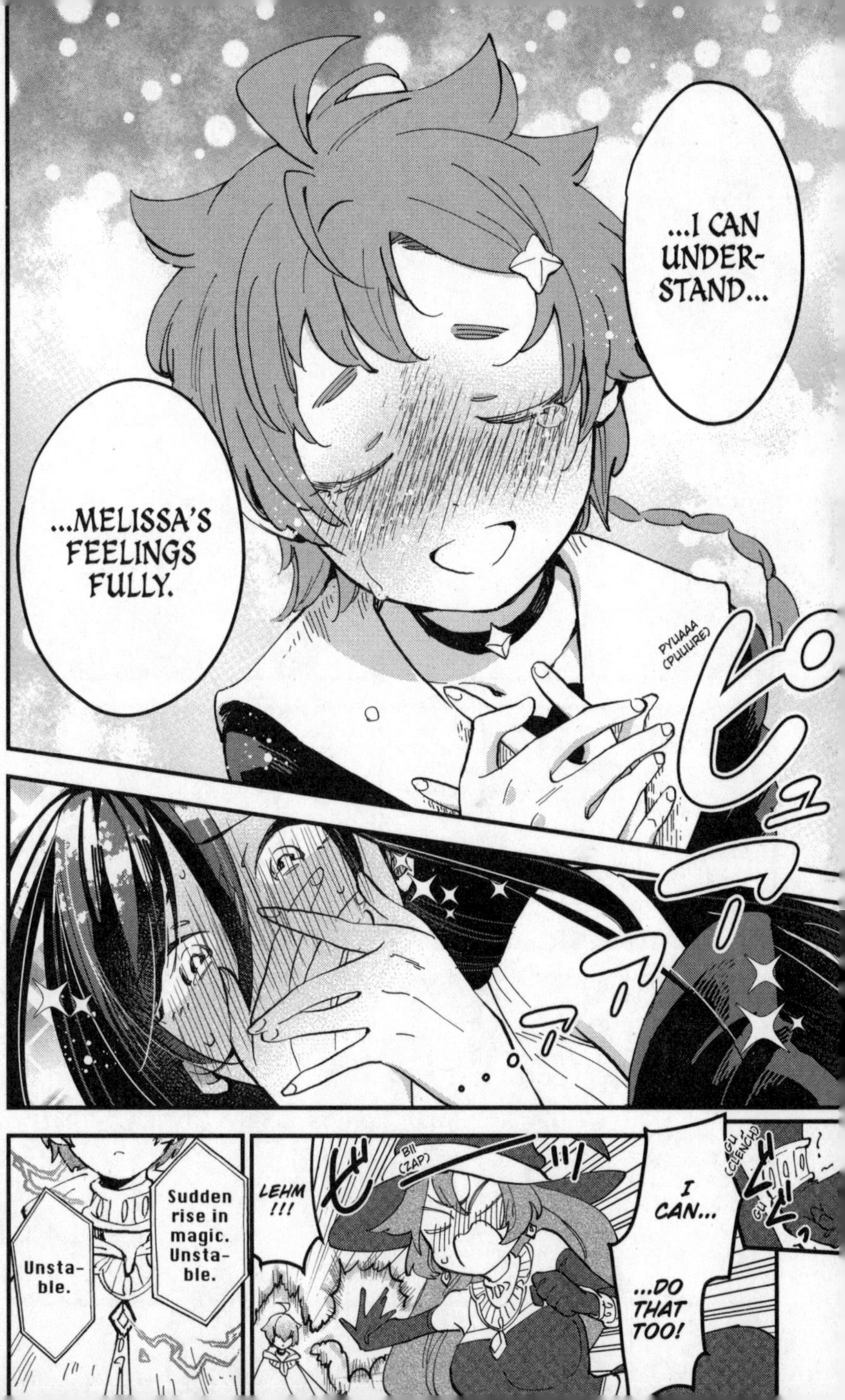
...I CAN UNDER-STAND...
...MELISSA'S FEELINGS FULLY.
PYUAAA (PUUURE)
GU (CLENCH)
I CAN...
...DO THAT TOO!
BII (ZAP)
LEHM !!!
Sudden rise in magic. Unsta-ble.
Unsta-ble.

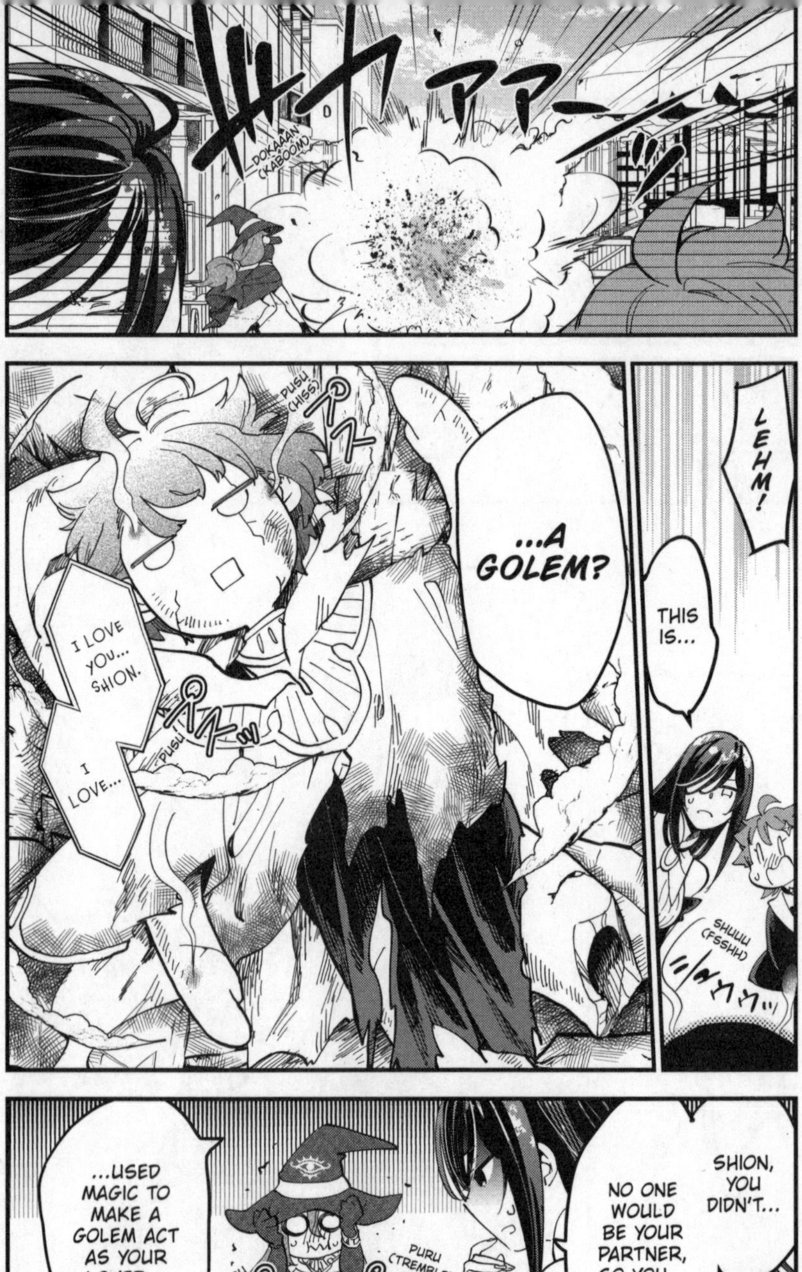
DOKAAAN (KABOOM)
LEHM!
THIS IS...
SHUUU (FSSHH)
...A GOLEM?
PUSU (HISS)
I LOVE YOU... SHION.
I LOVE...
PUSU
SHION, YOU DIDN'T...
NO ONE WOULD BE YOUR PARTNER, SO YOU...
...USED MAGIC TO MAKE A GOLEM ACT AS YOUR LOVER...
PURU (TREMBLE)
PURU

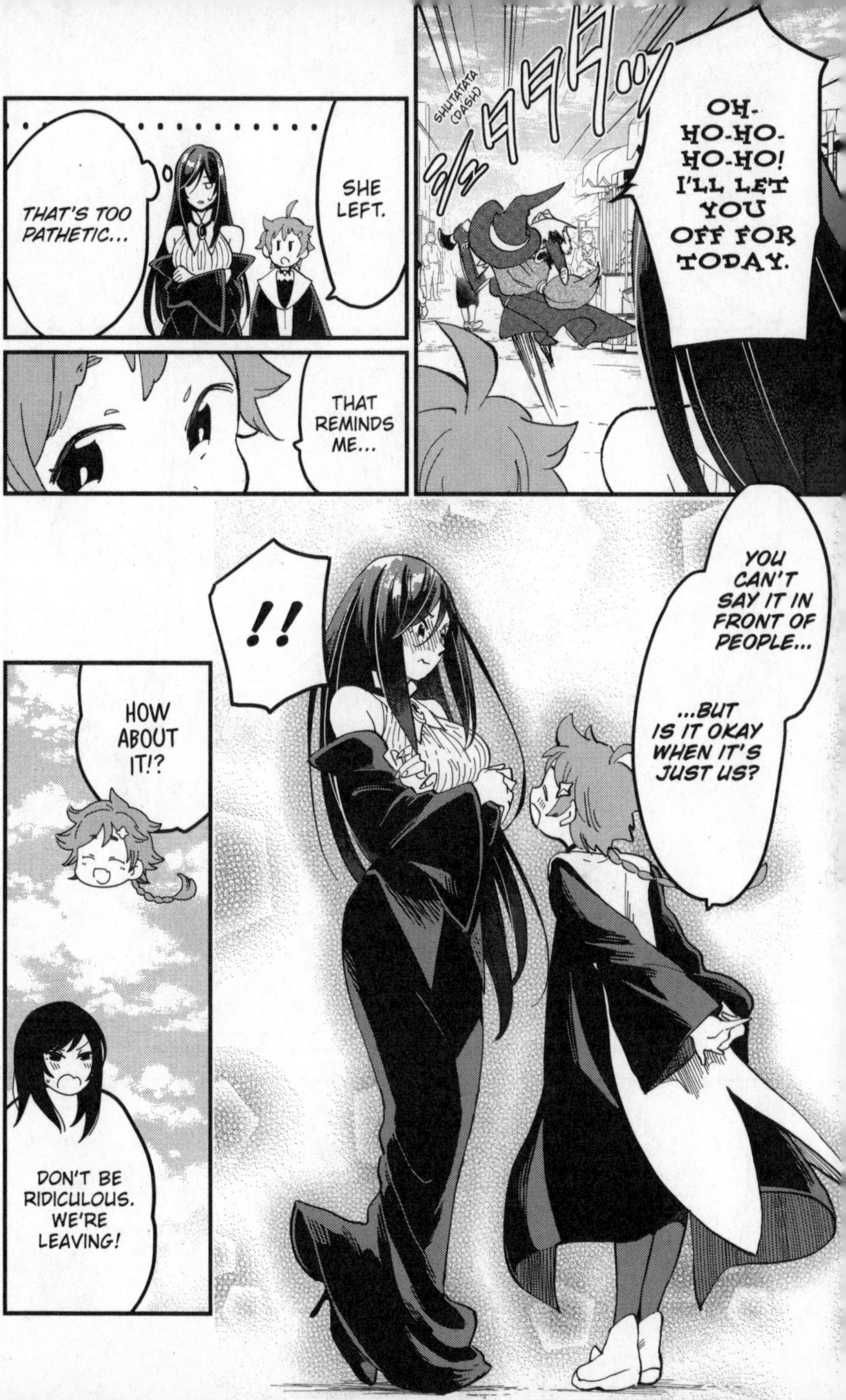
OH-HO-HO-HO-HO! I'LL LET YOU OFF FOR TODAY.
SHUTATATA (DASH)
SHE LEFT.
....
THAT'S TOO PATHETIC...
THAT REMINDS ME...
YOU CAN'T SAY IT IN FRONT OF PEOPLE...
...BUT IS IT OKAY WHEN IT'S JUST US?
!!
HOW ABOUT IT!?
DON'T BE RIDICULOUS. WE'RE LEAVING!

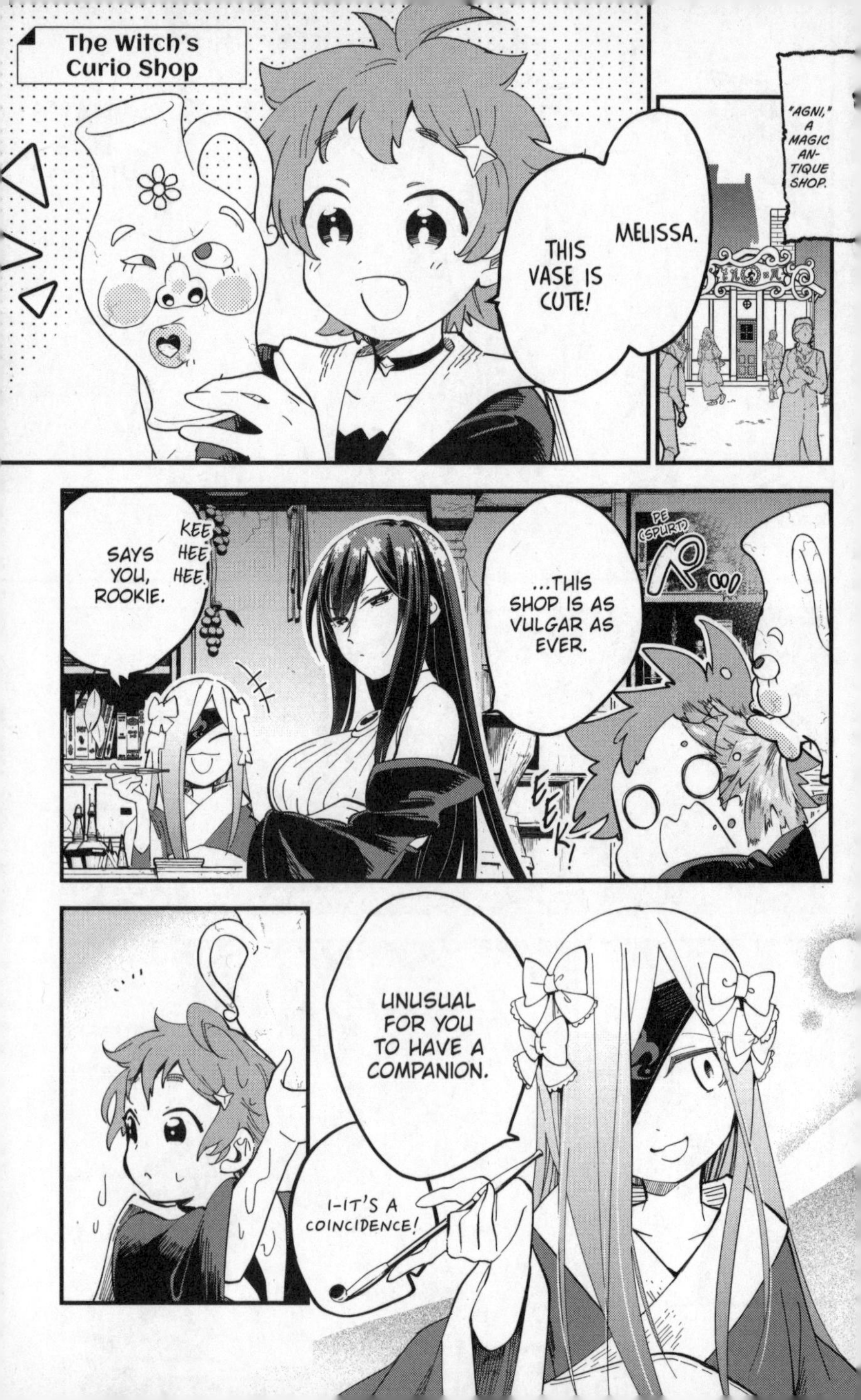
The Witch's Curio Shop
"AGNI," A MAGIC ANTIQUE SHOP.
MELISSA.
THIS VASE IS CUTE!
PE (SPURT)
ペ
...THIS SHOP IS AS VULGAR AS EVER.
EEK!
SAYS YOU, ROOKIE.
KEE HEE HEE.
UNUSUAL FOR YOU TO HAVE A COMPANION.
I-IT'S A COINCIDENCE!
...

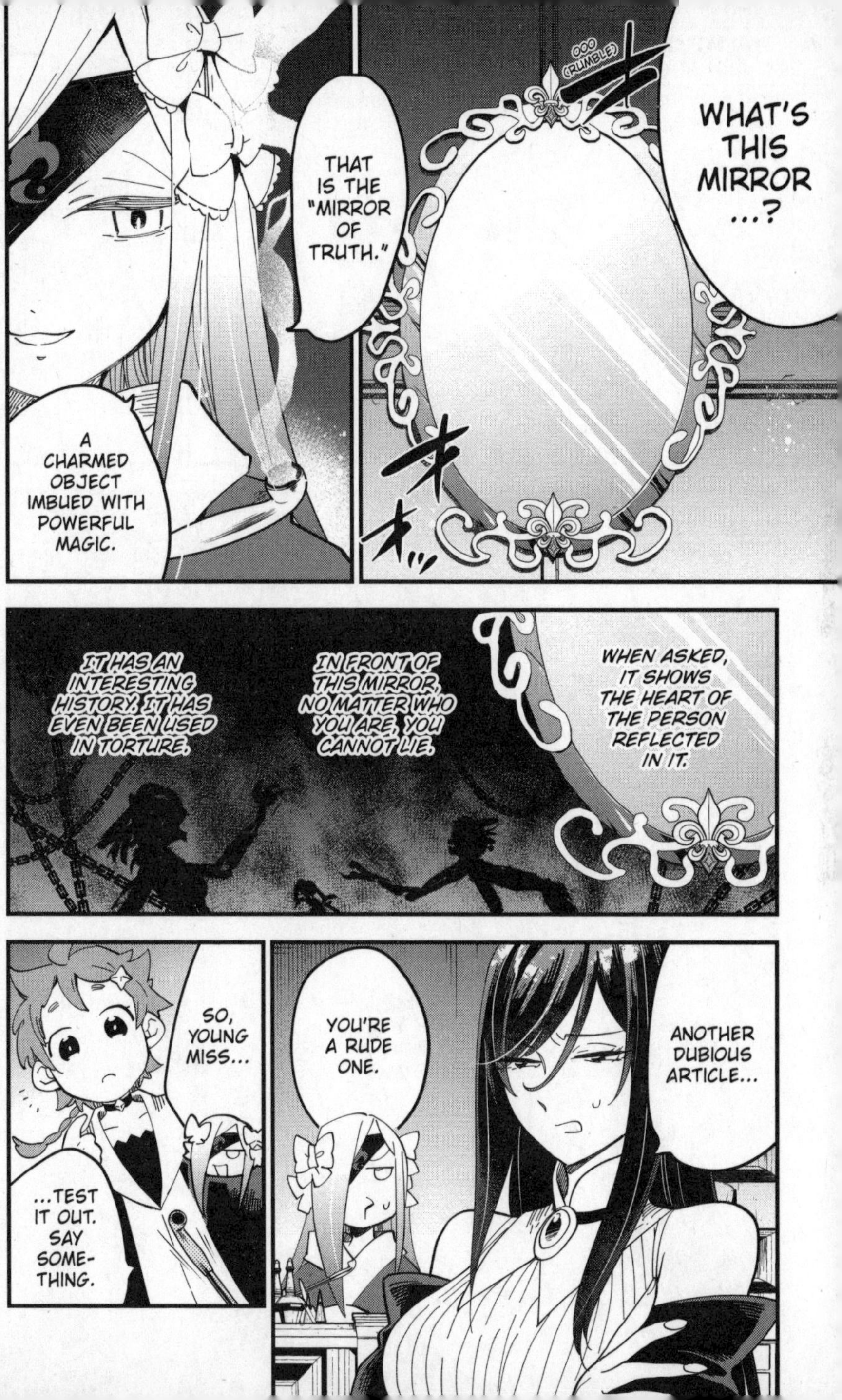
(RUMBLE)
WHAT'S THIS MIRROR ...?
THAT IS THE "MIRROR OF TRUTH."
A CHARMED OBJECT IMBUED WITH POWERFUL MAGIC.
WHEN ASKED, IT SHOWS THE HEART OF THE PERSON REFLECTED IN IT.
IN FRONT OF THIS MIRROR, NO MATTER WHO YOU ARE, YOU CANNOT LIE.
IT HAS AN INTERESTING HISTORY. IT HAS EVEN BEEN USED IN TORTURE.
ANOTHER DUBIOUS ARTICLE...
YOU'RE A RUDE ONE.
SO, YOUNG MISS...
...TEST IT OUT. SAY SOME-THING.

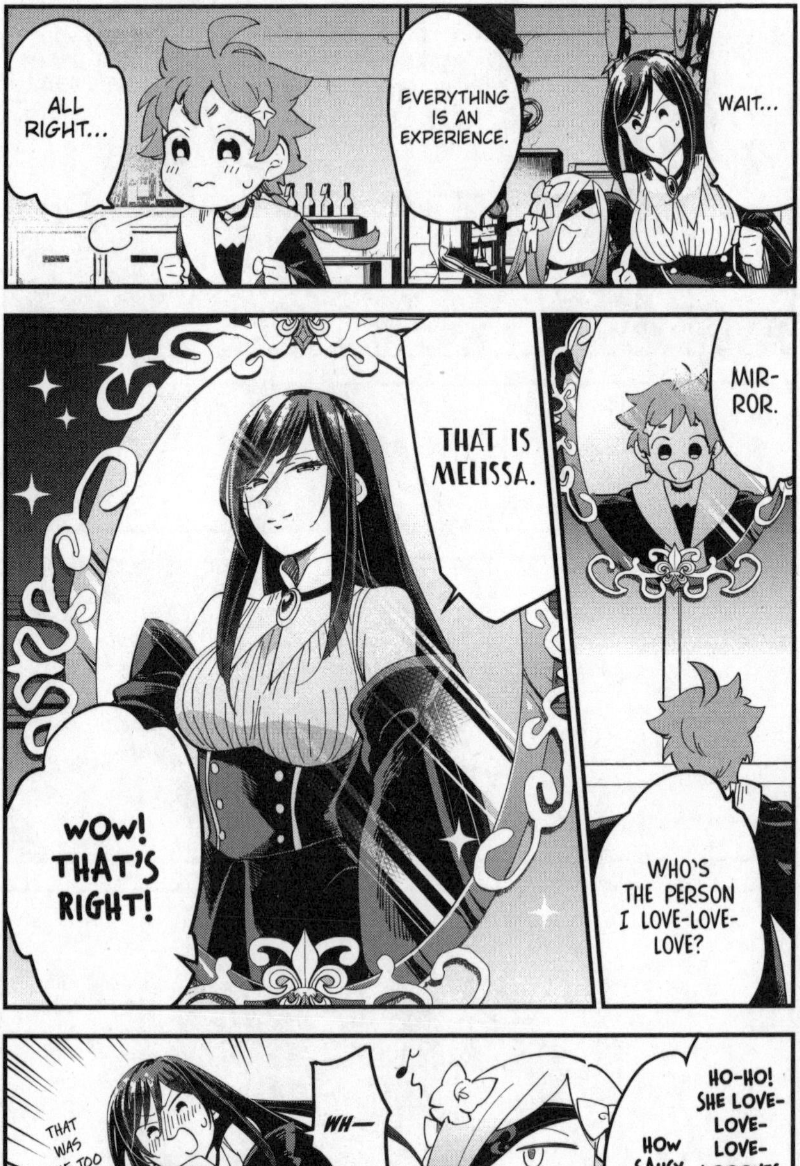
WAIT...
EVERYTHING IS AN EXPERIENCE.
ALL RIGHT...
MIRROR.
WHO'S THE PERSON I LOVE-LOVE-LOVE?
THAT IS MELISSA.
WOW! THAT'S RIGHT!
HO-HO! SHE LOVE-LOVE-LOVE-LOOOVES YOU...
HOW SAUCY.
WH—
THAT WAS ONE TOO MANY "LOVES"!!

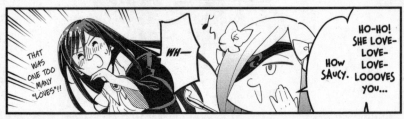

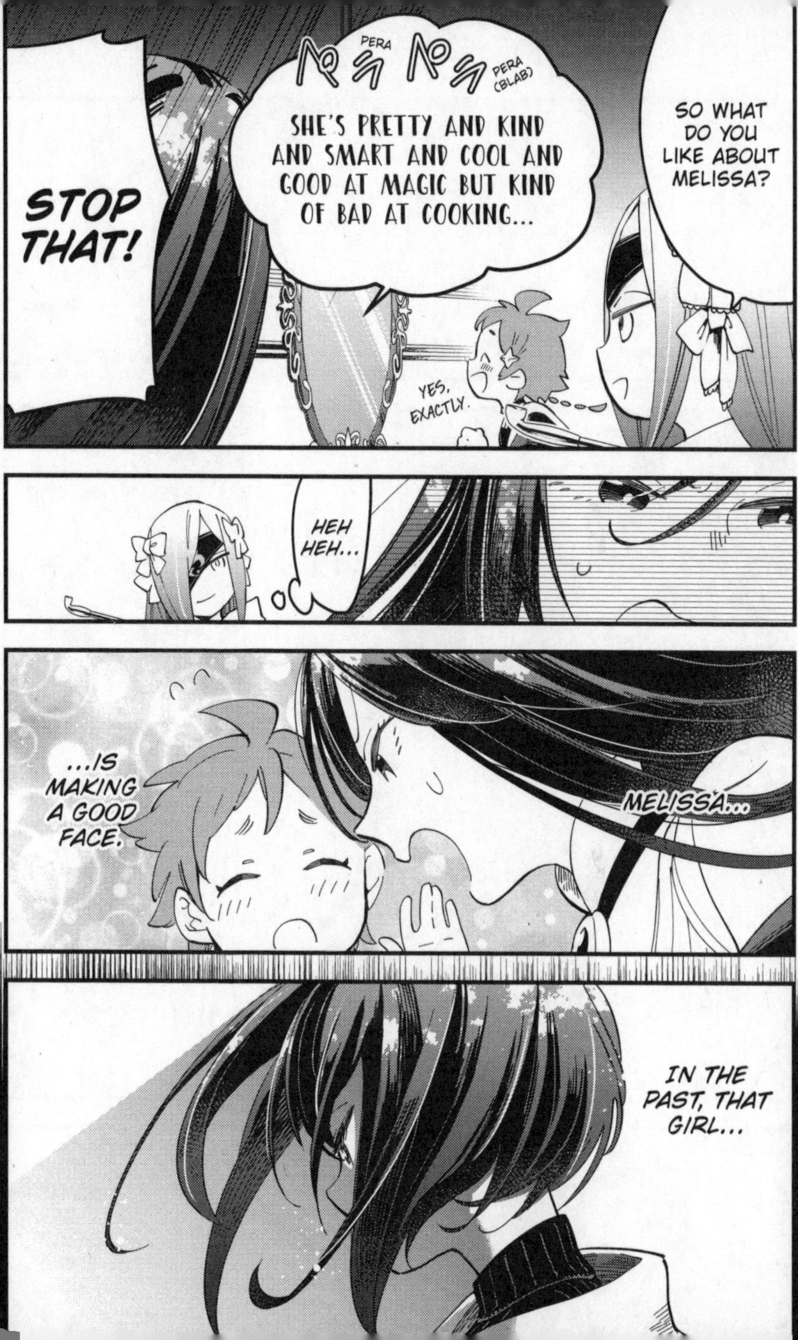
SO WHAT DO YOU LIKE ABOUT MELISSA?
PERA PERA PERA (BLAB)
SHE'S PRETTY AND KIND AND SMART AND COOL AND GOOD AT MAGIC BUT KIND OF BAD AT COOKING...
YES, EXACTLY.
STOP THAT!
HEH HEH...
MELISSA...
...IS MAKING A GOOD FACE.
IN THE PAST, THAT GIRL...

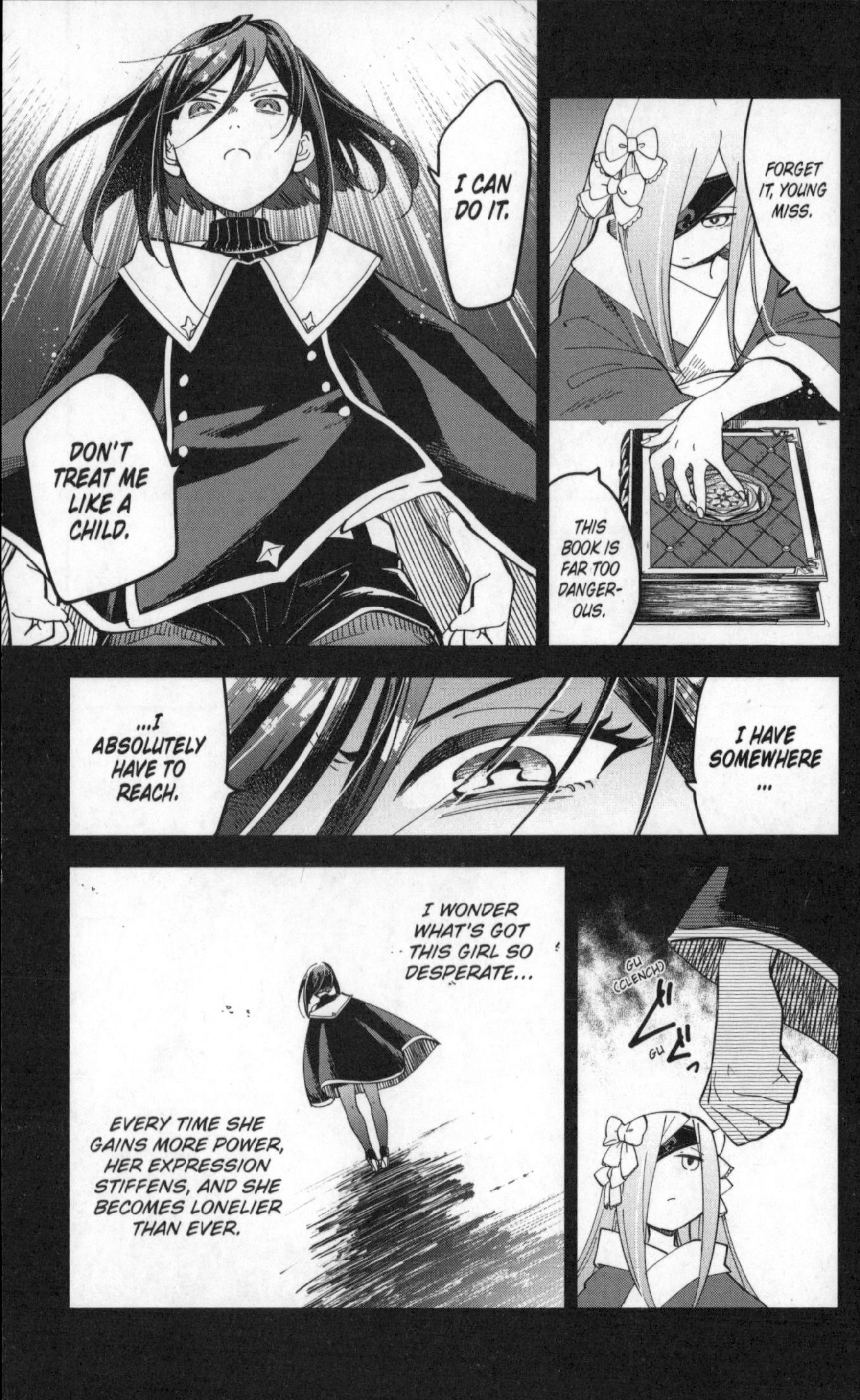
FORGET IT, YOUNG MISS.
THIS BOOK IS FAR TOO DANGER-OUS.
I CAN DO IT.
DON'T TREAT ME LIKE A CHILD.
I HAVE SOMEWHERE...
...I ABSOLUTELY HAVE TO REACH.
GU (CLENCH)
GU
I WONDER WHAT'S GOT THIS GIRL SO DESPERATE...
EVERY TIME SHE GAINS MORE POWER, HER EXPRESSION STIFFENS, AND SHE BECOMES LONELIER THAN EVER.

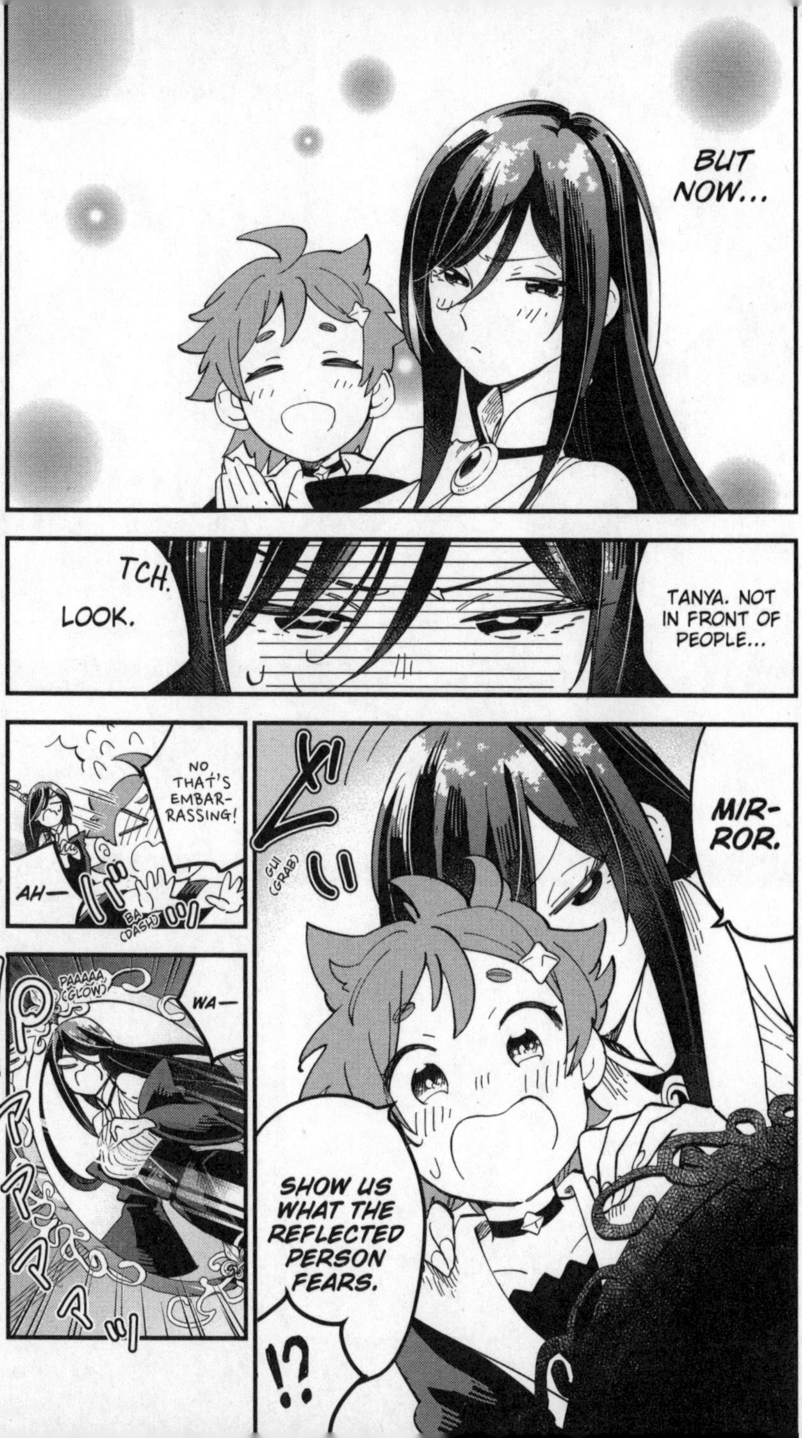
BUT NOW...
TANYA. NOT IN FRONT OF PEOPLE...
TCH.
LOOK.
MIR-ROR.
GUI (GRAB)
SHOW US WHAT THE REFLECTED PERSON FEARS.
!?
NO THAT'S EMBARRASSING!
AH—
BA (DASH)
WA—
PAAAAA (GLOW)

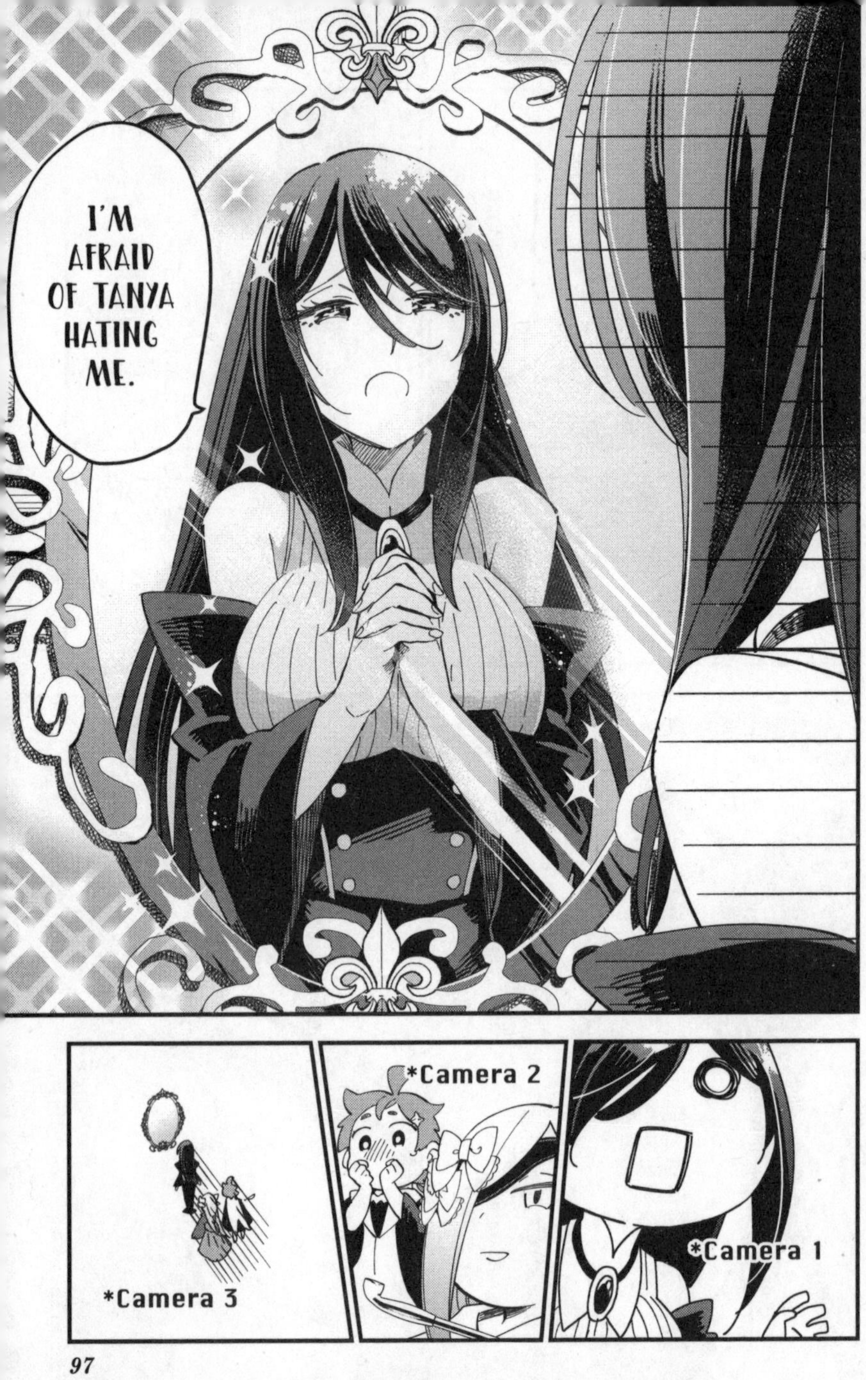
I'M AFRAID OF TANYA HATING ME.
*Camera 1
*Camera 2
*Camera 3

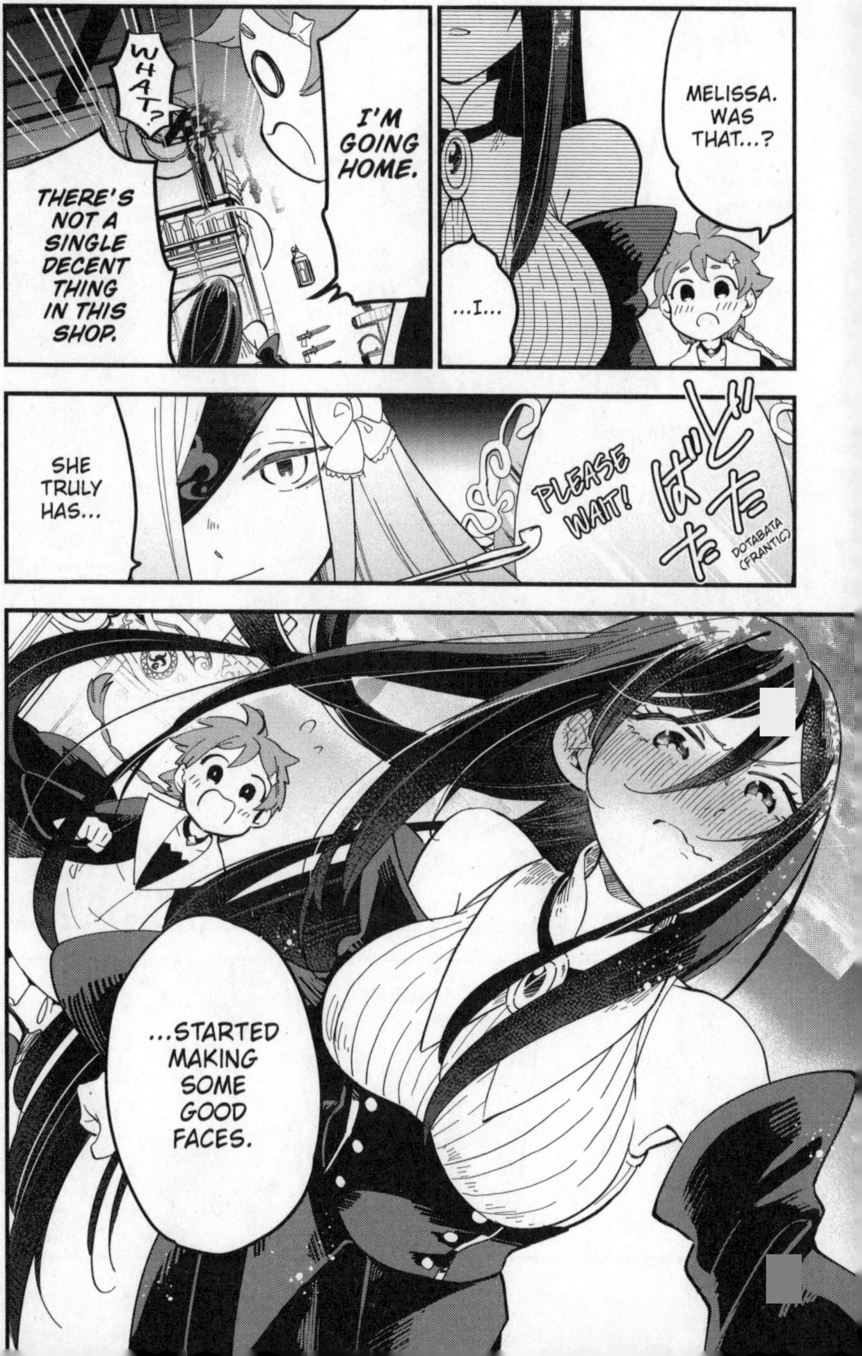
MELISSA. WAS THAT...?
...I...
I'M GOING HOME.
THERE'S NOT A SINGLE DECENT THING IN THIS SHOP.
WHAT?
どたばた
DOTABATA (FRANTIC)
PLEASE WAIT!
SHE TRULY HAS...
...STARTED MAKING SOME GOOD FACES.

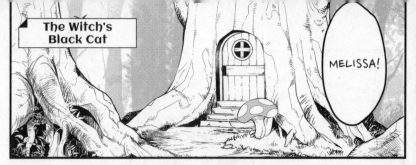

The Witch's Black Cat

MELISSA!

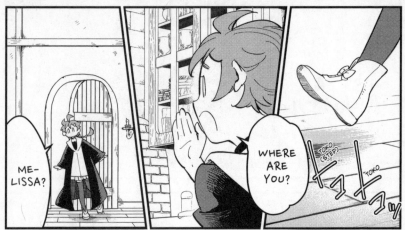

ME-LISSA?

WHERE ARE YOU?

TOKO (STEP)

TOKO

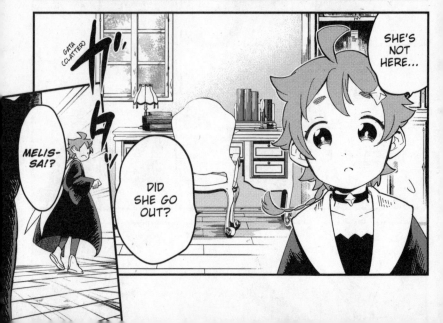

GATA (CLATTER)

SHE'S NOT HERE...

MELIS-SA!?

DID SHE GO OUT?

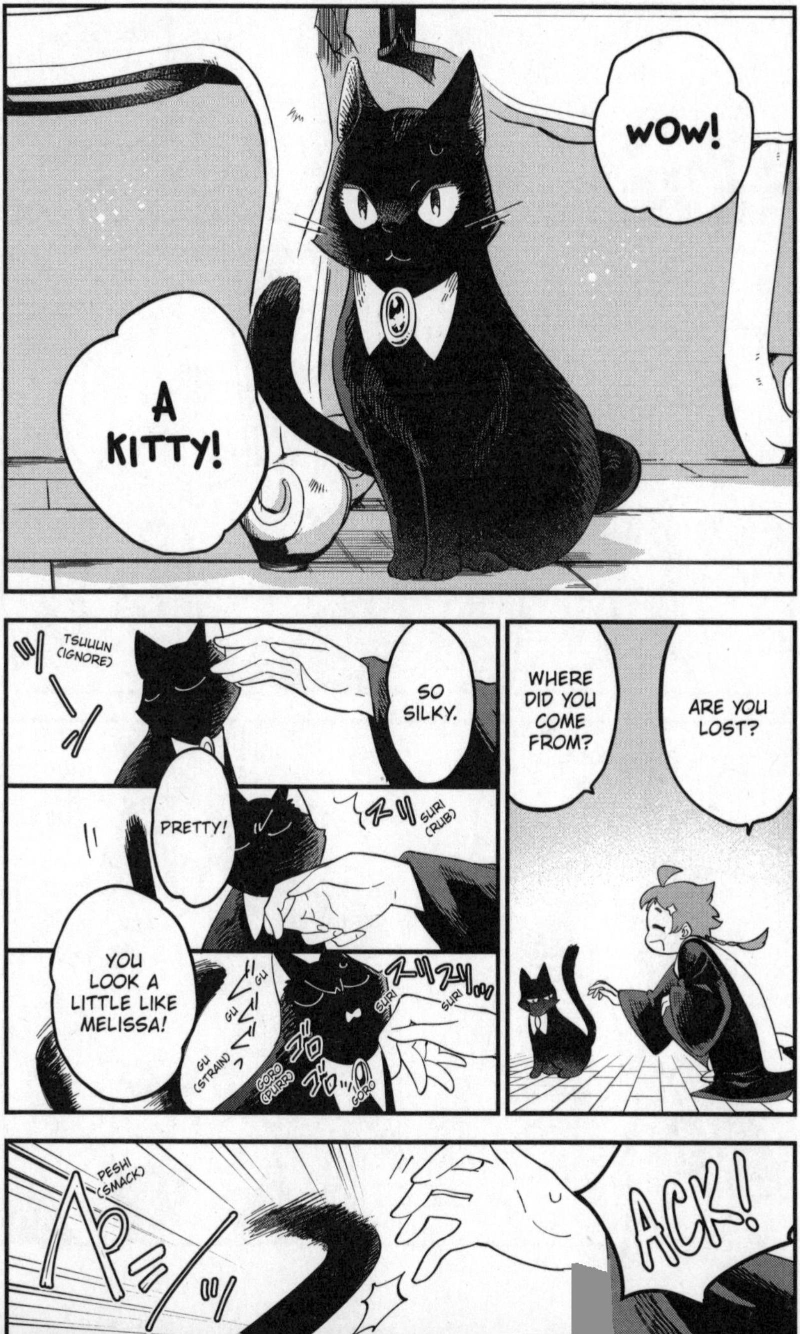
WOW!
A KITTY!
ARE YOU LOST?
WHERE DID YOU COME FROM?
SO SILKY.
TSUUUN (IGNORE)
SURI (RUB)
PRETTY!
SURI SURI
GU GU GU (STRAIN)
GORO (PURR) GORO
YOU LOOK A LITTLE LIKE MELISSA!
ACK!
PESHI (SMACK)

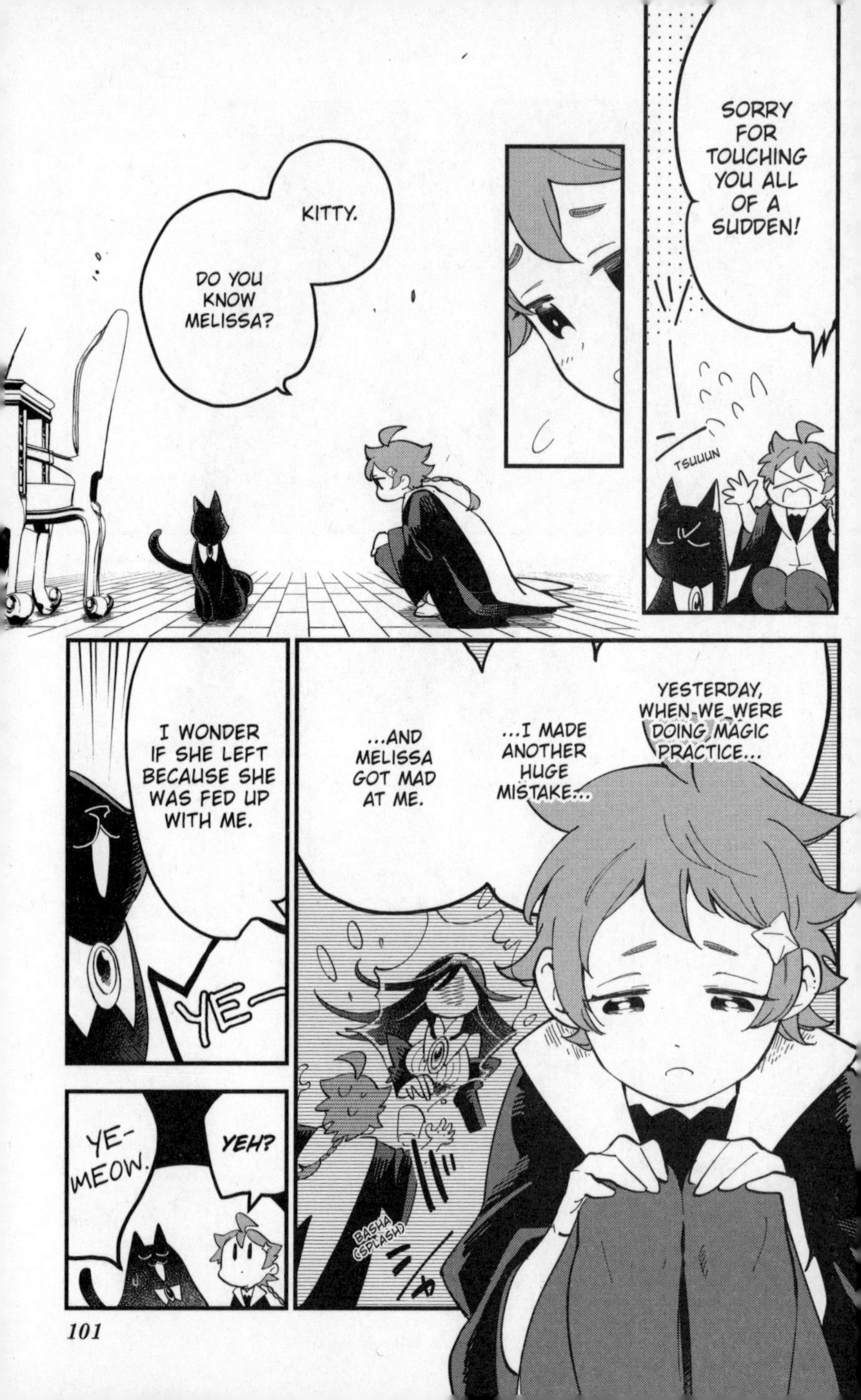
SORRY FOR TOUCHING YOU ALL OF A SUDDEN!
TSUUUN
KITTY.
DO YOU KNOW MELISSA?
YESTERDAY, WHEN WE WERE DOING MAGIC PRACTICE...
...I MADE ANOTHER HUGE MISTAKE...
...AND MELISSA GOT MAD AT ME.
BASHA (SPLASH)
I WONDER IF SHE LEFT BECAUSE SHE WAS FED UP WITH ME.
YE—
YEH?
YE-MEOW.

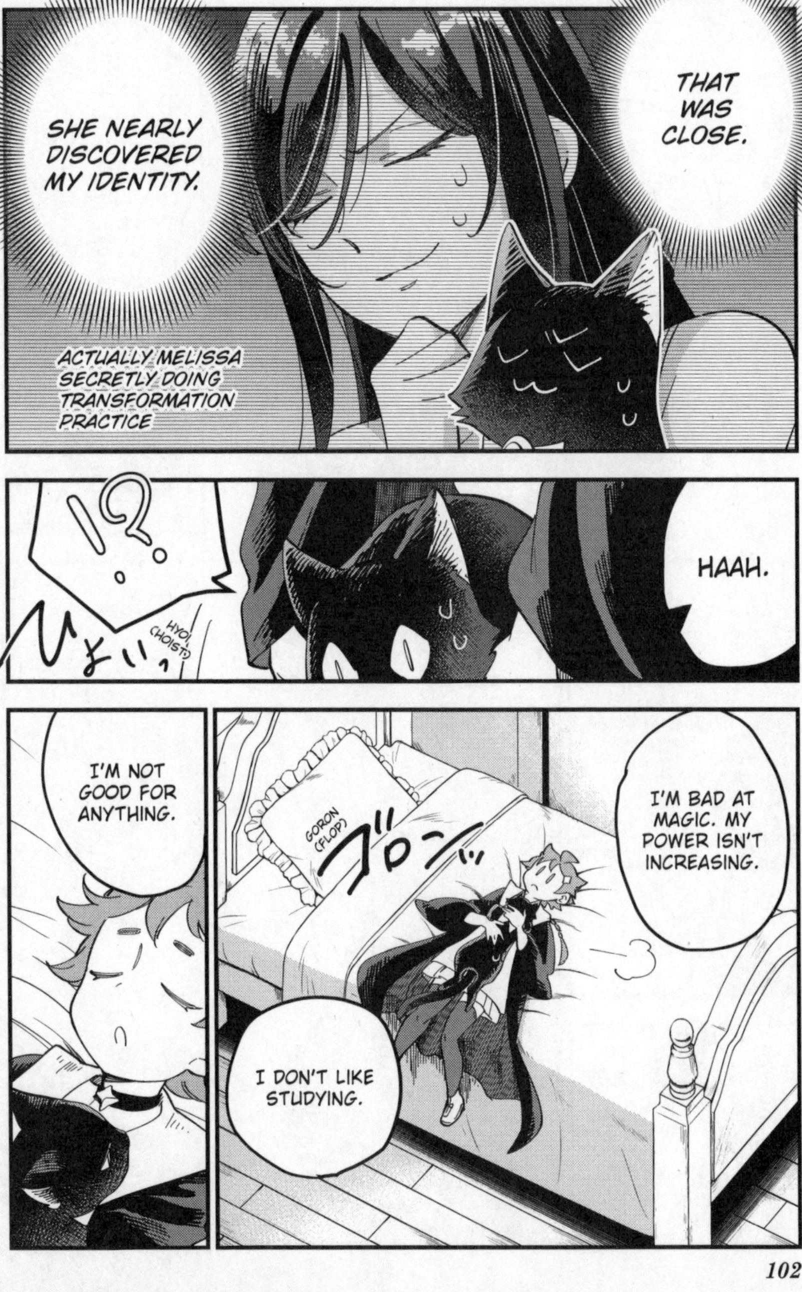
THAT WAS CLOSE.
SHE NEARLY DISCOVERED MY IDENTITY.
ACTUALLY MELISSA SECRETLY DOING TRANSFORMATION PRACTICE
HAAH.
!?
HYOI (HOIST)
I'M BAD AT MAGIC. MY POWER ISN'T INCREASING.
GORON (FLOP)
I DON'T LIKE STUDYING.
I'M NOT GOOD FOR ANYTHING.

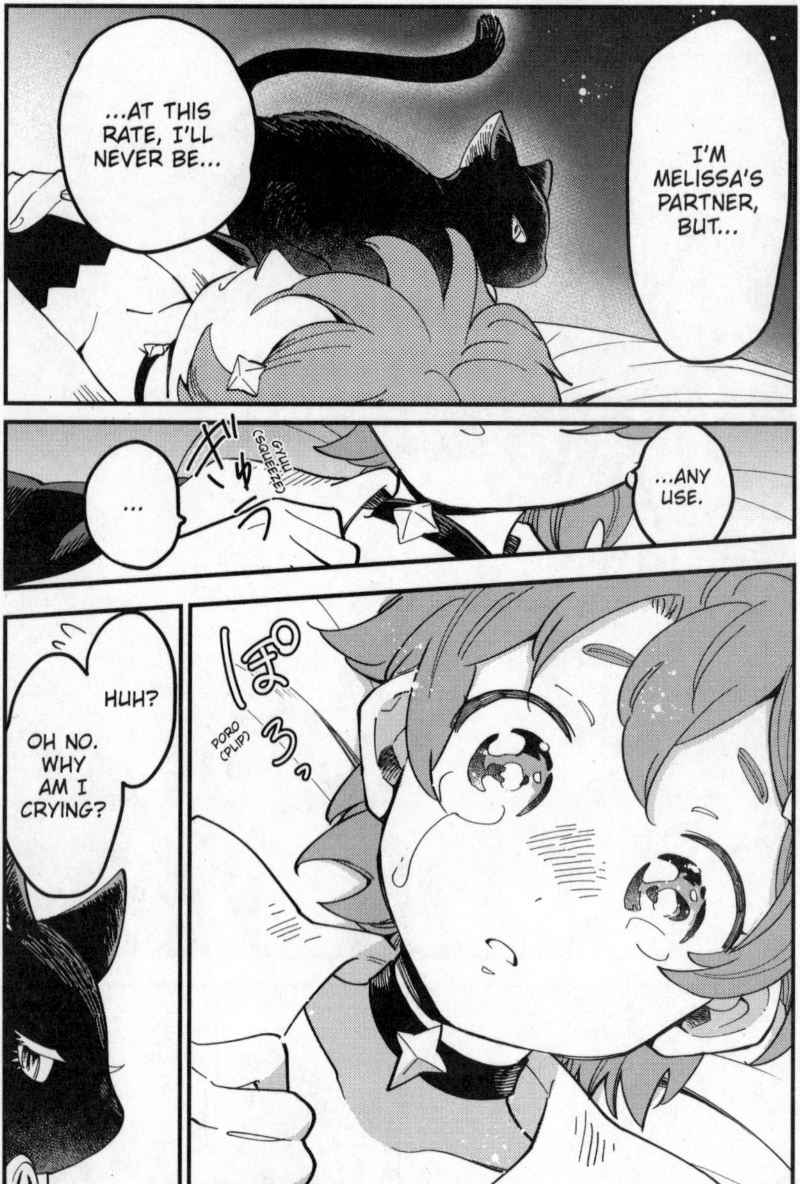
I'M MELISSA'S PARTNER, BUT...
...AT THIS RATE, I'LL NEVER BE...
...ANY USE.
GYUU (SQUEEZE)
...
PORO (PLIP)
HUH?
OH NO. WHY AM I CRYING?

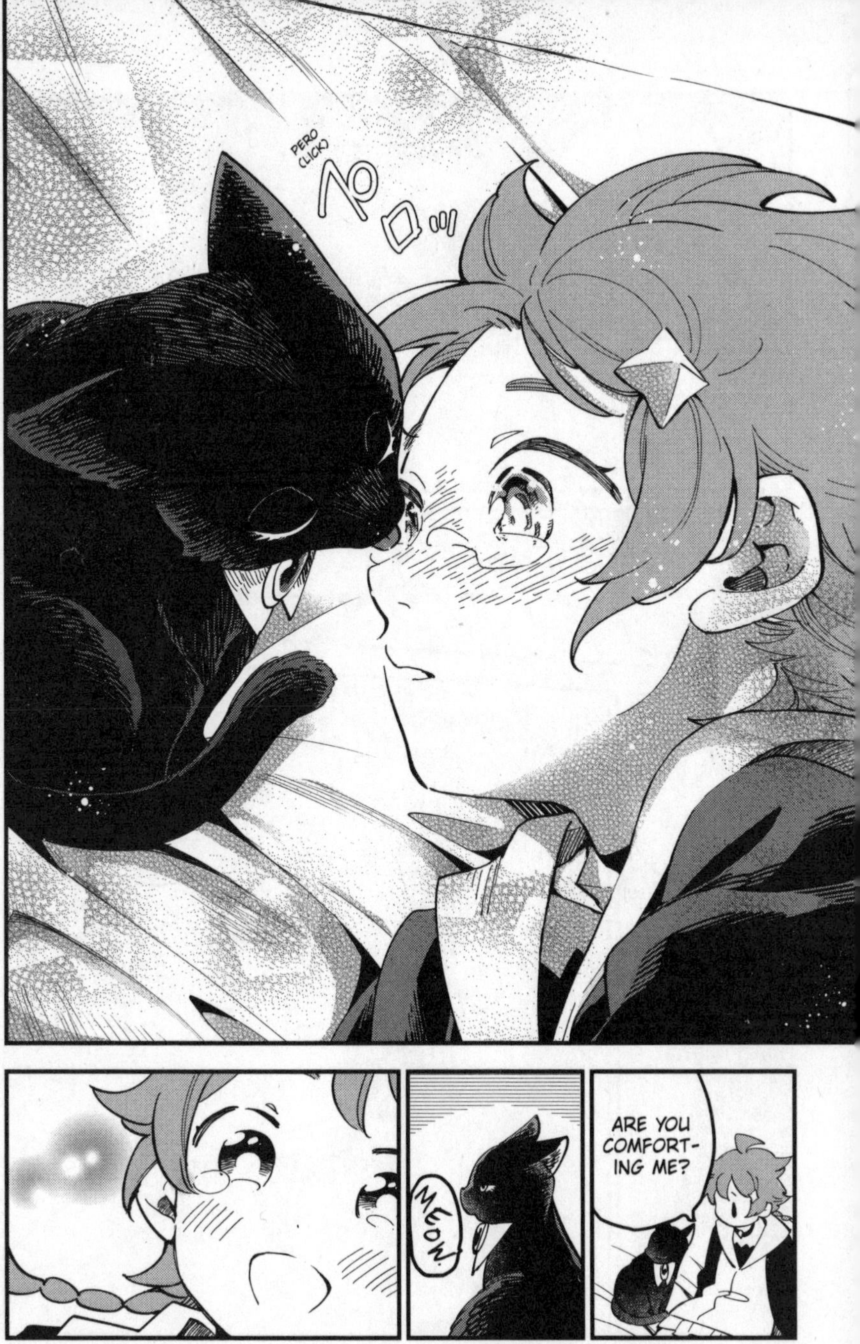
PERO (LICK)
ARE YOU COMFORTING ME?
MEOW.

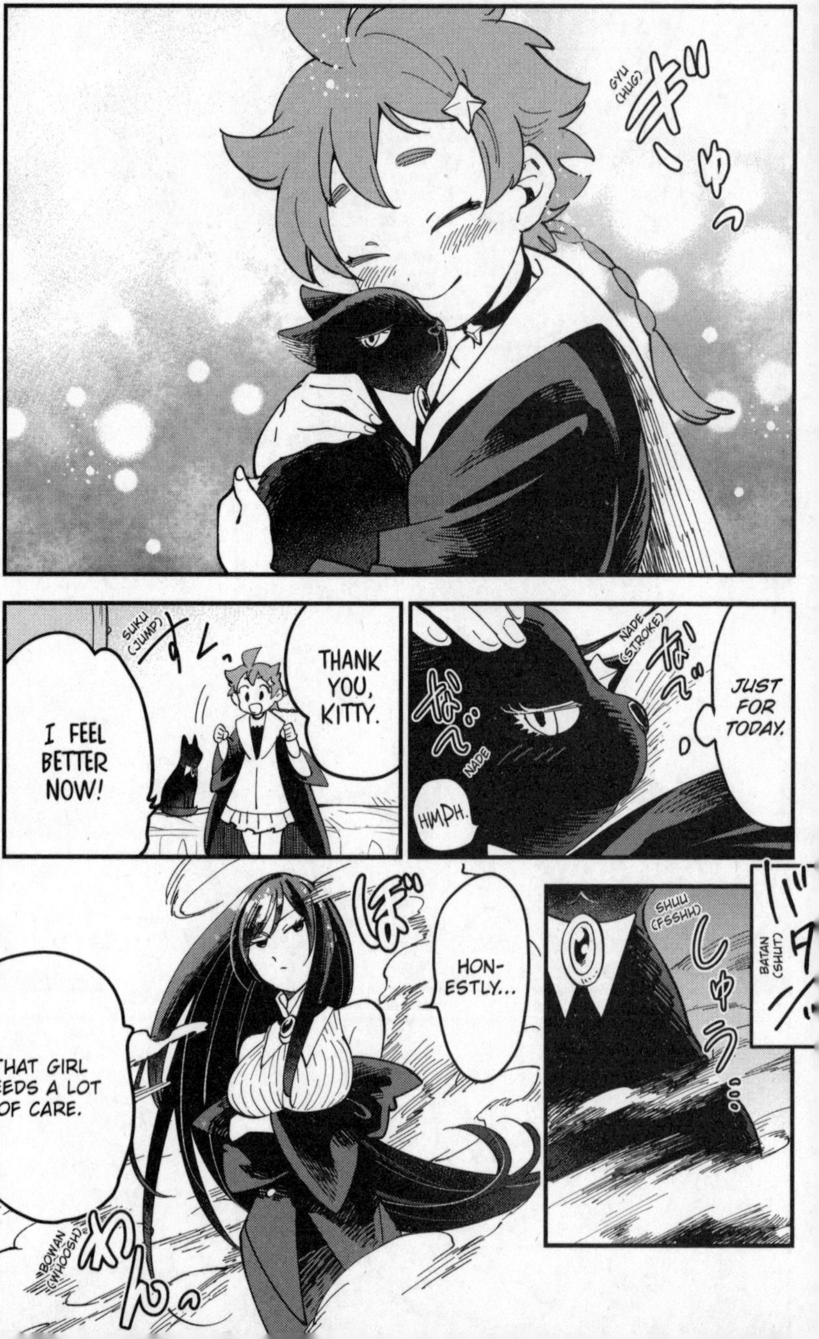
GYU (HUG)
ぎゅっ
NADE (STROKE)
なで
なで
NADE
JUST FOR TODAY.
HMPH.
THANK YOU, KITTY.
SUKU (JUMP)
すくっ
I FEEL BETTER NOW!
BATAN (SHUT)
バタン
SHUU (FSSHH)
しゅう…
HON-ESTLY...
ぼ
THAT GIRL NEEDS A LOT OF CARE.
BOWAN (WHOOSH)
わんっ

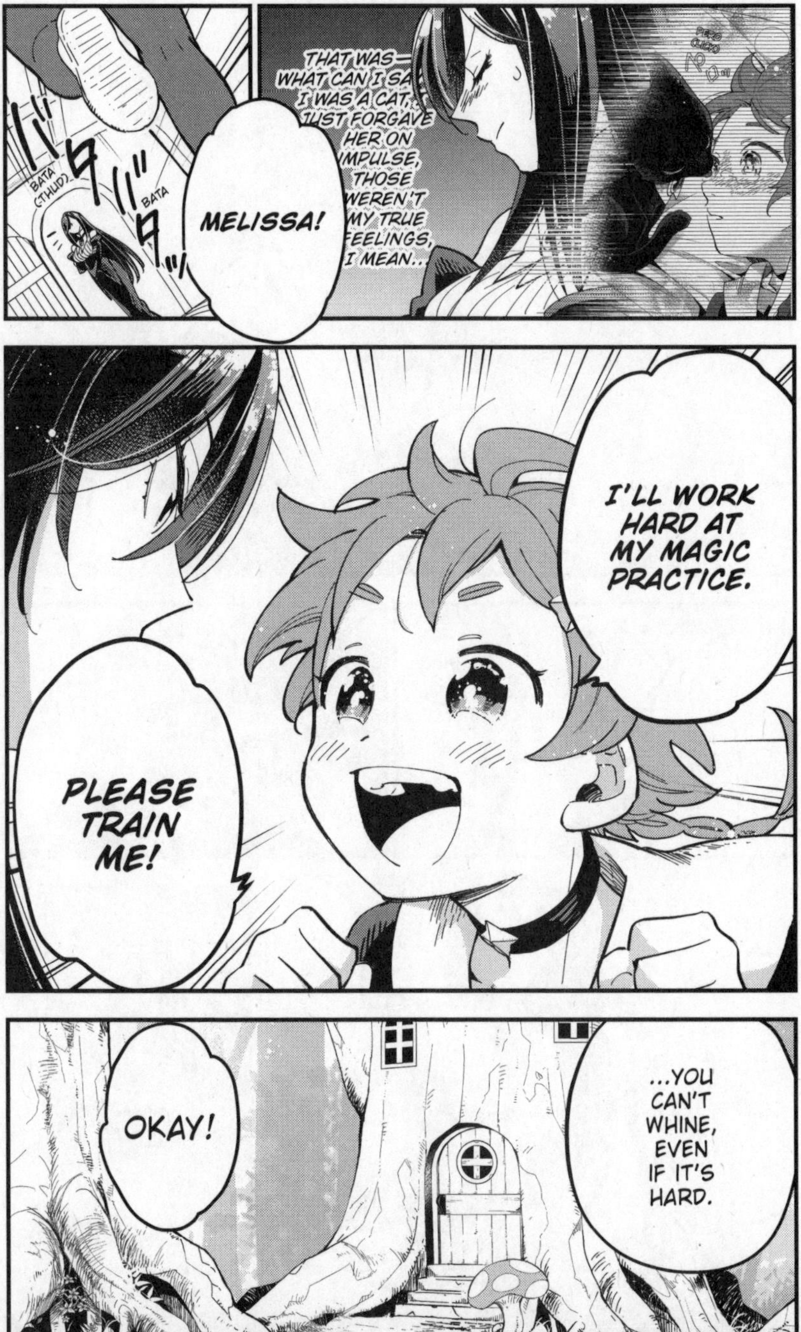
PERO CLICK
THAT WAS— WHAT CAN I SA I WAS A CAT, JUST FORGAVE HER ON IMPULSE, THOSE WEREN'T MY TRUE FEELINGS, I MEAN...
MELISSA!
BATA (THUD)
BATA
I'LL WORK HARD AT MY MAGIC PRACTICE.
PLEASE TRAIN ME!
...YOU CAN'T WHINE, EVEN IF IT'S HARD.
OKAY!

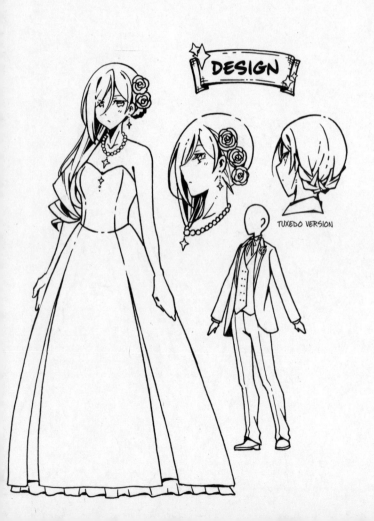

DESIGN

TUXEDO VERSION

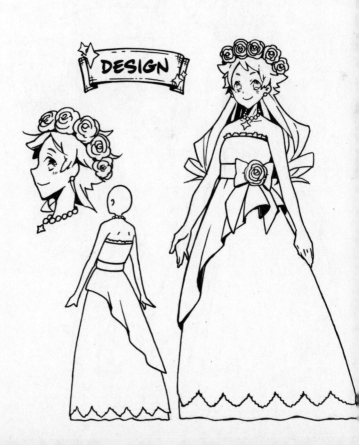

DESIGN

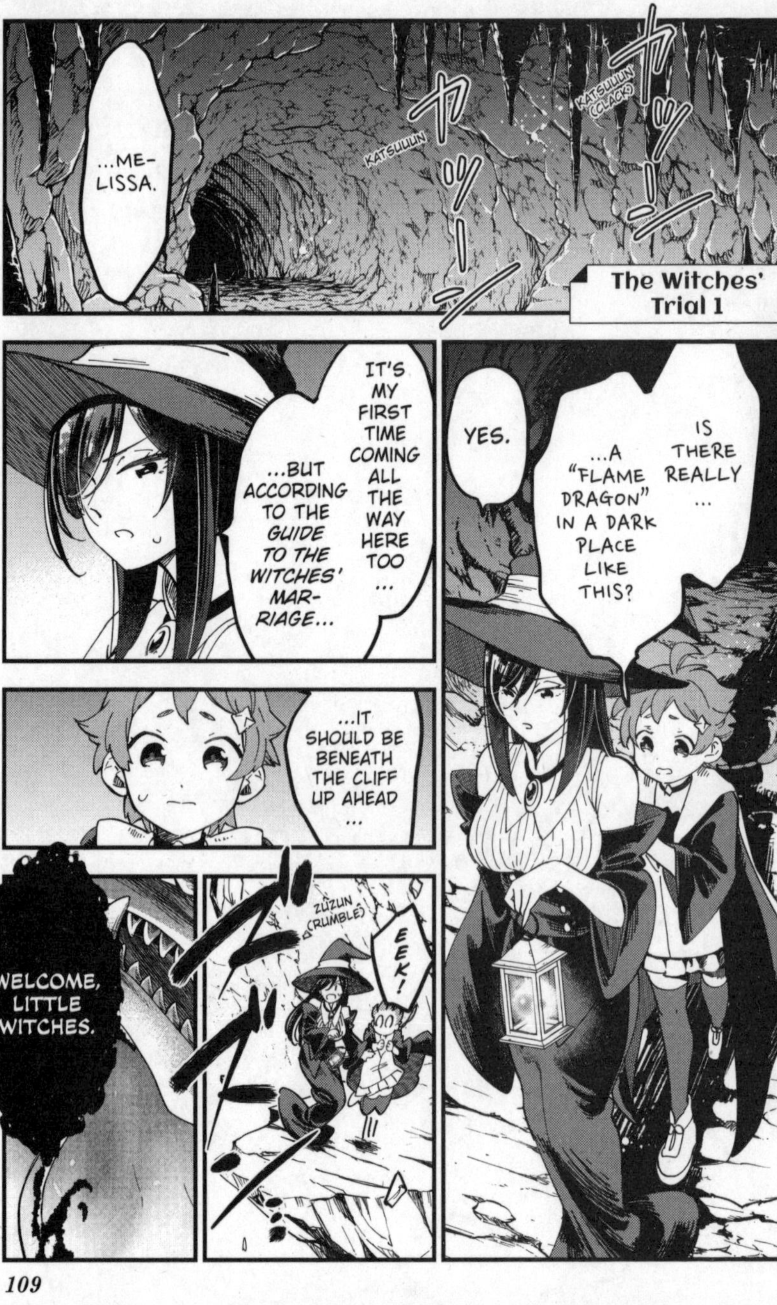
KATSUUUN (CLACK)
KATSUUUN
...ME-LISSA.
The Witches' Trial 1
IS THERE REALLY ...
...A "FLAME DRAGON" IN A DARK PLACE LIKE THIS?
YES.
IT'S MY FIRST TIME COMING ALL THE WAY HERE TOO ...
...BUT ACCORDING TO THE GUIDE TO THE WITCHES' MARRIAGE...
...IT SHOULD BE BENEATH THE CLIFF UP AHEAD ...
ZUZUN (RUMBLE)
EEK!
WELCOME, LITTLE WITCHES.

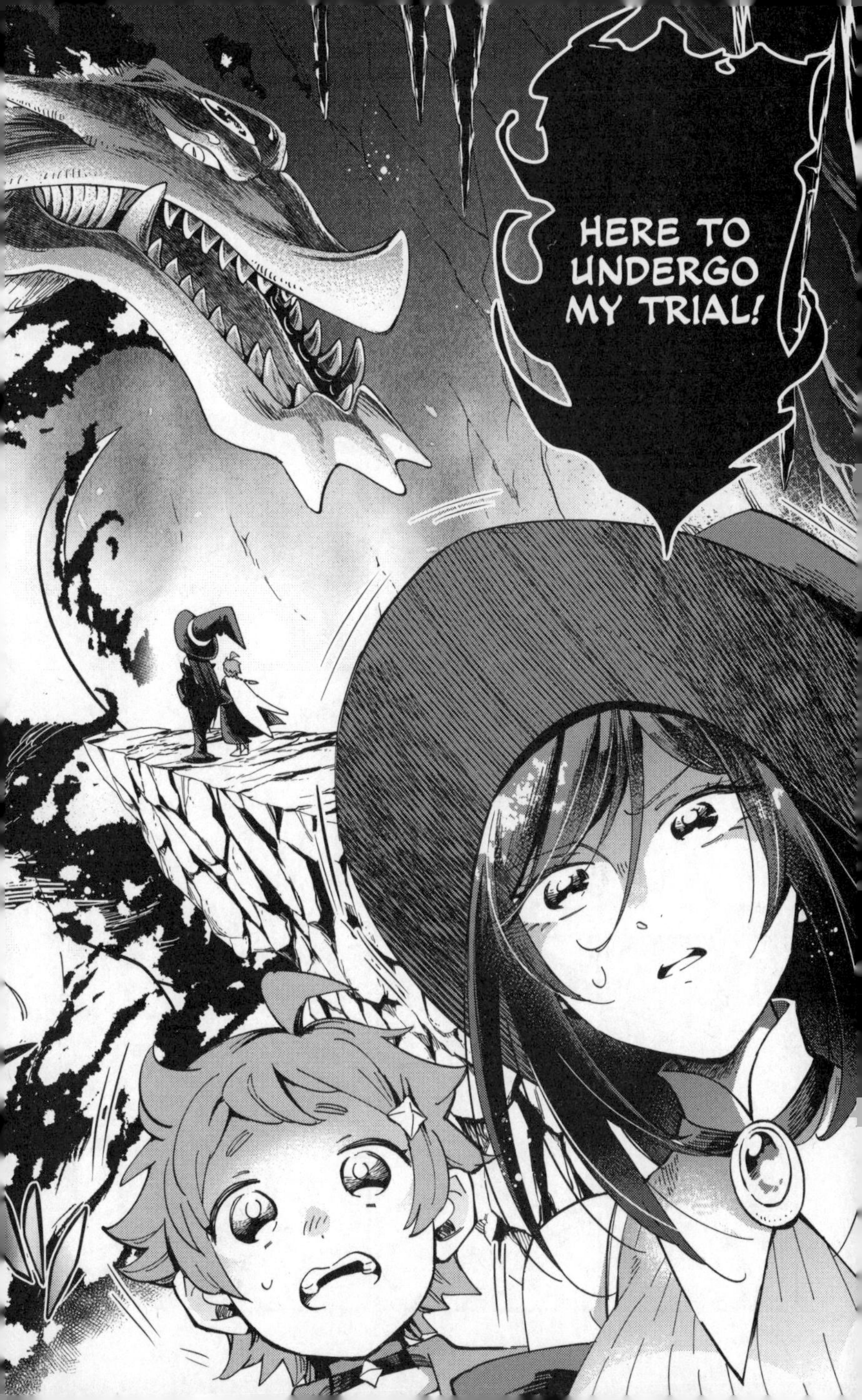
HERE TO UNDERGO MY TRIAL!

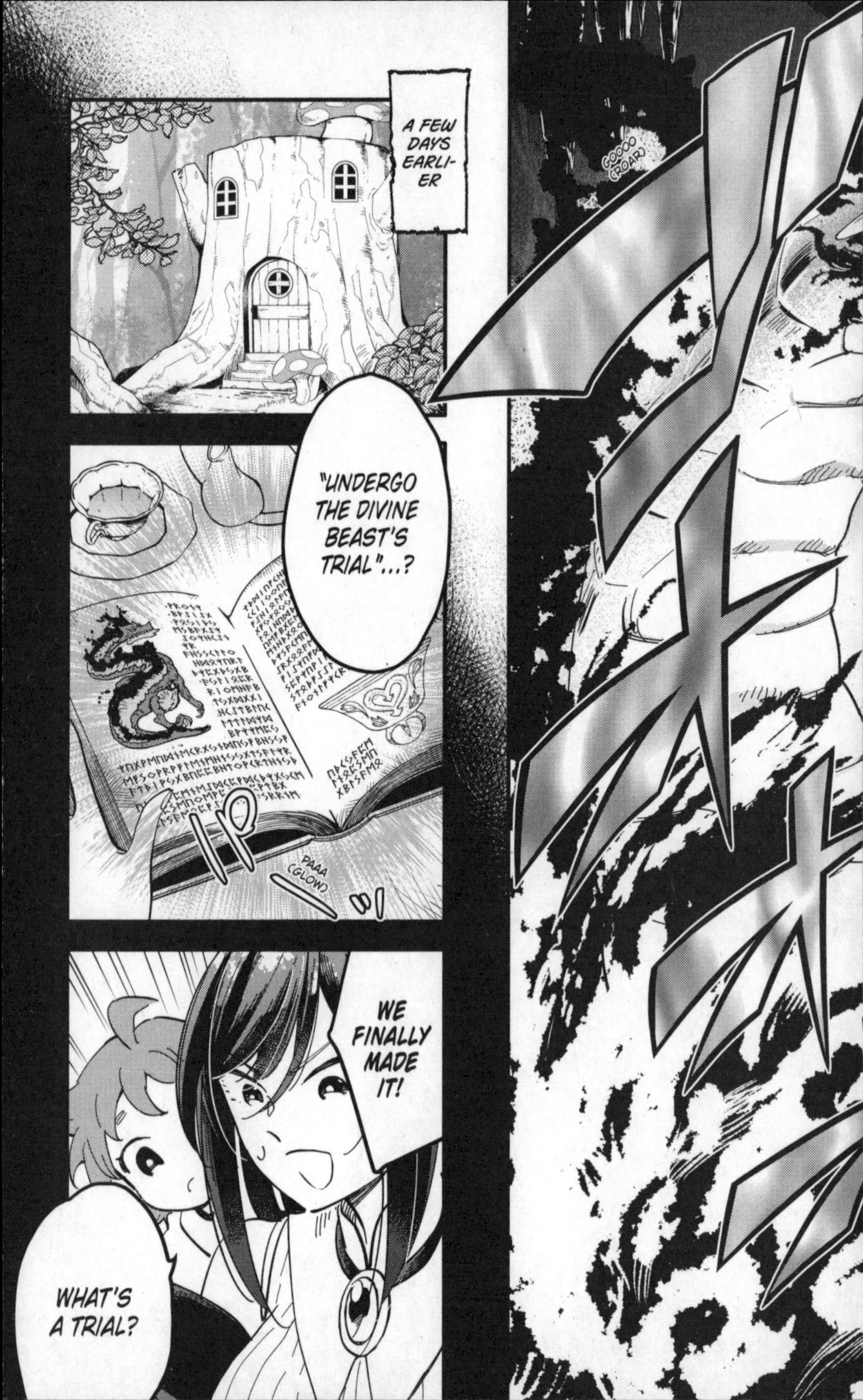
GOOOO (ROAR)
A FEW DAYS EARLIER
"UNDERGO THE DIVINE BEAST'S TRIAL"...?
PAAA (GLOW)
WE FINALLY MADE IT!
WHAT'S A TRIAL?

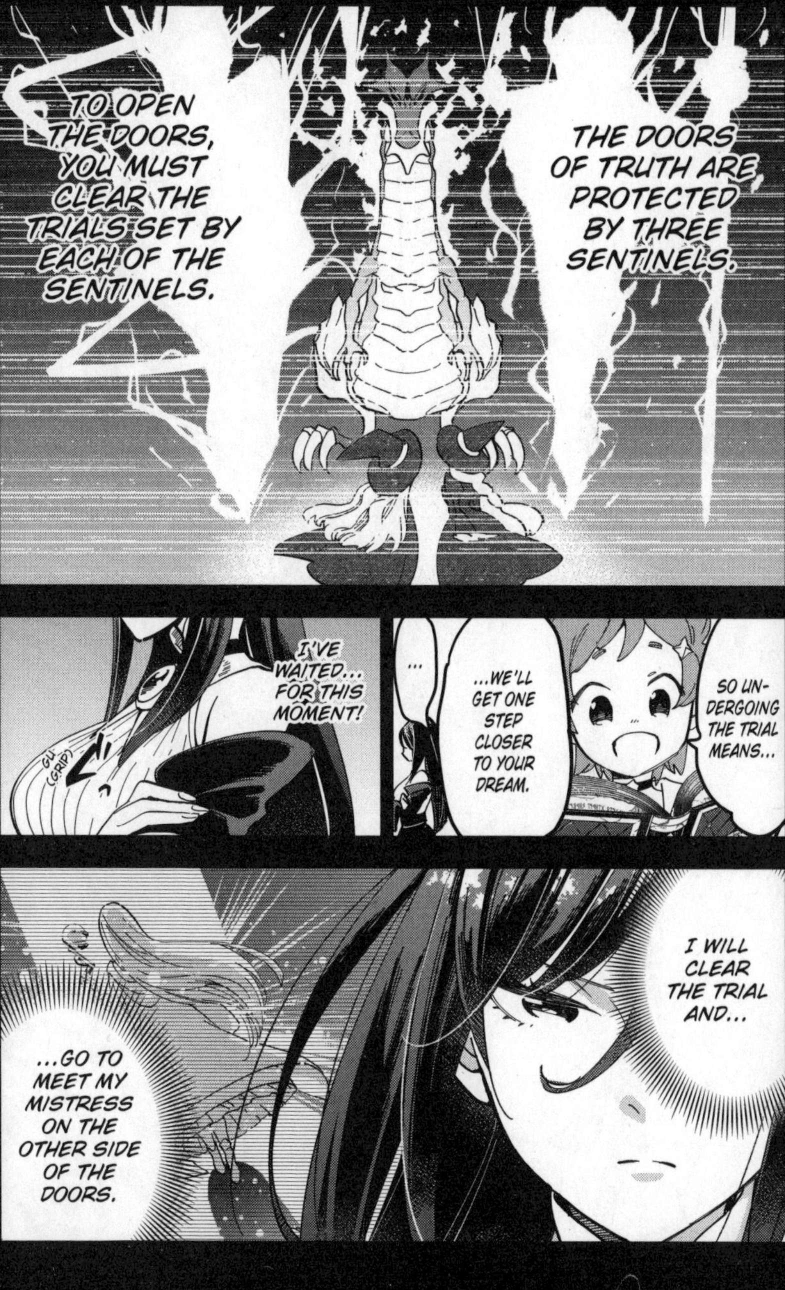
THE DOORS OF TRUTH ARE PROTECTED BY THREE SENTINELS.
TO OPEN THE DOORS, YOU MUST CLEAR THE TRIALS SET BY EACH OF THE SENTINELS.
SO UN-DERGOING THE TRIAL MEANS...
...WE'LL GET ONE STEP CLOSER TO YOUR DREAM.
...
I'VE WAITED... FOR THIS MOMENT!
GU (GRIP)
I WILL CLEAR THE TRIAL AND...
...GO TO MEET MY MISTRESS ON THE OTHER SIDE OF THE DOORS.

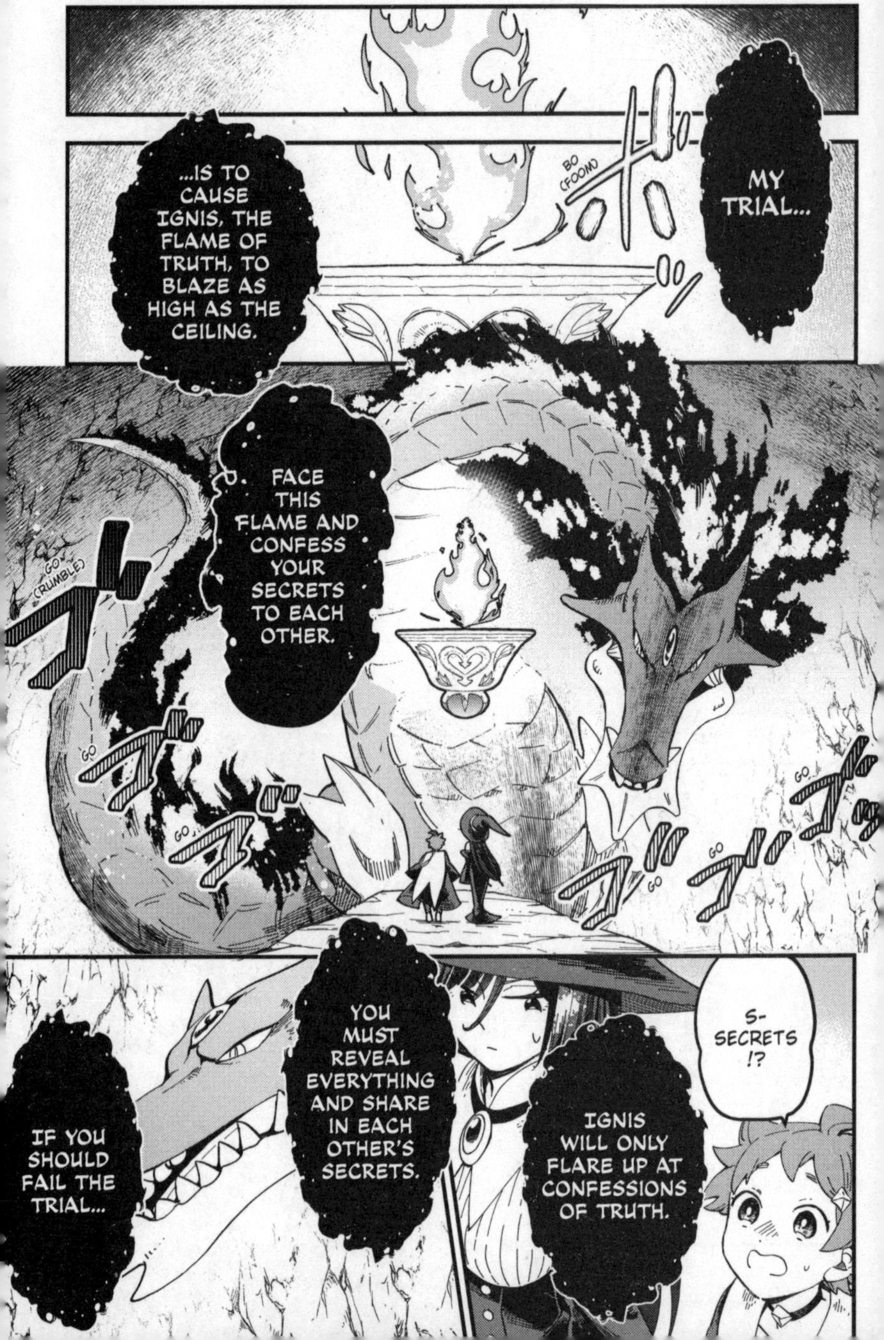
MY TRIAL...
BO (FOOM)
...IS TO CAUSE IGNIS, THE FLAME OF TRUTH, TO BLAZE AS HIGH AS THE CEILING.
GO GO GO
FACE THIS FLAME AND CONFESS YOUR SECRETS TO EACH OTHER.
GO (RUMBLE)
GO
GO
S-SECRETS!?
IGNIS WILL ONLY FLARE UP AT CONFESSIONS OF TRUTH.
YOU MUST REVEAL EVERYTHING AND SHARE IN EACH OTHER'S SECRETS.
IF YOU SHOULD FAIL THE TRIAL...

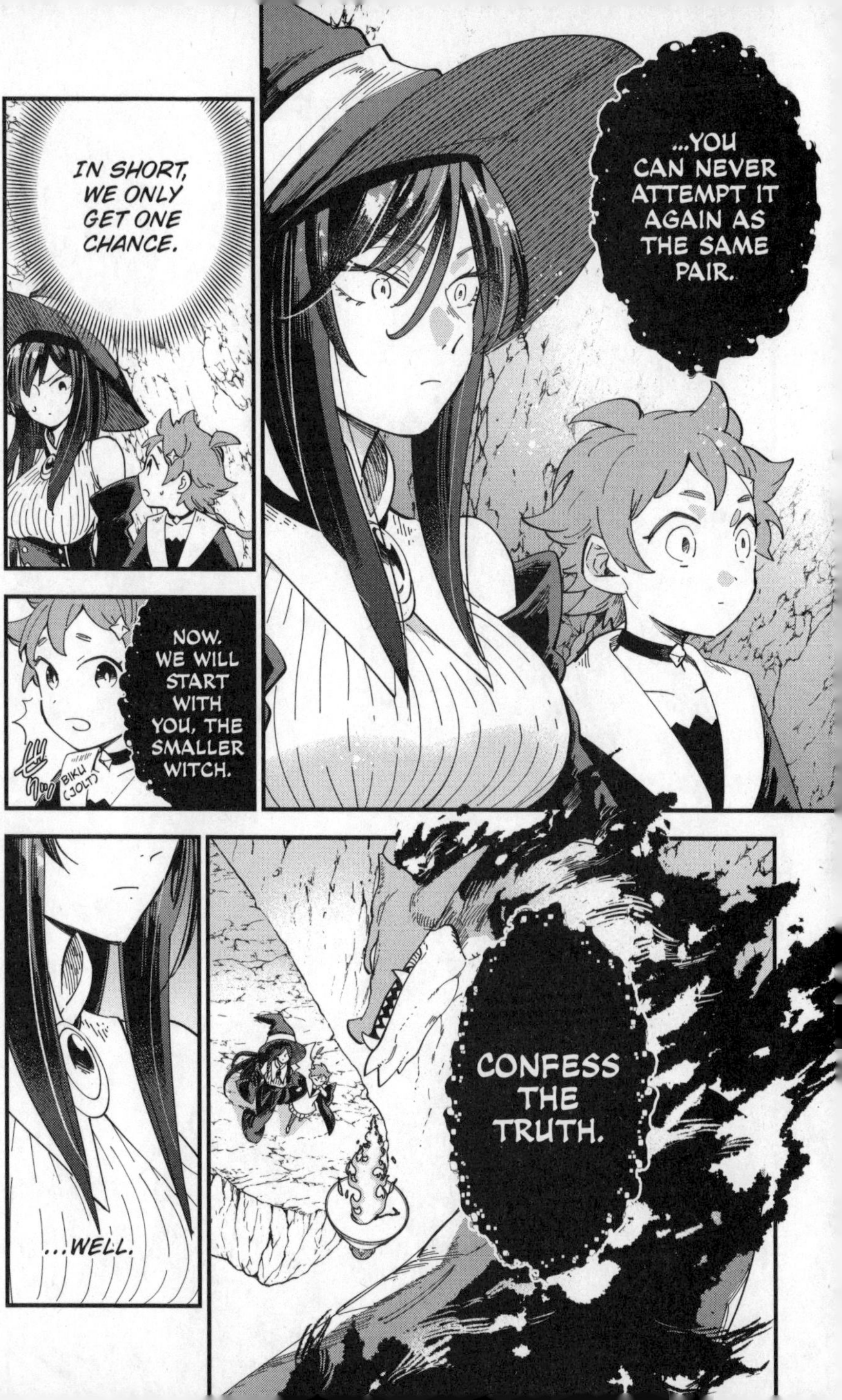
...YOU CAN NEVER ATTEMPT IT AGAIN AS THE SAME PAIR.
IN SHORT, WE ONLY GET ONE CHANCE.
NOW. WE WILL START WITH YOU, THE SMALLER WITCH.
BIKU (JOLT)
CONFESS THE TRUTH.
...WELL.

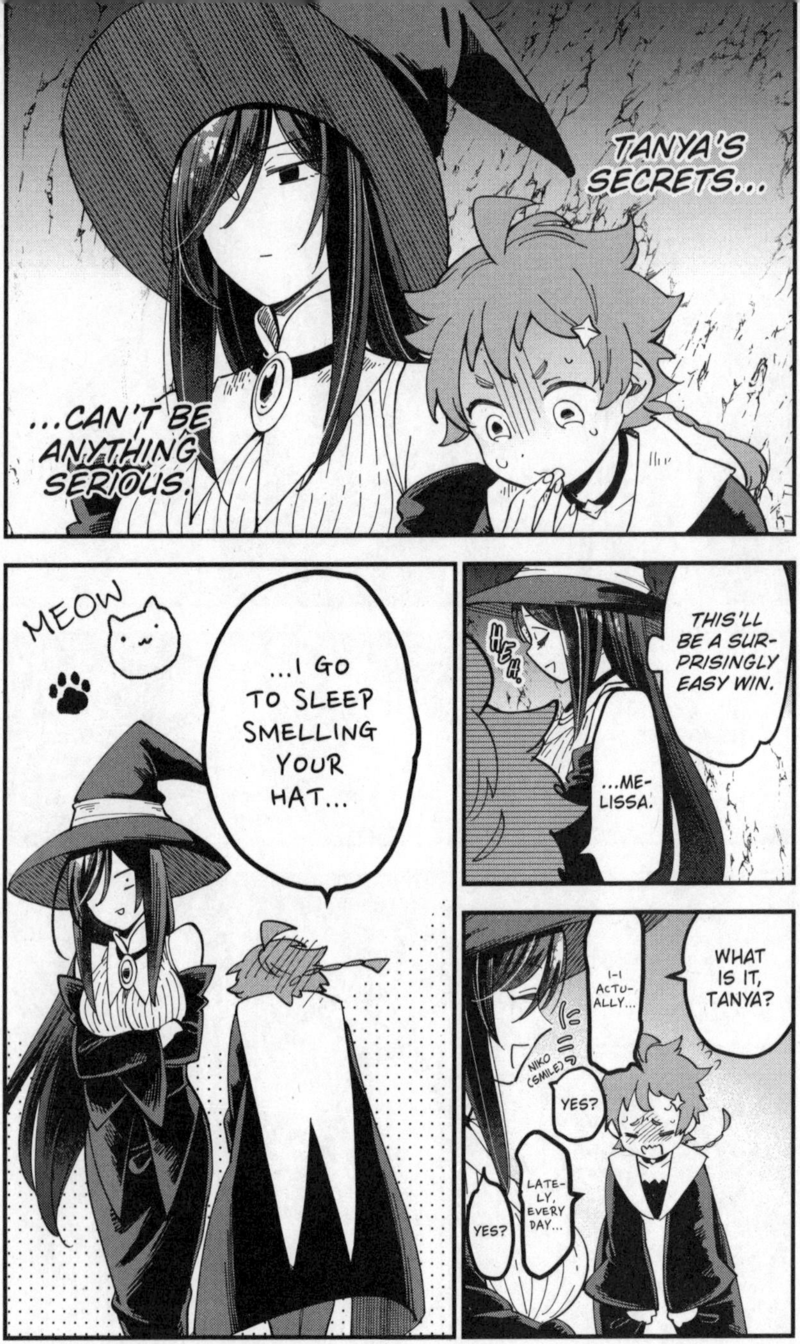
TANYA'S SECRETS...
...CAN'T BE ANYTHING SERIOUS.
THIS'LL BE A SUR-PRISINGLY EASY WIN.
HEH.
...ME-LISSA.
WHAT IS IT, TANYA?
I-I ACTU-ALLY...
NIKO (SMILE)
YES?
LATE-LY, EVERY DAY...
YES?
MEOW
...I GO TO SLEEP SMELLING YOUR HAT...

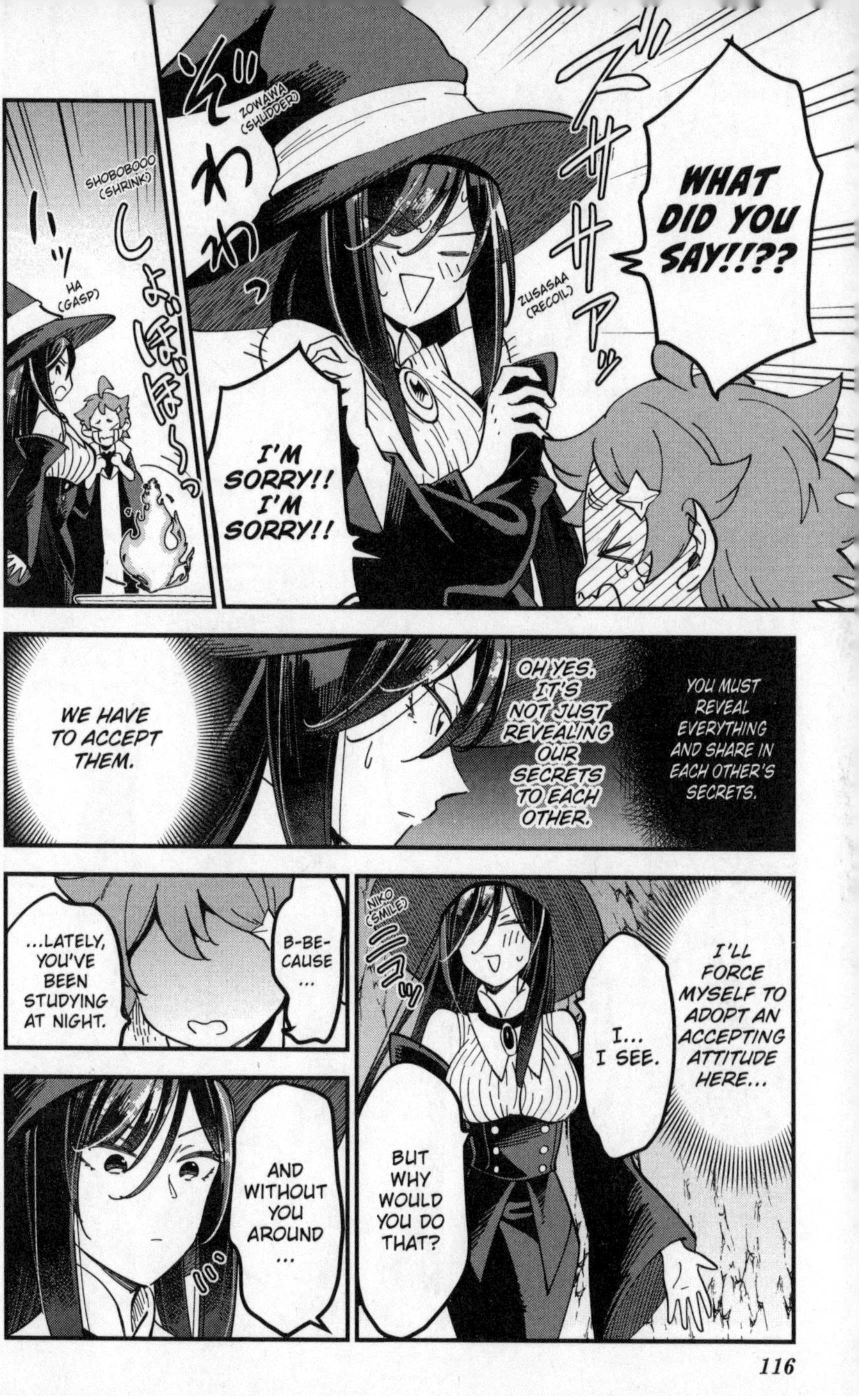
WHAT DID YOU SAY!!??
ZUSASAA (RECOIL)
ZOWAWA (SHUDDER)
I'M SORRY!! I'M SORRY!!
SHOBOBOOO (SHRINK)
HA (GASP)
YOU MUST REVEAL EVERYTHING AND SHARE IN EACH OTHER'S SECRETS.
OH YES. IT'S NOT JUST REVEALING OUR SECRETS TO EACH OTHER.
WE HAVE TO ACCEPT THEM.
I'LL FORCE MYSELF TO ADOPT AN ACCEPTING ATTITUDE HERE...
I... I SEE.
NIKO (SMILE)
BUT WHY WOULD YOU DO THAT?
B-BE-CAUSE...
...LATELY, YOU'VE BEEN STUDYING AT NIGHT.
AND WITHOUT YOU AROUND...

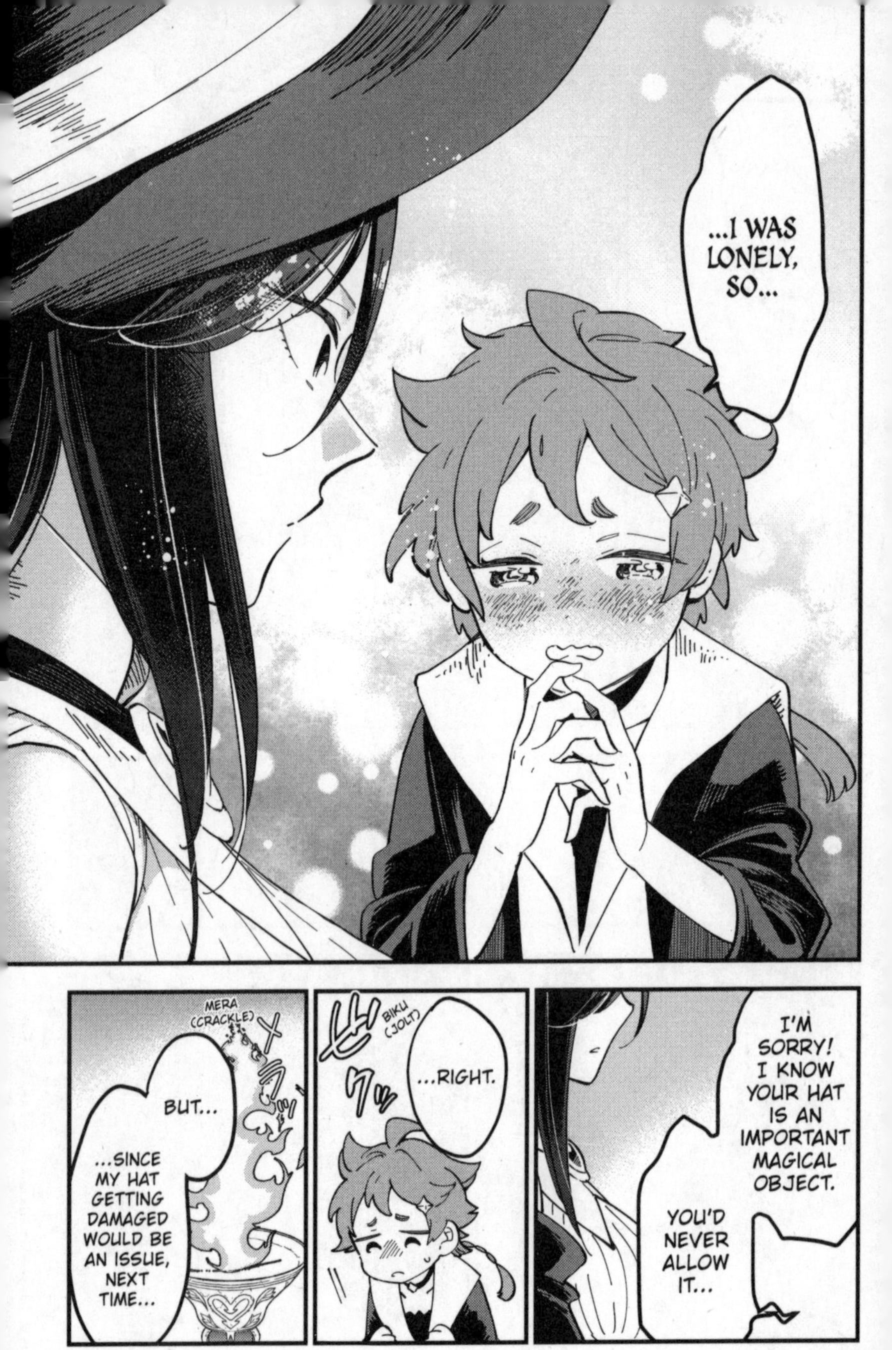
...I WAS LONELY, SO...
I'M SORRY! I KNOW YOUR HAT IS AN IMPORTANT MAGICAL OBJECT.
YOU'D NEVER ALLOW IT...
BIKU (JOLT)
...RIGHT.
MERA (CRACKLE)
BUT...
...SINCE MY HAT GETTING DAMAGED WOULD BE AN ISSUE, NEXT TIME...

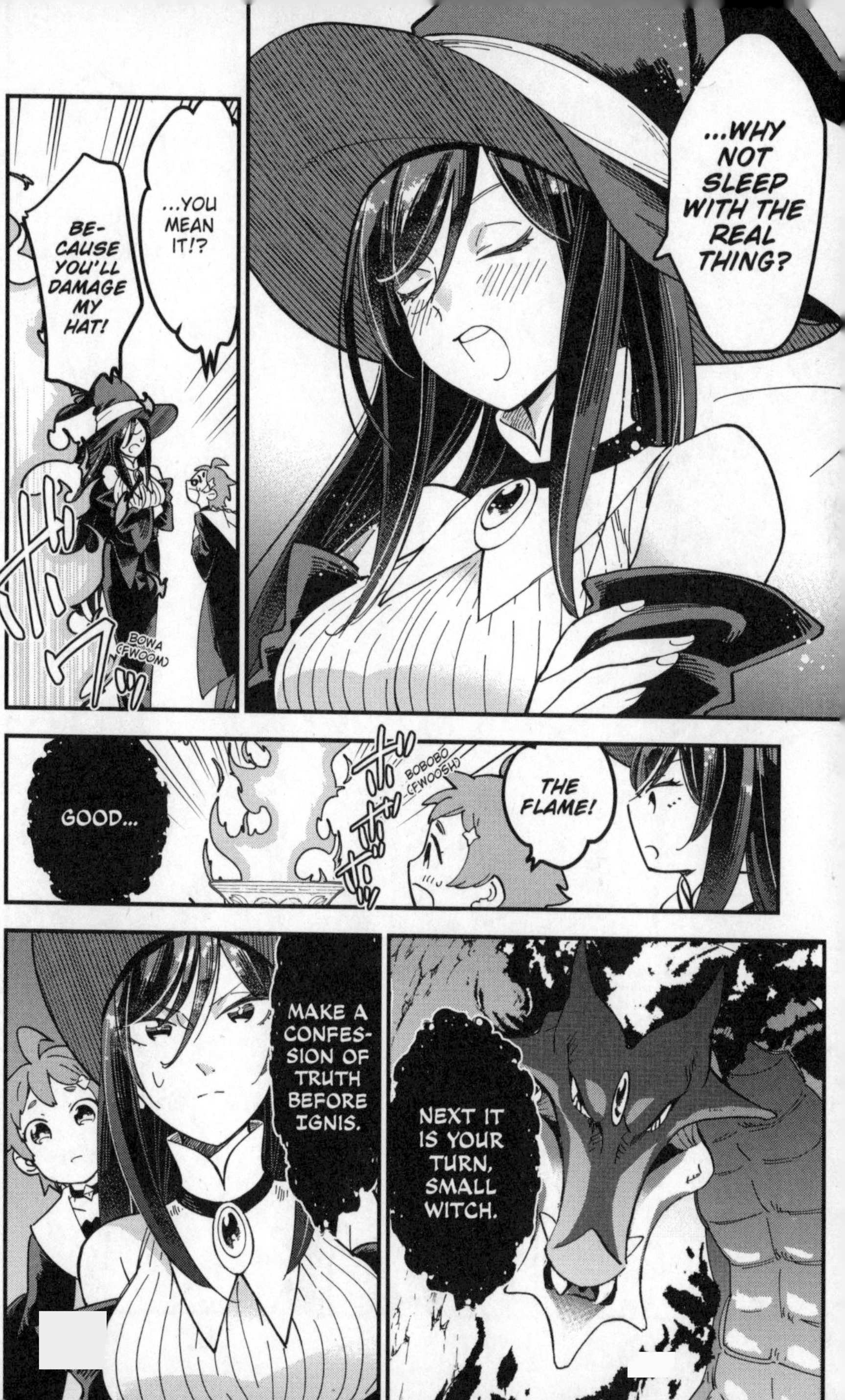
...WHY NOT SLEEP WITH THE REAL THING?
...YOU MEAN IT!?
BE-CAUSE YOU'LL DAMAGE MY HAT!
BOWA (FWOOM)
THE FLAME!
BOBOBO (FWOOSH)
GOOD...
NEXT IT IS YOUR TURN, SMALL WITCH.
MAKE A CONFES-SION OF TRUTH BEFORE IGNIS.

The Witches' Trial 2

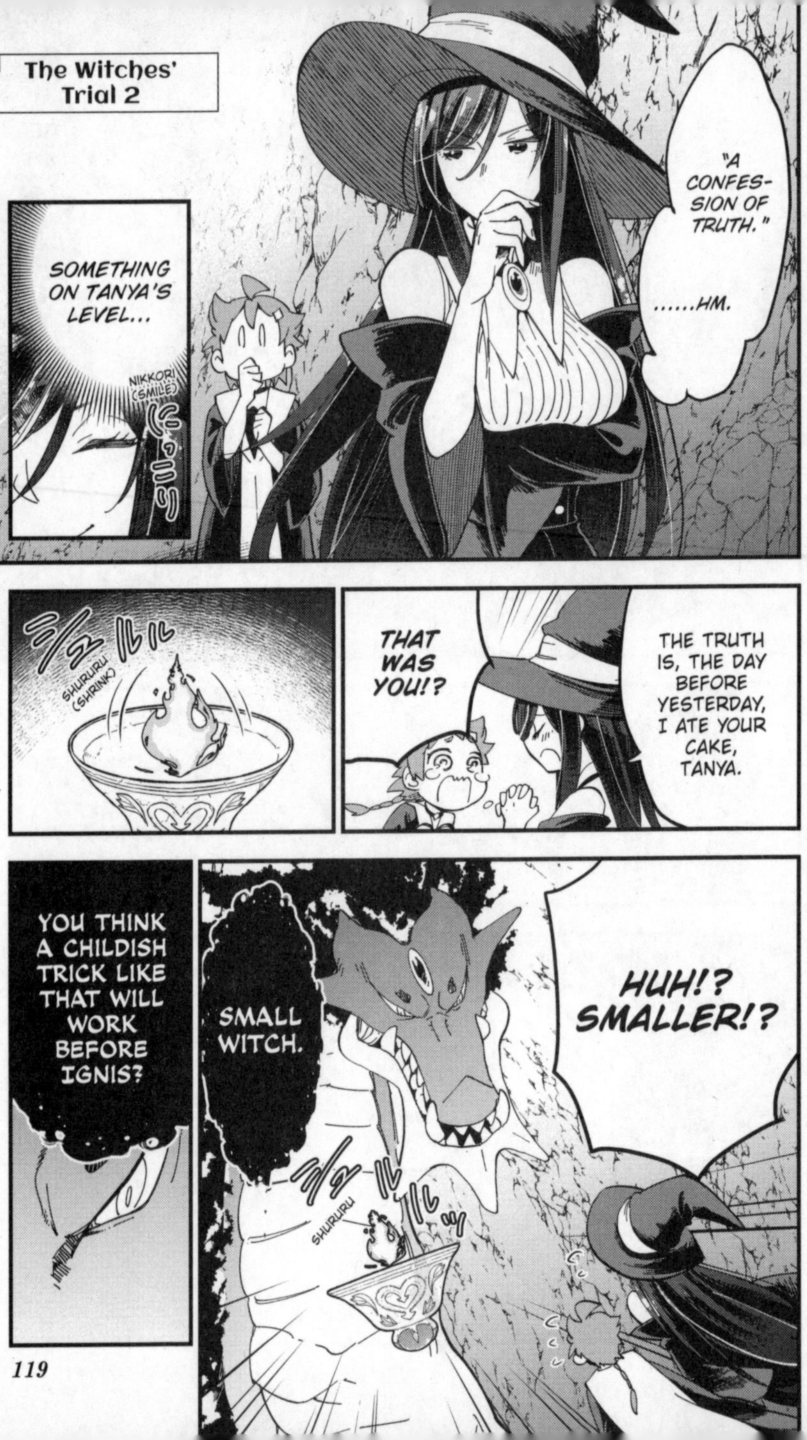
"A CONFESSION OF TRUTH."
......HM.
SOMETHING ON TANYA'S LEVEL...
NIKKORI (SMILE)
THE TRUTH IS, THE DAY BEFORE YESTERDAY, I ATE YOUR CAKE, TANYA.
THAT WAS YOU!?
SHURURU (SHRINK)
HUH!? SMALLER!?
SMALL WITCH.
SHURURU
YOU THINK A CHILDISH TRICK LIKE THAT WILL WORK BEFORE IGNIS?

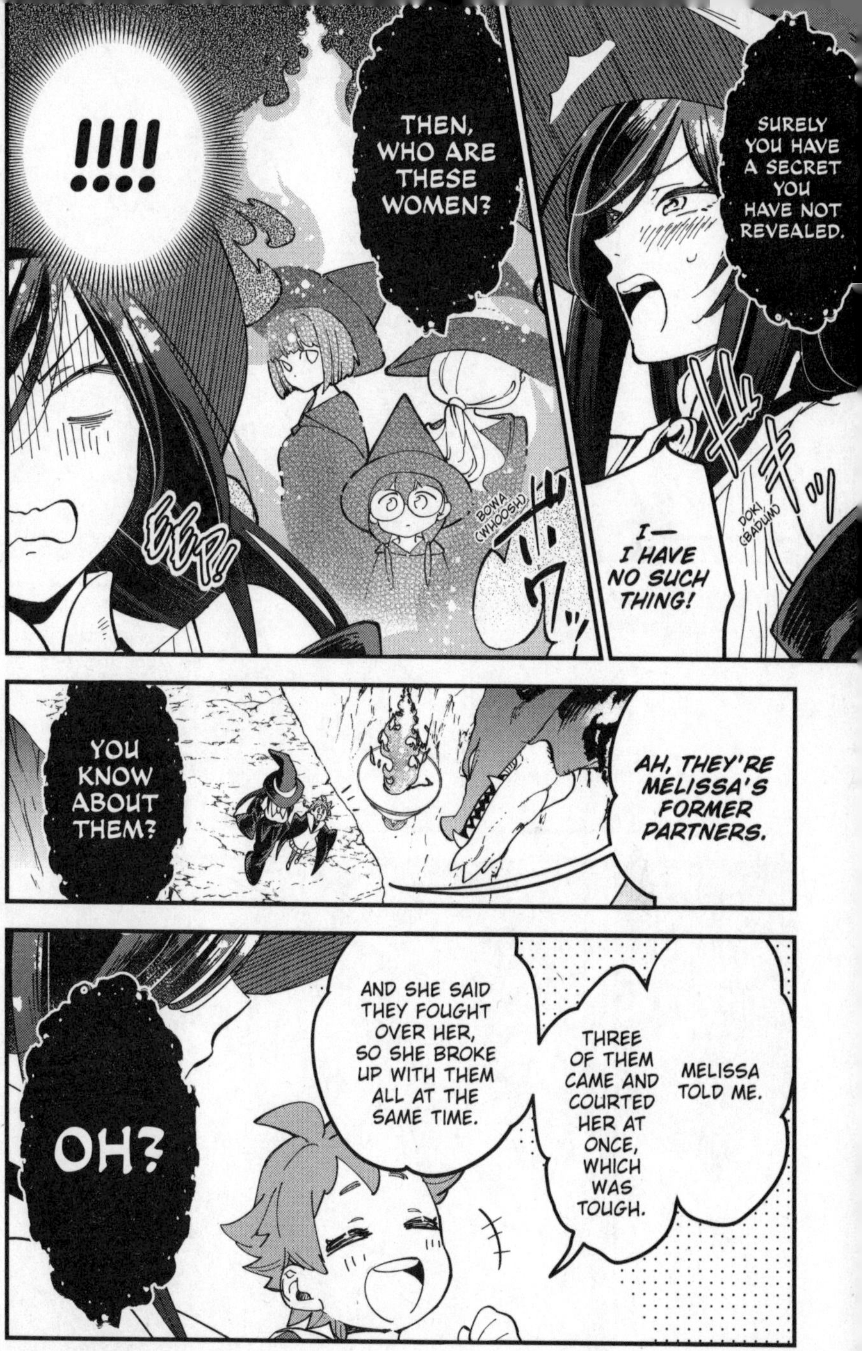
SURELY YOU HAVE A SECRET YOU HAVE NOT REVEALED.
DOKI (BADUMP)
I— I HAVE NO SUCH THING!
THEN, WHO ARE THESE WOMEN?
BOWA (WHOOSH)
!!!!
EEP!
AH, THEY'RE MELISSA'S FORMER PARTNERS.
YOU KNOW ABOUT THEM?
MELISSA TOLD ME.
THREE OF THEM CAME AND COURTED HER AT ONCE, WHICH WAS TOUGH.
AND SHE SAID THEY FOUGHT OVER HER, SO SHE BROKE UP WITH THEM ALL AT THE SAME TIME.
OH?

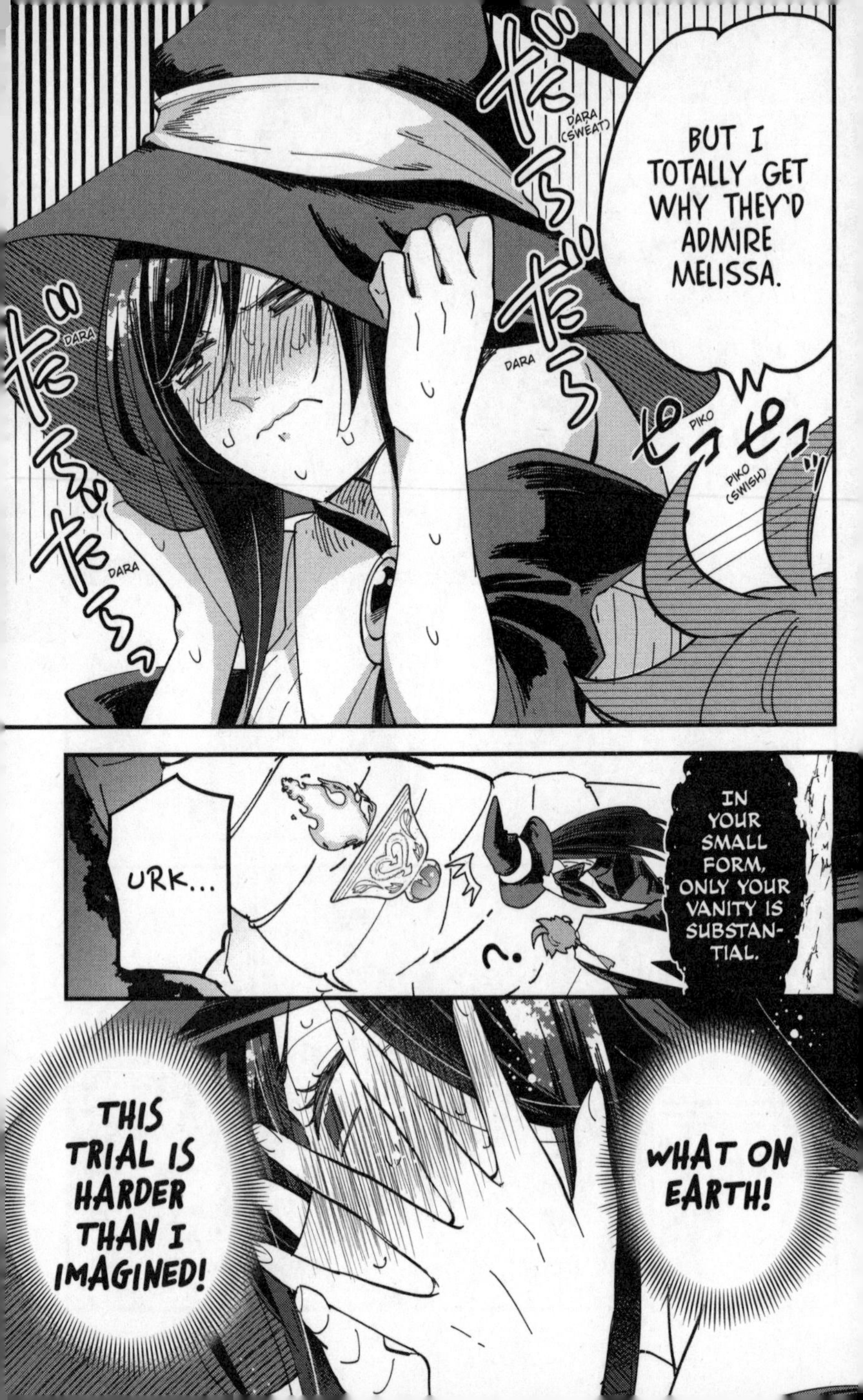
BUT I TOTALLY GET WHY THEY'D ADMIRE MELISSA.
DARA (SWEAT)
DARA
DARA
DARA
PIKO
PIKO (SWISH)
IN YOUR SMALL FORM, ONLY YOUR VANITY IS SUBSTANTIAL.
URK...
?
WHAT ON EARTH!
THIS TRIAL IS HARDER THAN I IMAGINED!

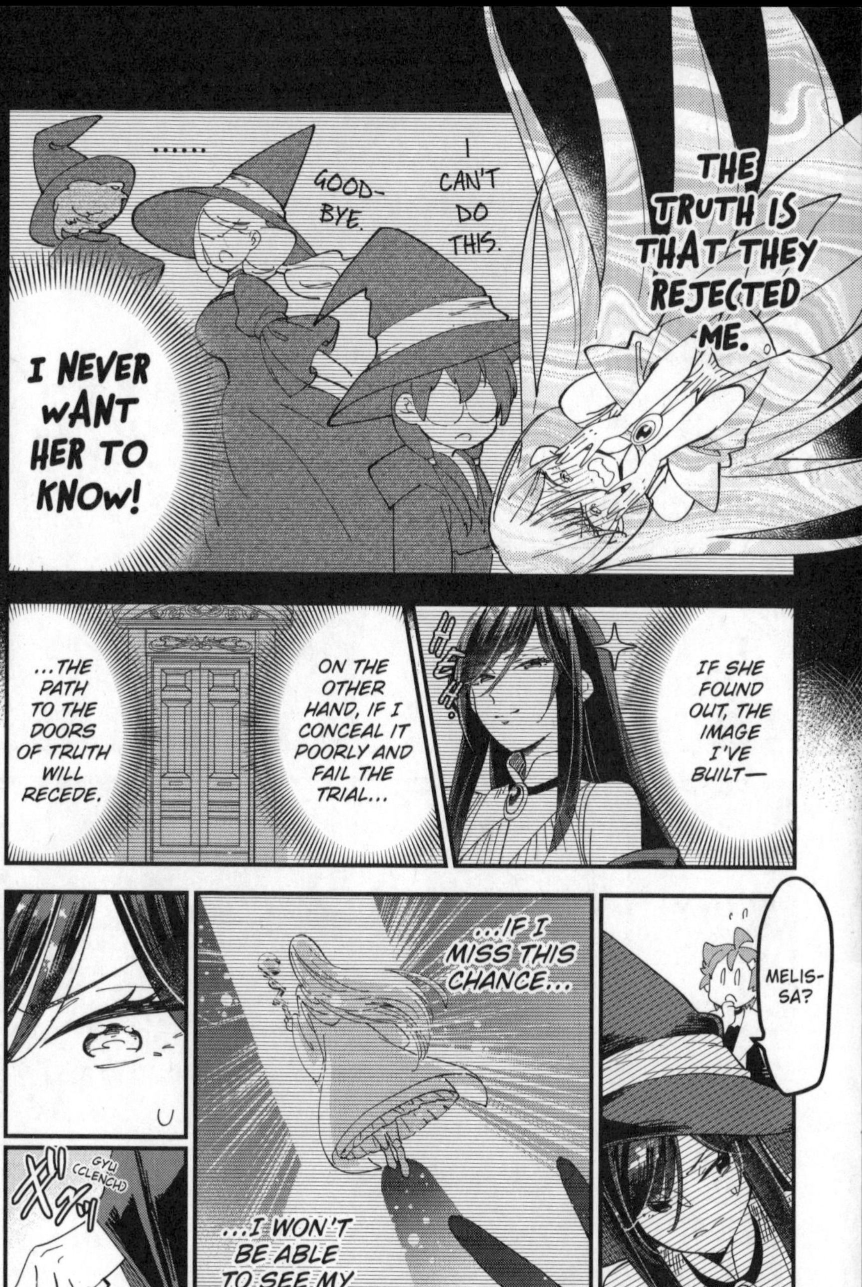
THE TRUTH IS THAT THEY REJECTED ME.
I CAN'T DO THIS.
GOOD-BYE.
......
I NEVER WANT HER TO KNOW!
IF SHE FOUND OUT, THE IMAGE I'VE BUILT—
ON THE OTHER HAND, IF I CONCEAL IT POORLY AND FAIL THE TRIAL...
...THE PATH TO THE DOORS OF TRUTH WILL RECEDE.
MELIS-SA?
...BUT...
...IF I MISS THIS CHANCE...
...I WON'T BE ABLE TO SEE MY MISTRESS.
GYU (CLENCH)

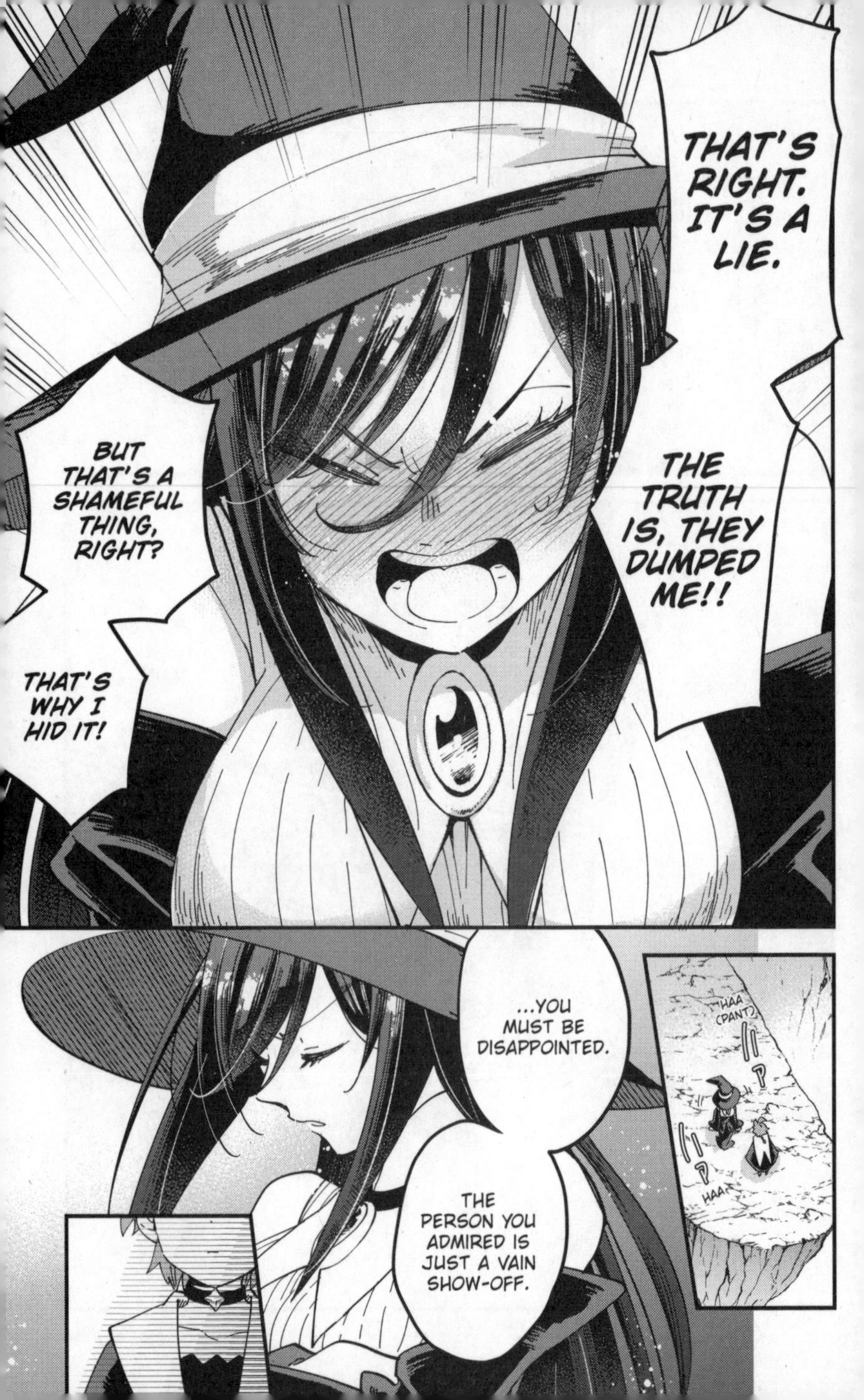
THAT'S RIGHT. IT'S A LIE.
THE TRUTH IS, THEY DUMPED ME!!
BUT THAT'S A SHAMEFUL THING, RIGHT?
THAT'S WHY I HID IT!
HAA (PANT)
HAA
...YOU MUST BE DISAPPOINTED.
THE PERSON YOU ADMIRED IS JUST A VAIN SHOW-OFF.

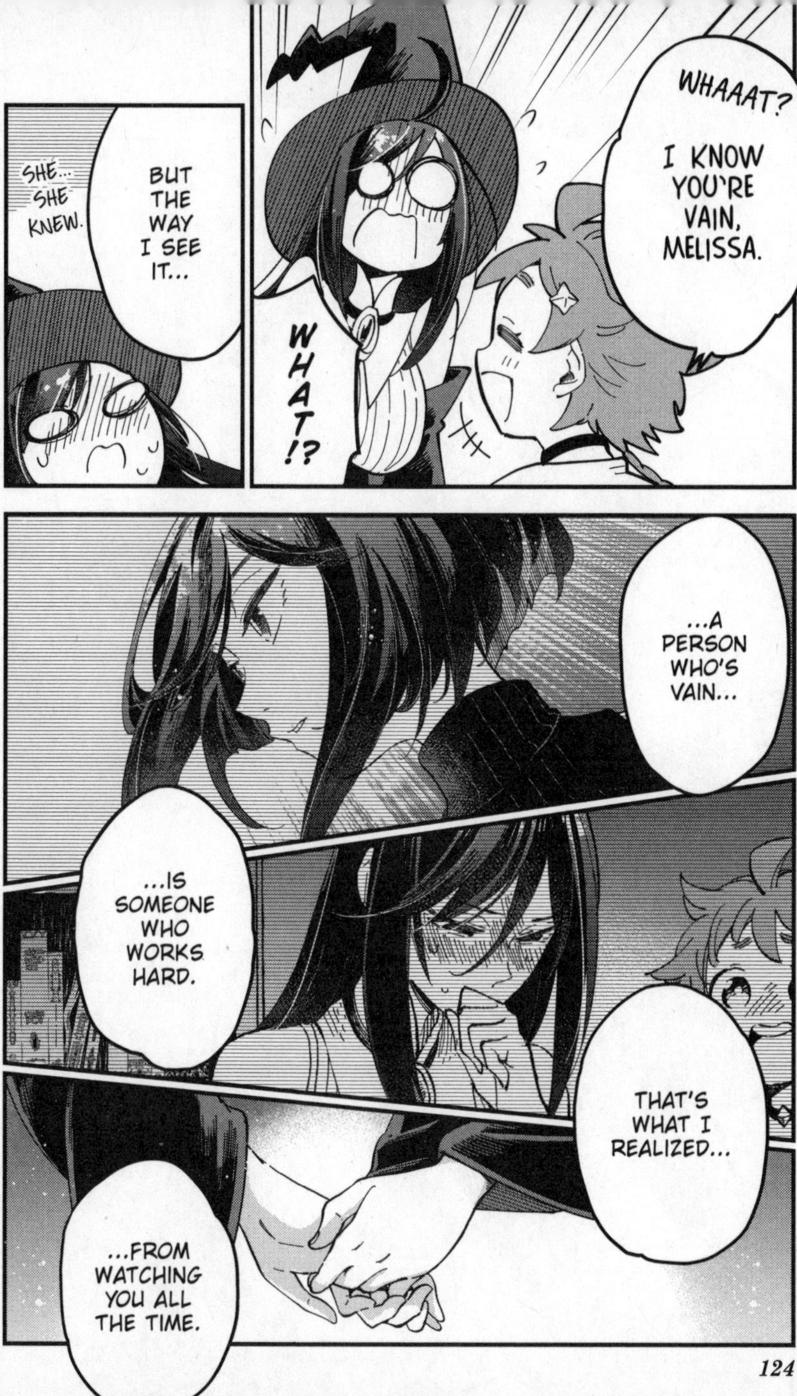
WHAAAT?
I KNOW YOU'RE VAIN, MELISSA.
WHAT!?
BUT THE WAY I SEE IT...
SHE... SHE KNEW.
...A PERSON WHO'S VAIN...
...IS SOMEONE WHO WORKS HARD.
THAT'S WHAT I REALIZED...
...FROM WATCHING YOU ALL THE TIME.

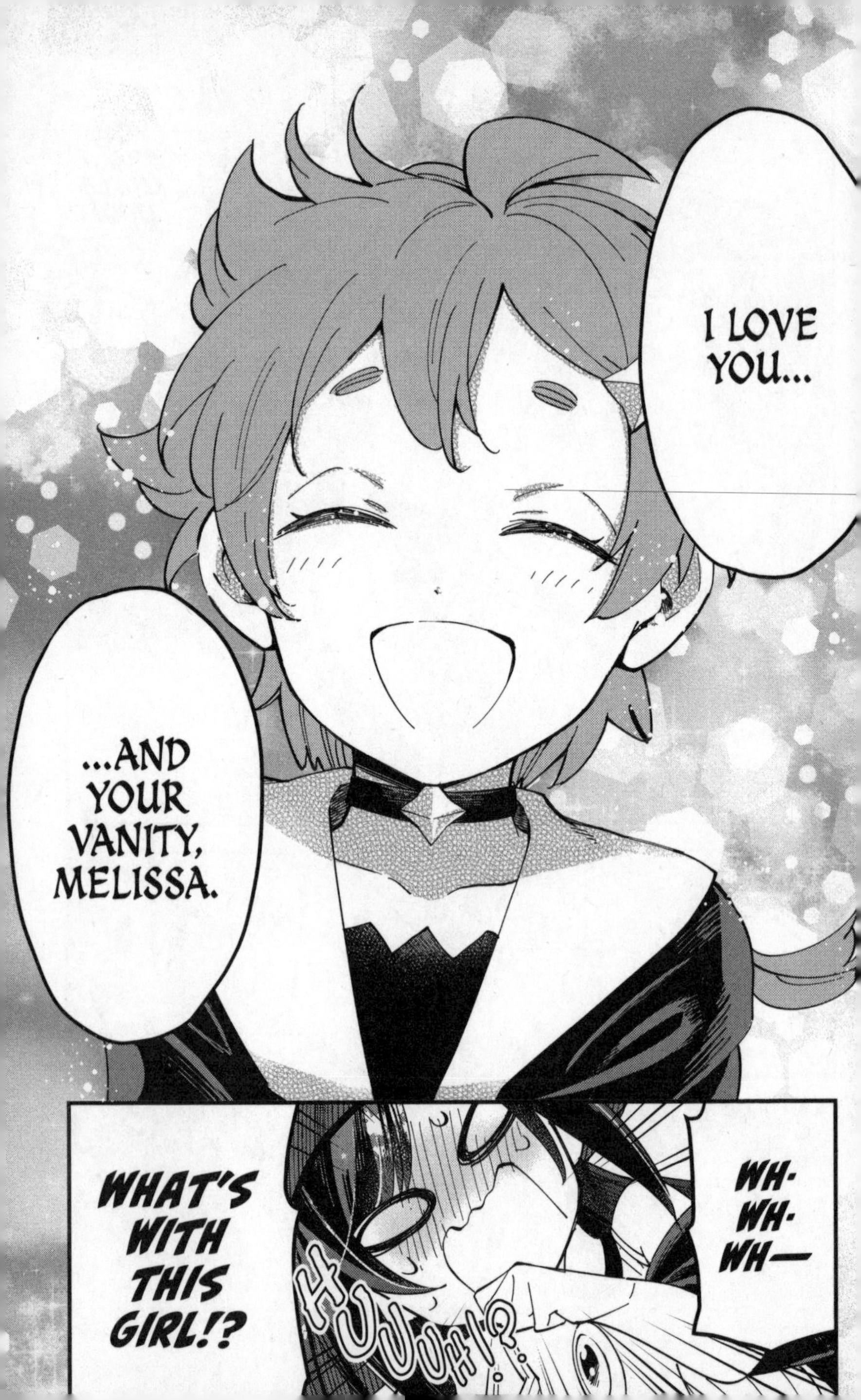
I LOVE YOU...
...AND YOUR VANITY, MELISSA.
WH-WH-WH—
WHAT'S WITH THIS GIRL!?
HUUUH!?

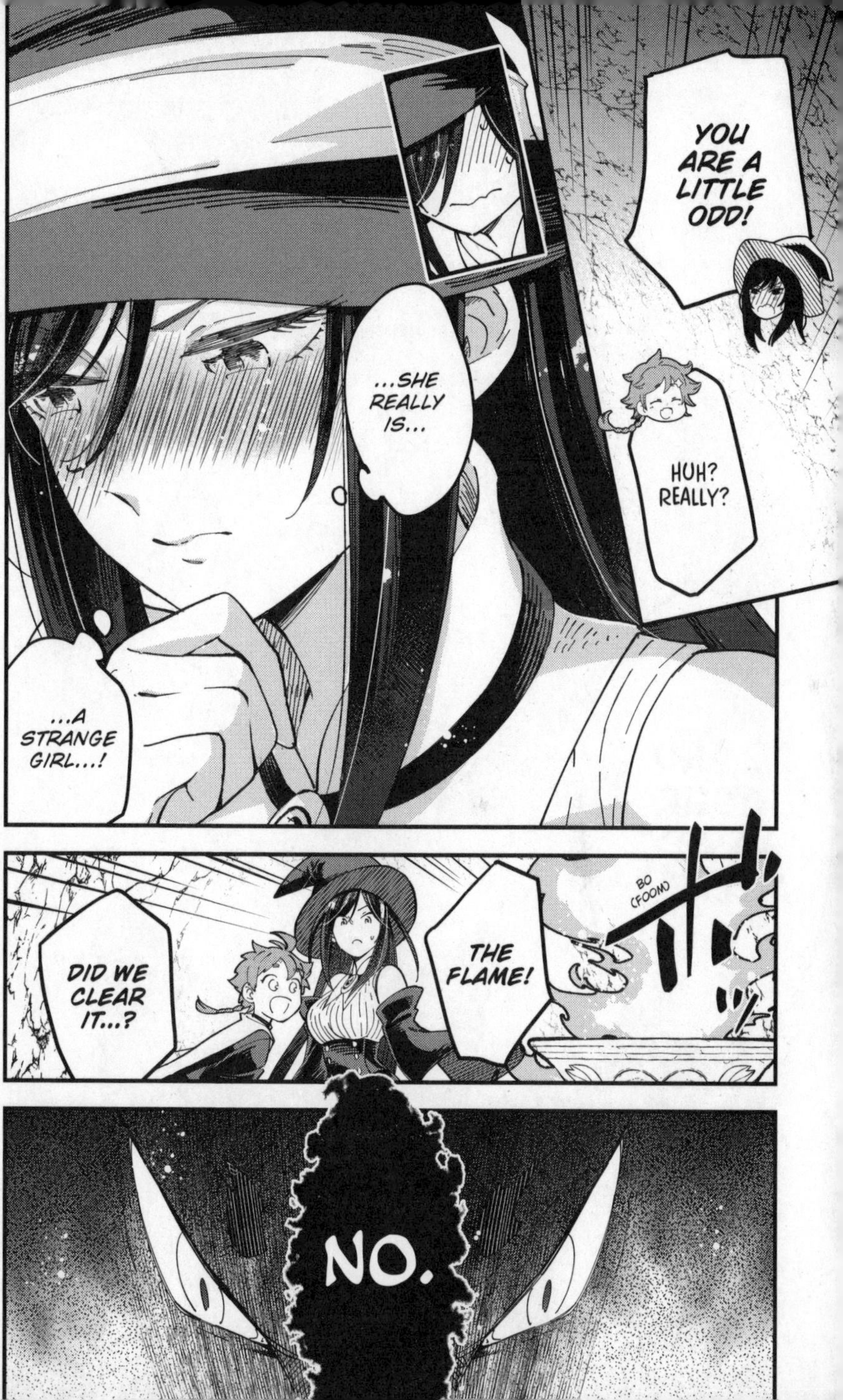
YOU ARE A LITTLE ODD!
HUH? REALLY?
...SHE REALLY IS...
...A STRANGE GIRL...!
BO (FOOM)
THE FLAME!
DID WE CLEAR IT...?
NO.

The Witches' Trial 3

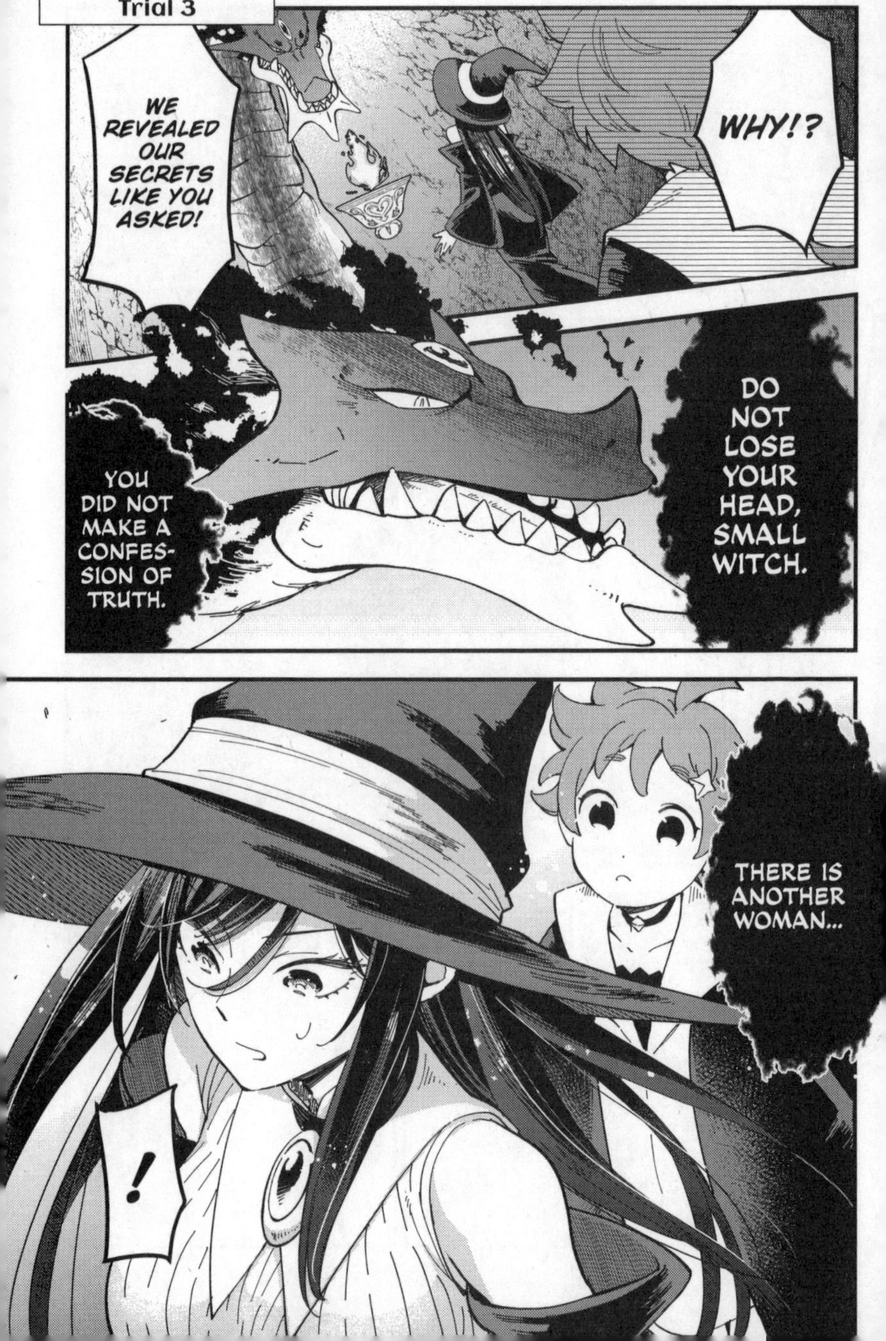
WHY!?
WE REVEALED OUR SECRETS LIKE YOU ASKED!
DO NOT LOSE YOUR HEAD, SMALL WITCH.
YOU DID NOT MAKE A CONFESSION OF TRUTH.
THERE IS ANOTHER WOMAN...
!

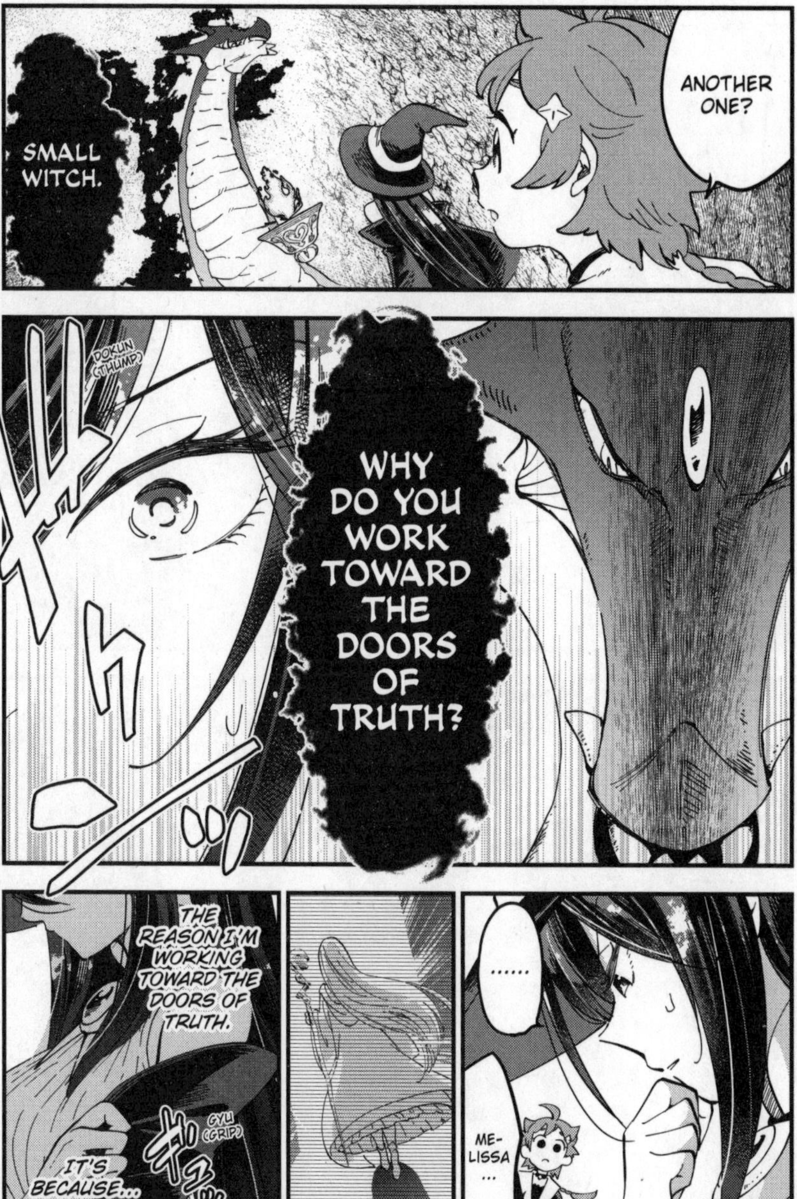
ANOTHER ONE?
SMALL WITCH.
WHY DO YOU WORK TOWARD THE DOORS OF TRUTH?
DOKUN (THUMP)
......
ME-LISSA...
THE REASON I'M WORKING TOWARD THE DOORS OF TRUTH.
GYU (GRIP)
IT'S BECAUSE...

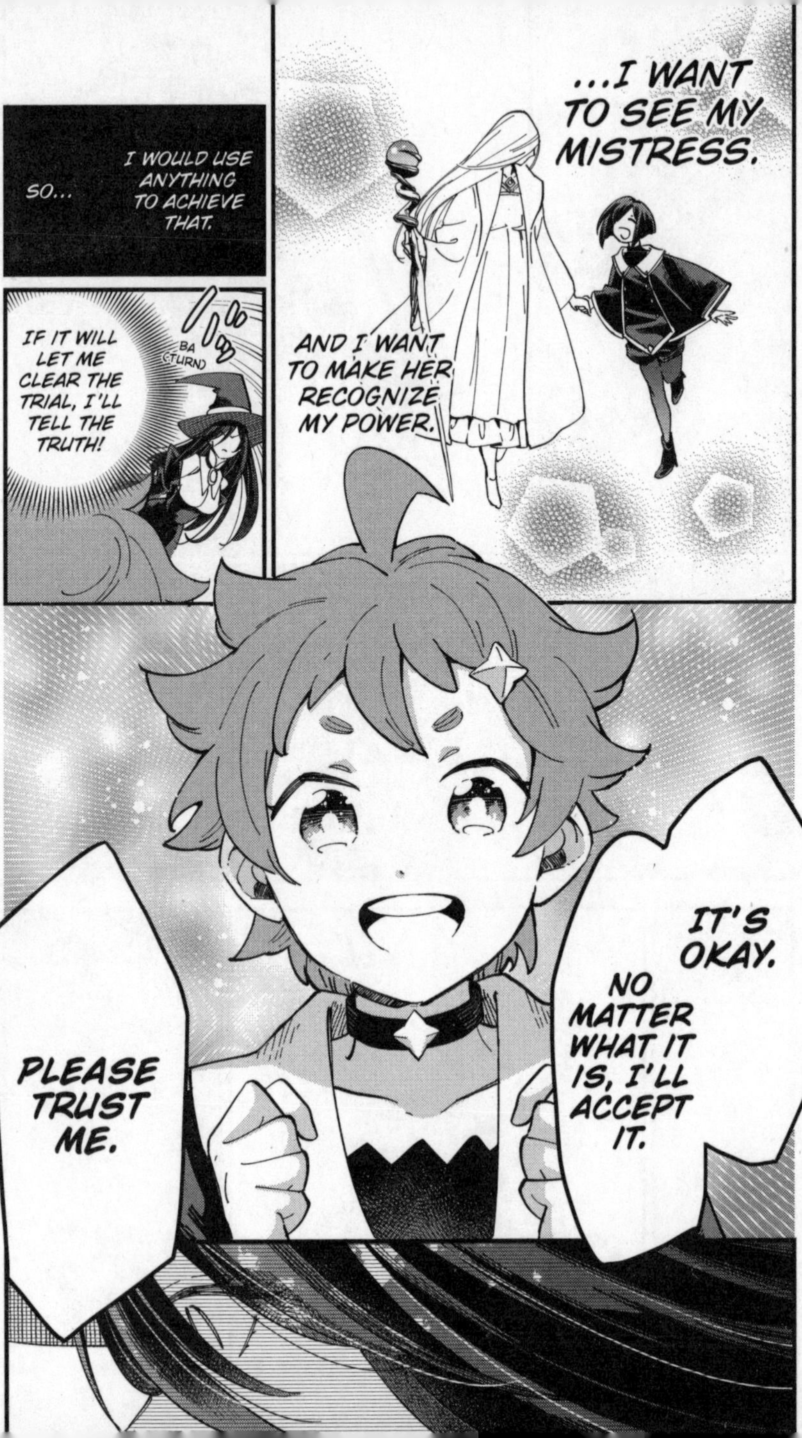
...I WANT TO SEE MY MISTRESS.
AND I WANT TO MAKE HER RECOGNIZE MY POWER.
I WOULD USE ANYTHING TO ACHIEVE THAT.
SO...
BA (TURN)
IF IT WILL LET ME CLEAR THE TRIAL, I'LL TELL THE TRUTH!
IT'S OKAY.
NO MATTER WHAT IT IS, I'LL ACCEPT IT.
PLEASE TRUST ME.

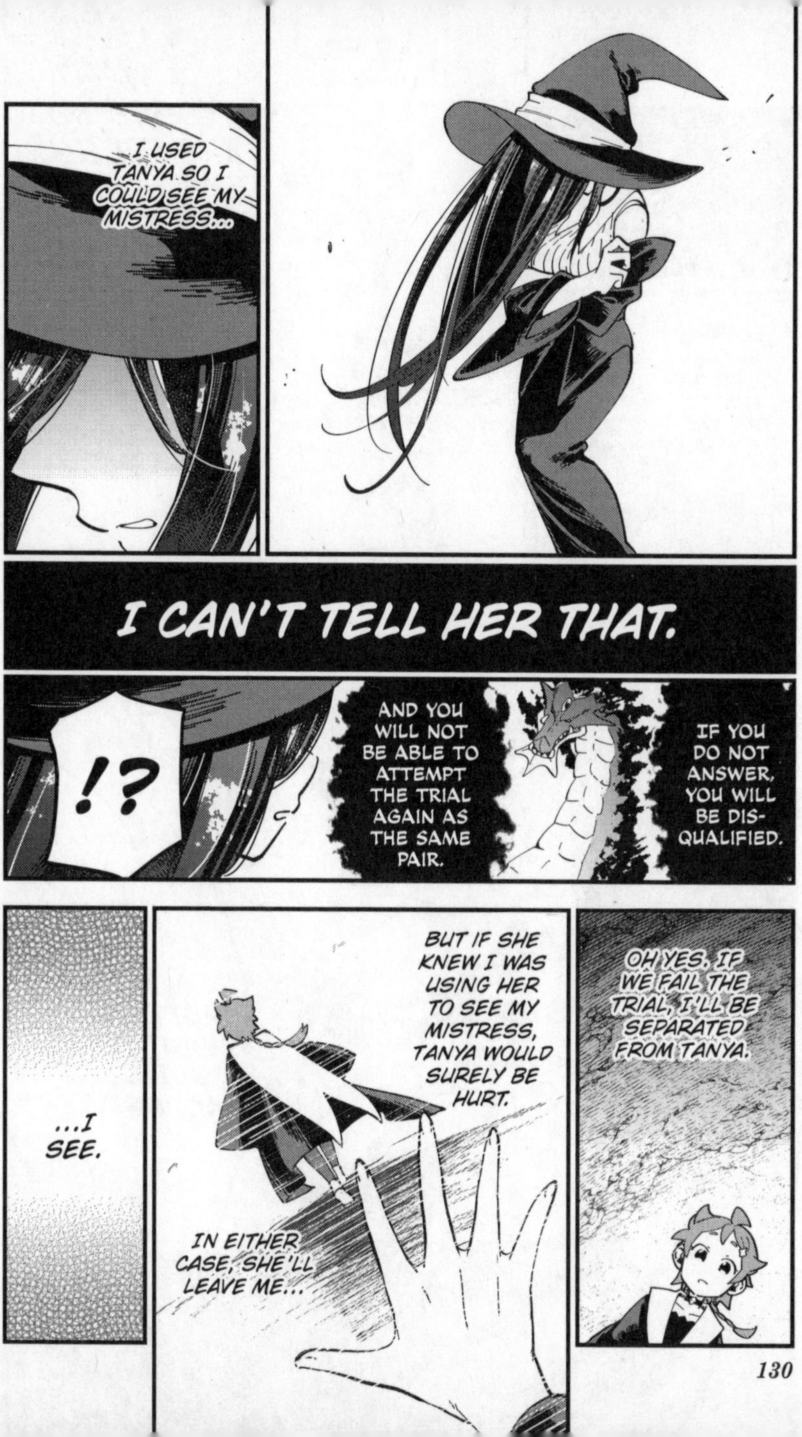
I USED TANYA SO I COULD SEE MY MISTRESS...
I CAN'T TELL HER THAT.
IF YOU DO NOT ANSWER, YOU WILL BE DIS-QUALIFIED.
AND YOU WILL NOT BE ABLE TO ATTEMPT THE TRIAL AGAIN AS THE SAME PAIR.
!?
OH YES. IF WE FAIL THE TRIAL, I'LL BE SEPARATED FROM TANYA.
BUT IF SHE KNEW I WAS USING HER TO SEE MY MISTRESS, TANYA WOULD SURELY BE HURT.
IN EITHER CASE, SHE'LL LEAVE ME...
...I SEE.

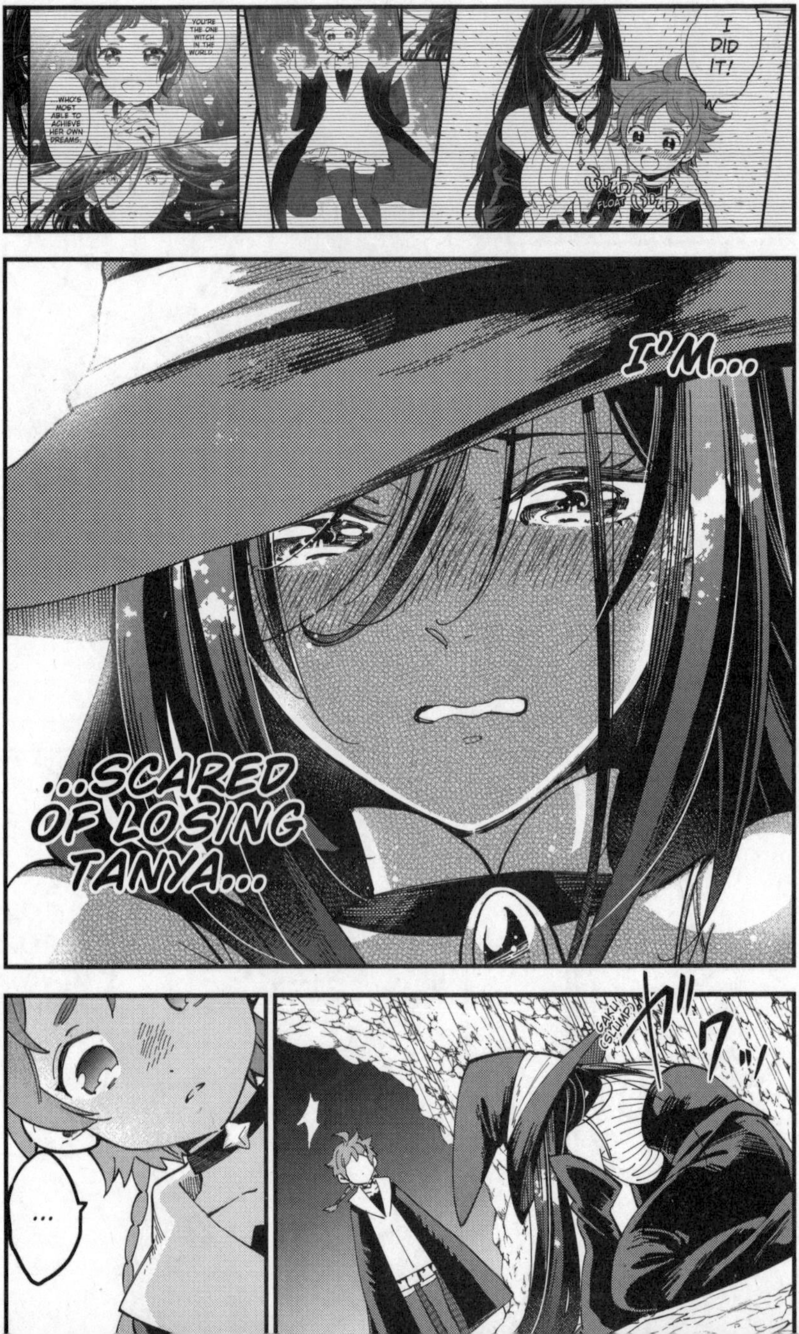
I DID IT!
FLOAT
YOU'RE THE ONE WITCH IN THE WORLD...
...WHO'S MOST ABLE TO ACHIEVE HER OWN DREAMS.
I'M...
...SCARED OF LOSING TANYA...
GAKU (SLUMP)
...

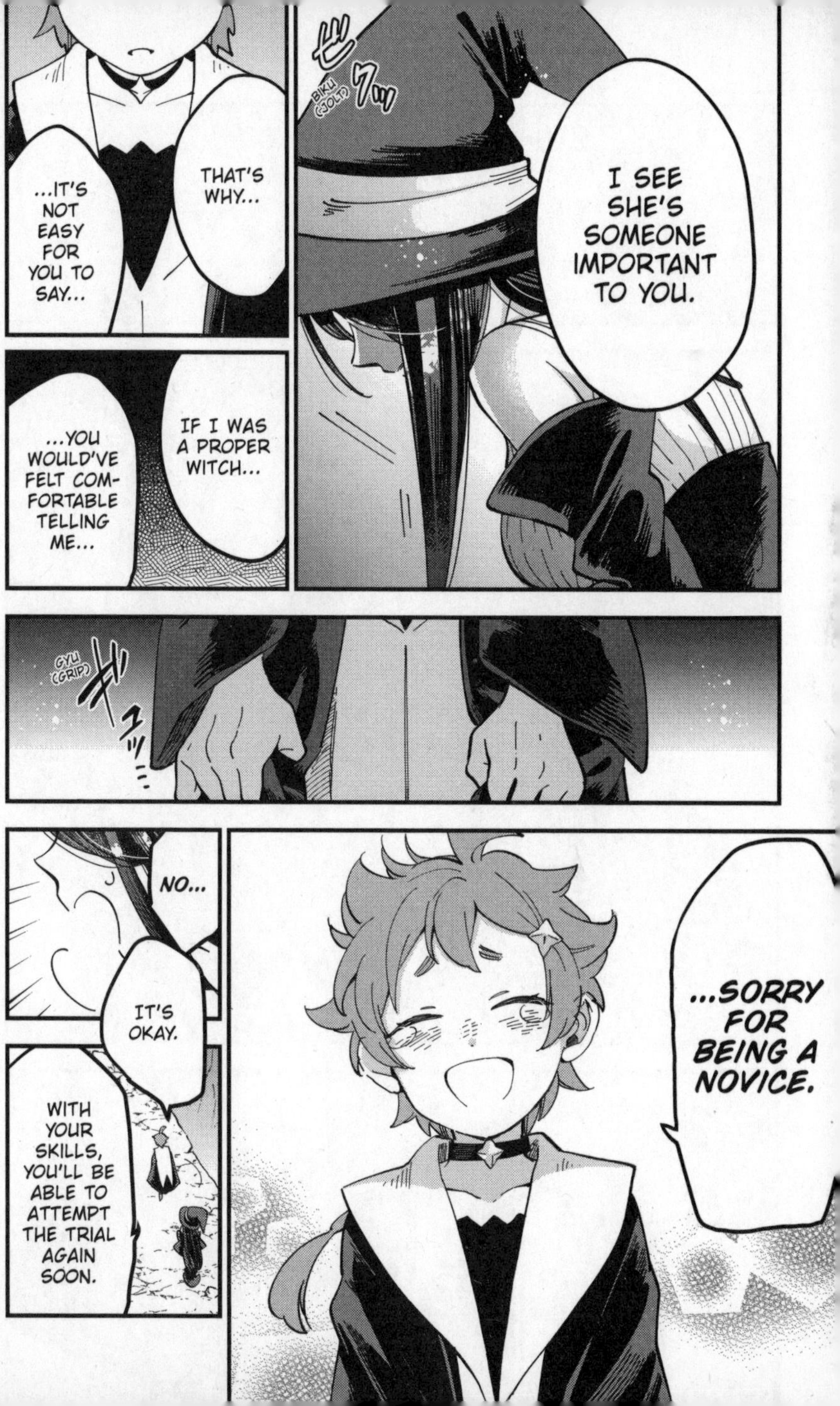
BIKU (JOLT)
I SEE SHE'S SOMEONE IMPORTANT TO YOU.
THAT'S WHY...
...IT'S NOT EASY FOR YOU TO SAY...
IF I WAS A PROPER WITCH...
...YOU WOULD'VE FELT COM-FORTABLE TELLING ME...
GYU (GRIP)
...SORRY FOR BEING A NOVICE.
NO...
IT'S OKAY.
WITH YOUR SKILLS, YOU'LL BE ABLE TO ATTEMPT THE TRIAL AGAIN SOON.

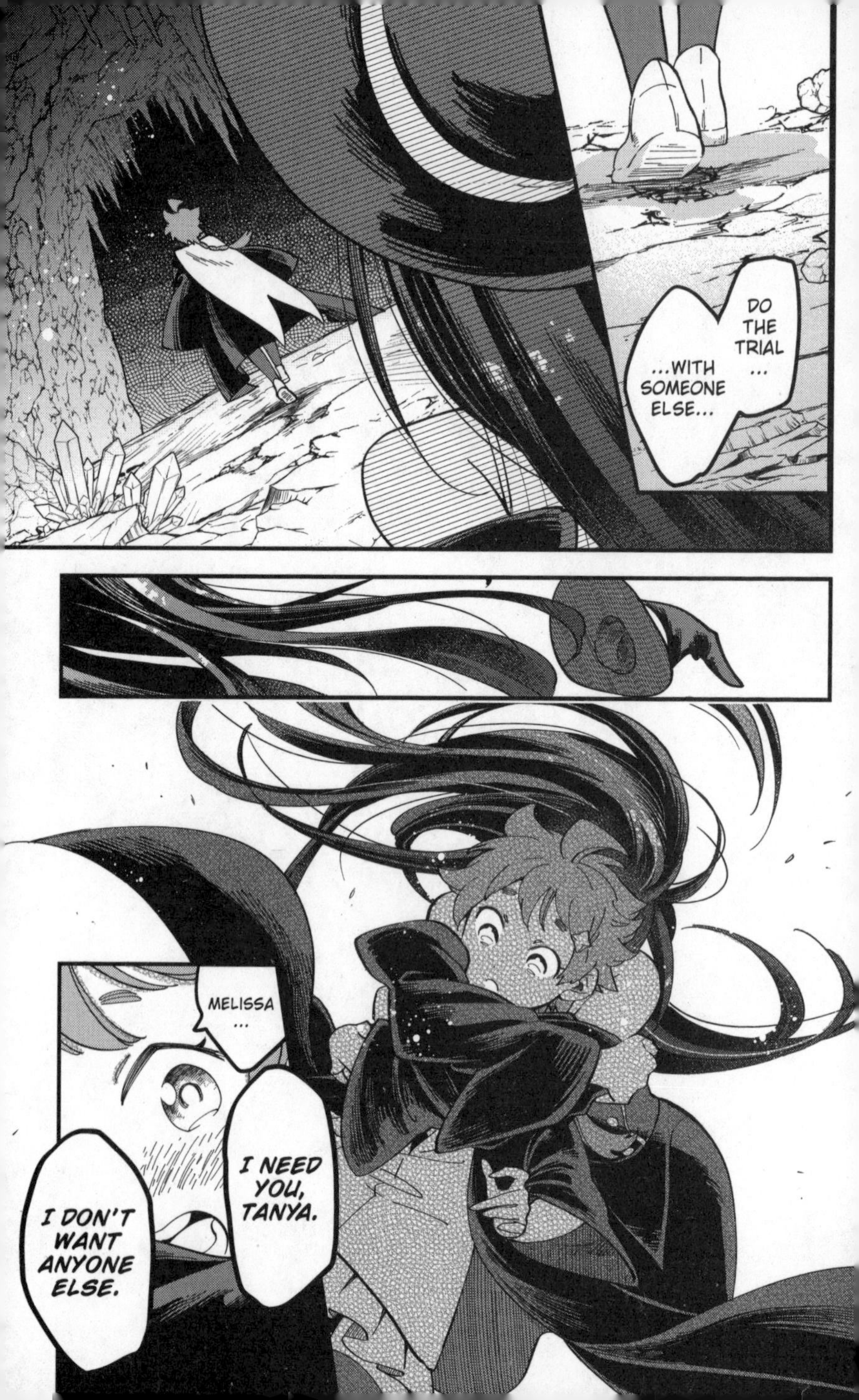
DO THE TRIAL ...
...WITH SOMEONE ELSE...
MELISSA ...
I NEED YOU, TANYA.
I DON'T WANT ANYONE ELSE.

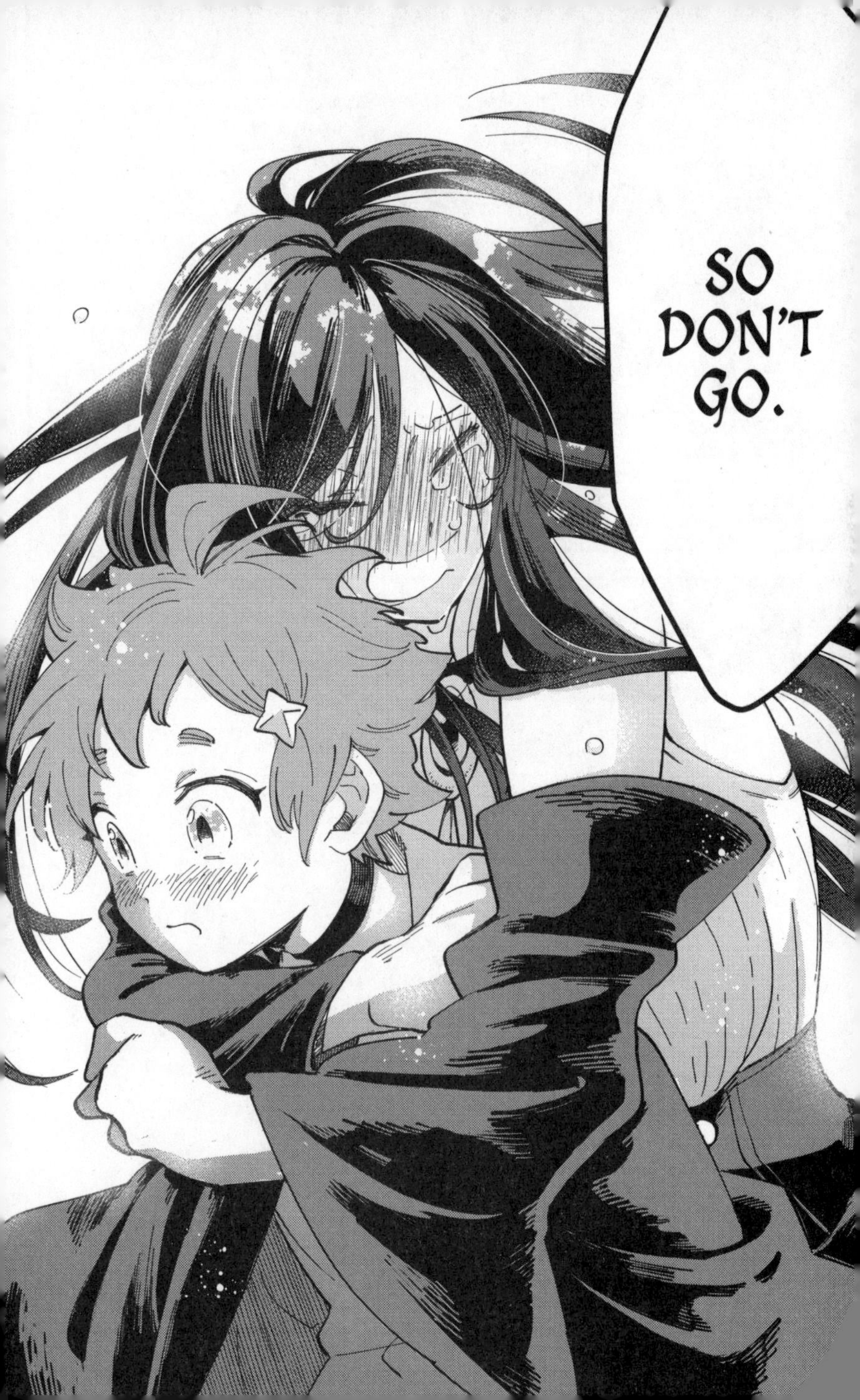
SO DON'T GO.

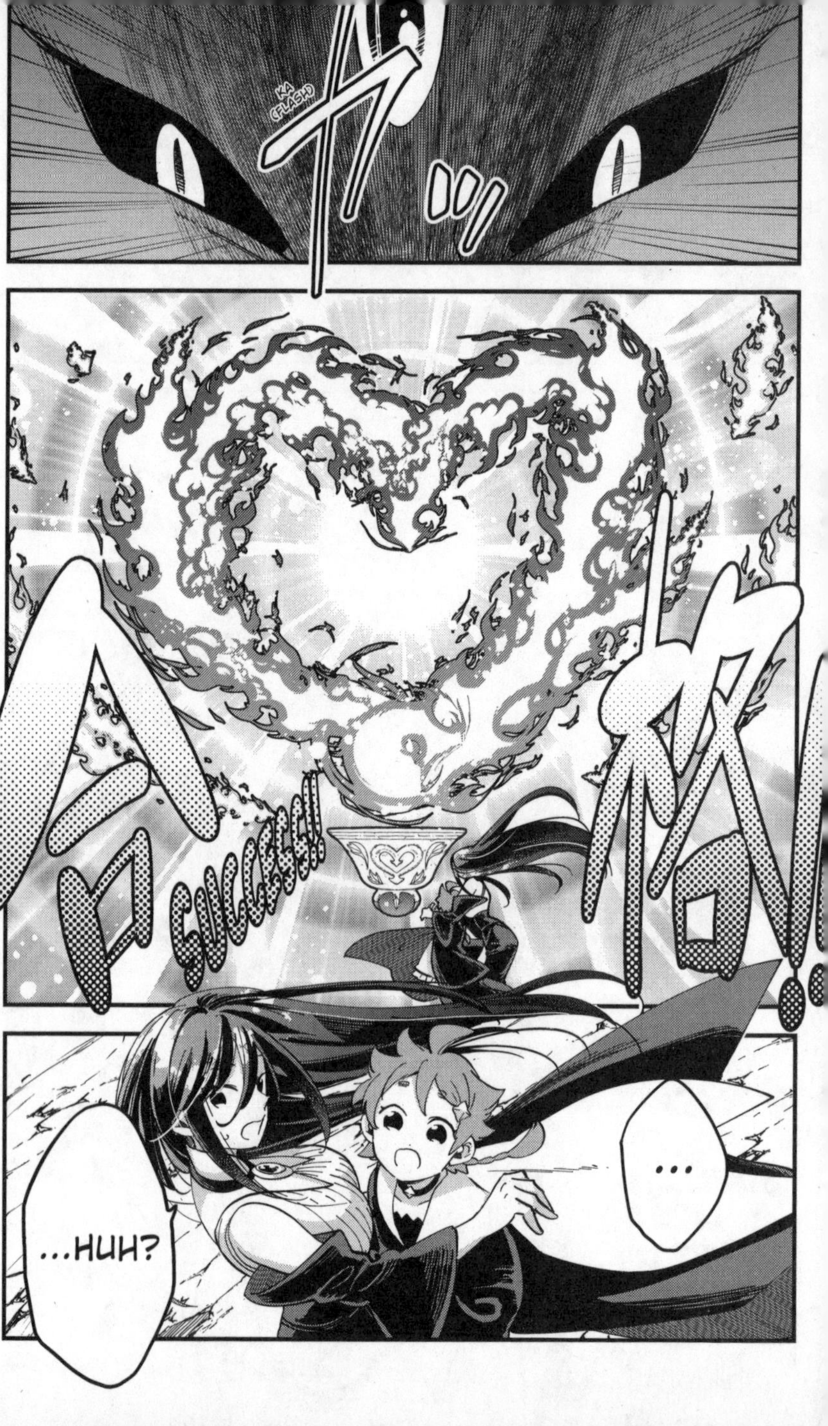
KA (FLASH)
SUCCESS!!
...
...HUH?

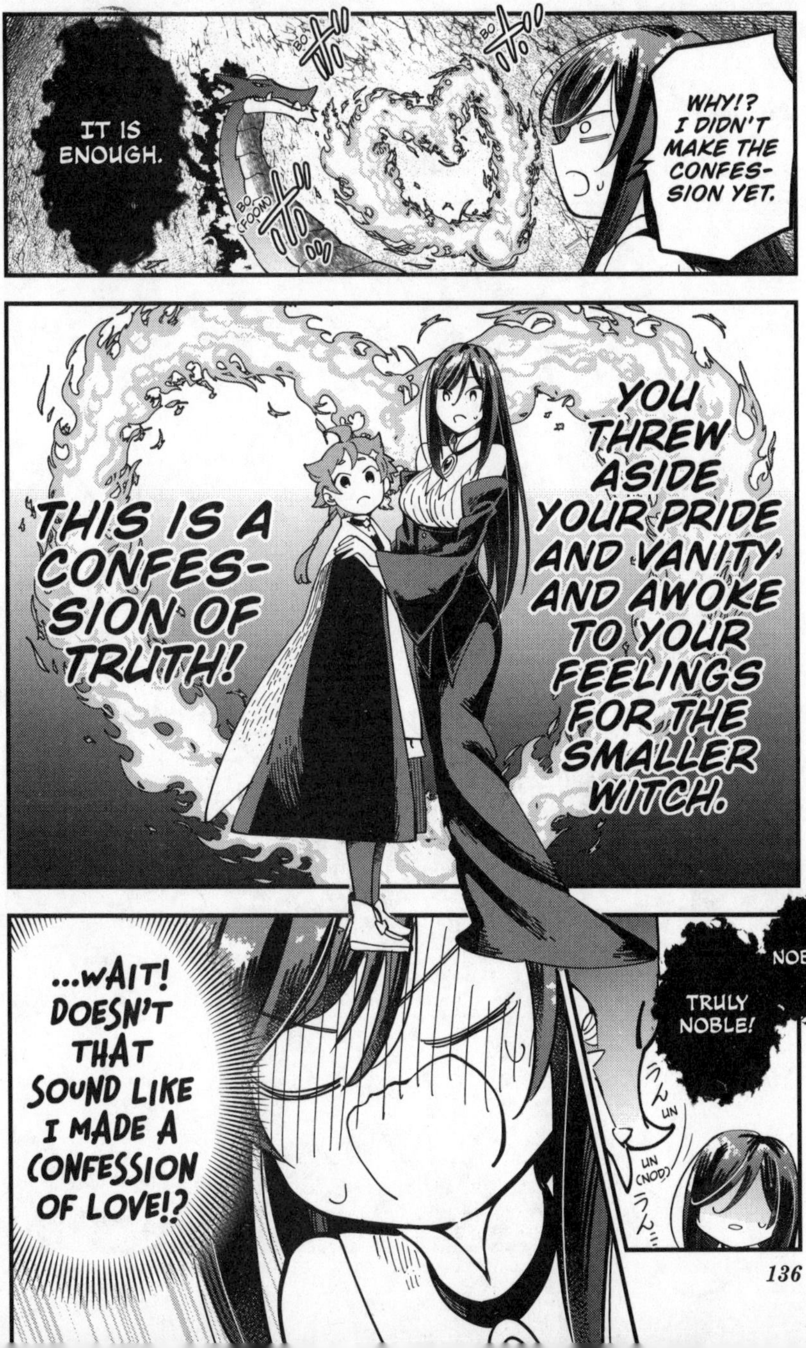
WHY!? I DIDN'T MAKE THE CONFES-SION YET.
BO
BO
IT IS ENOUGH.
BO (FOOM)
YOU THREW ASIDE YOUR PRIDE AND VANITY AND AWOKE TO YOUR FEELINGS FOR THE SMALLER WITCH.
THIS IS A CONFES-SION OF TRUTH!
NOBLE.
TRULY NOBLE!
UN
UN (NOD)
...WAIT! DOESN'T THAT SOUND LIKE I MADE A CONFESSION OF LOVE!?

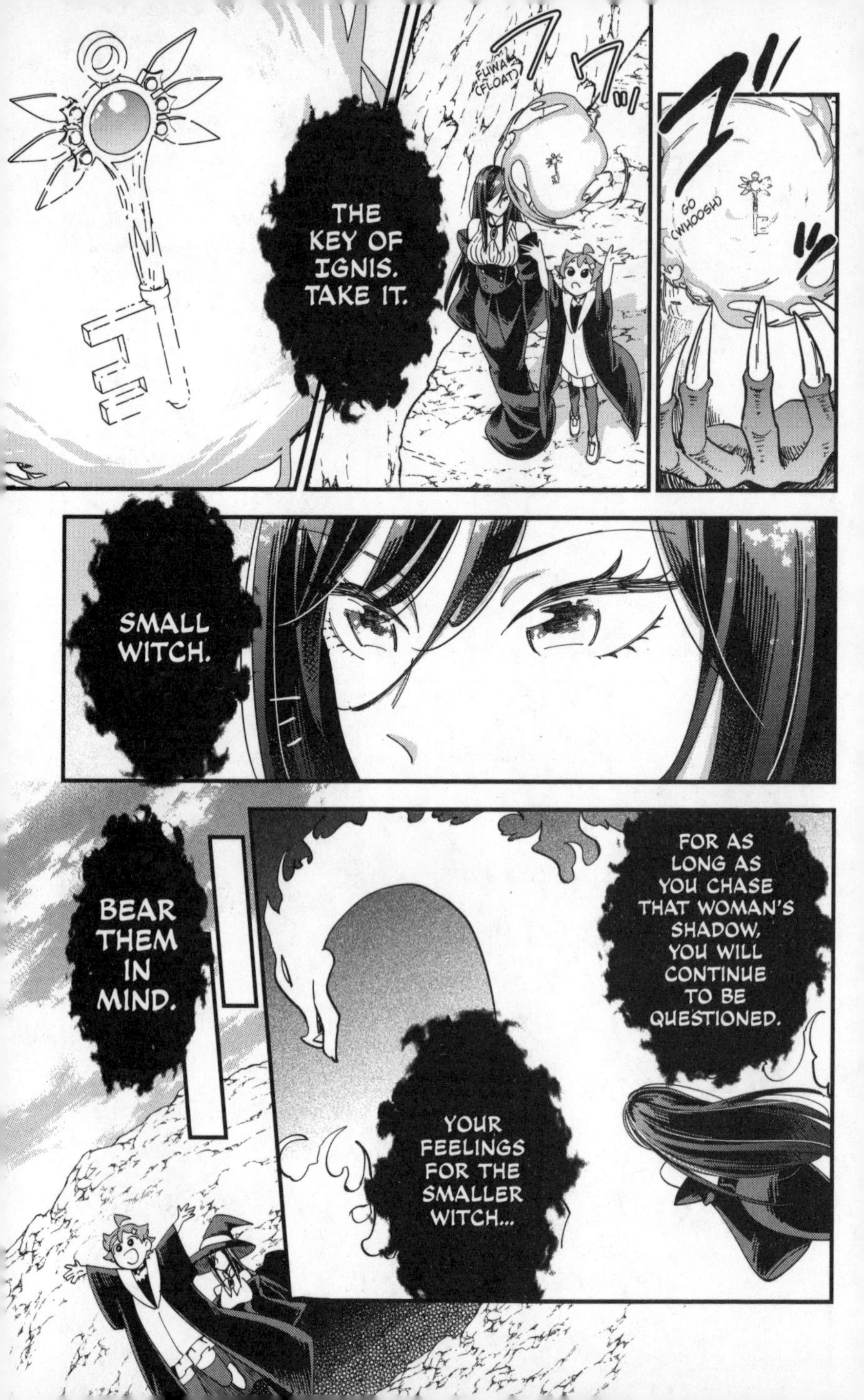
GO (WHOOSH)
FUWA (FLOAT)
THE KEY OF IGNIS. TAKE IT.
SMALL WITCH.
FOR AS LONG AS YOU CHASE THAT WOMAN'S SHADOW, YOU WILL CONTINUE TO BE QUESTIONED.
YOUR FEELINGS FOR THE SMALLER WITCH...
BEAR THEM IN MIND.

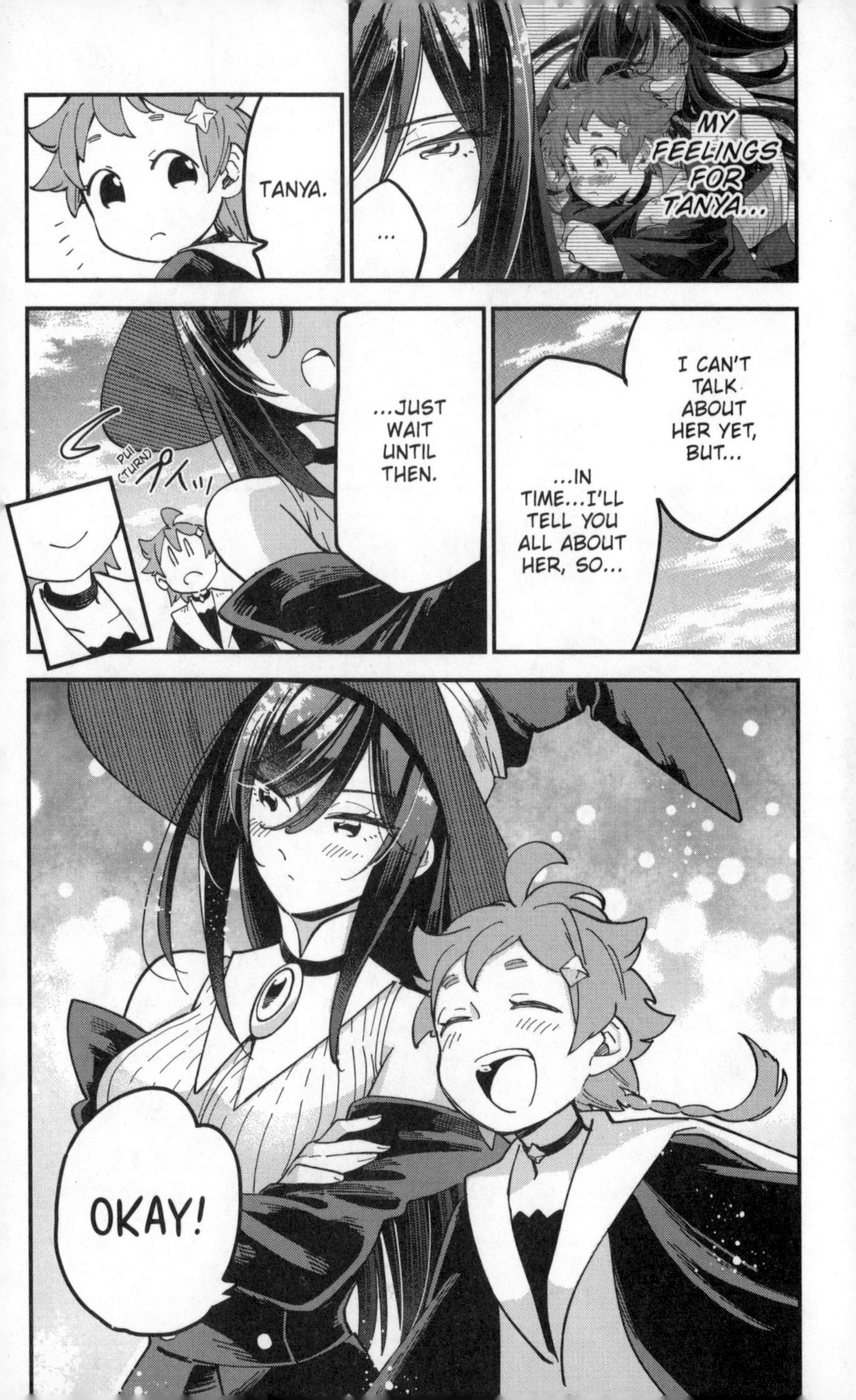
MY FEELINGS FOR TANYA...
...
TANYA.
I CAN'T TALK ABOUT HER YET, BUT...
...IN TIME...I'LL TELL YOU ALL ABOUT HER, SO...
...JUST WAIT UNTIL THEN.
PUI (TURN)
OKAY!

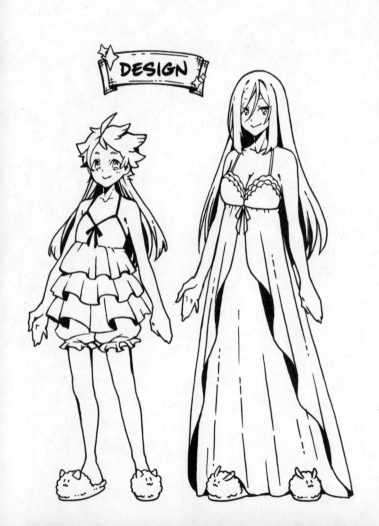
DESIGN

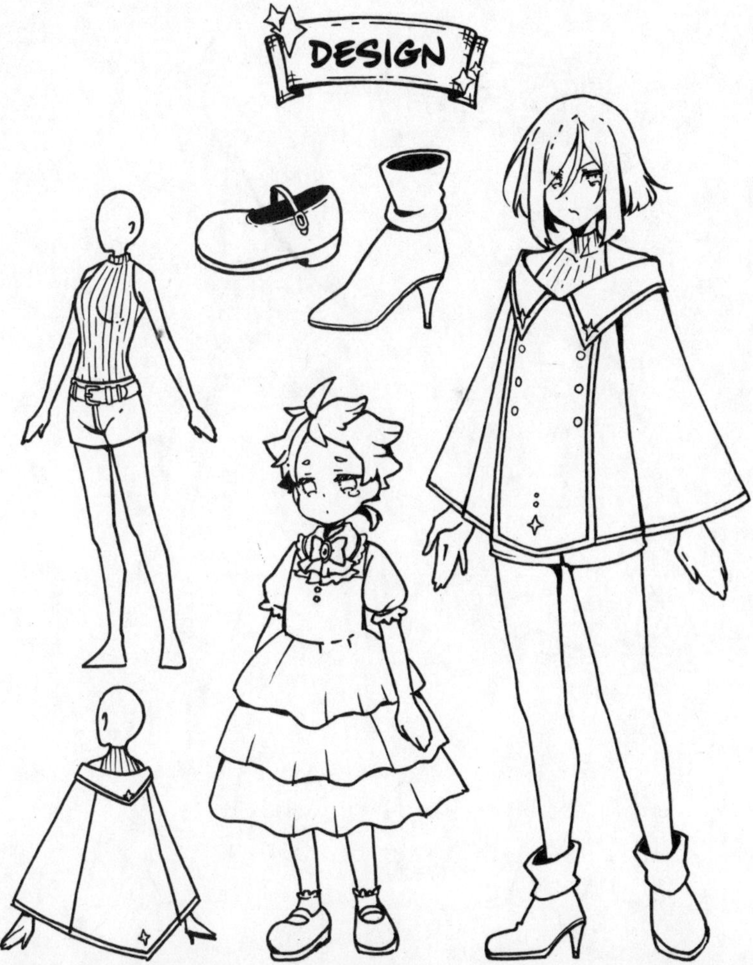
DESIGN

The Witch's Golem

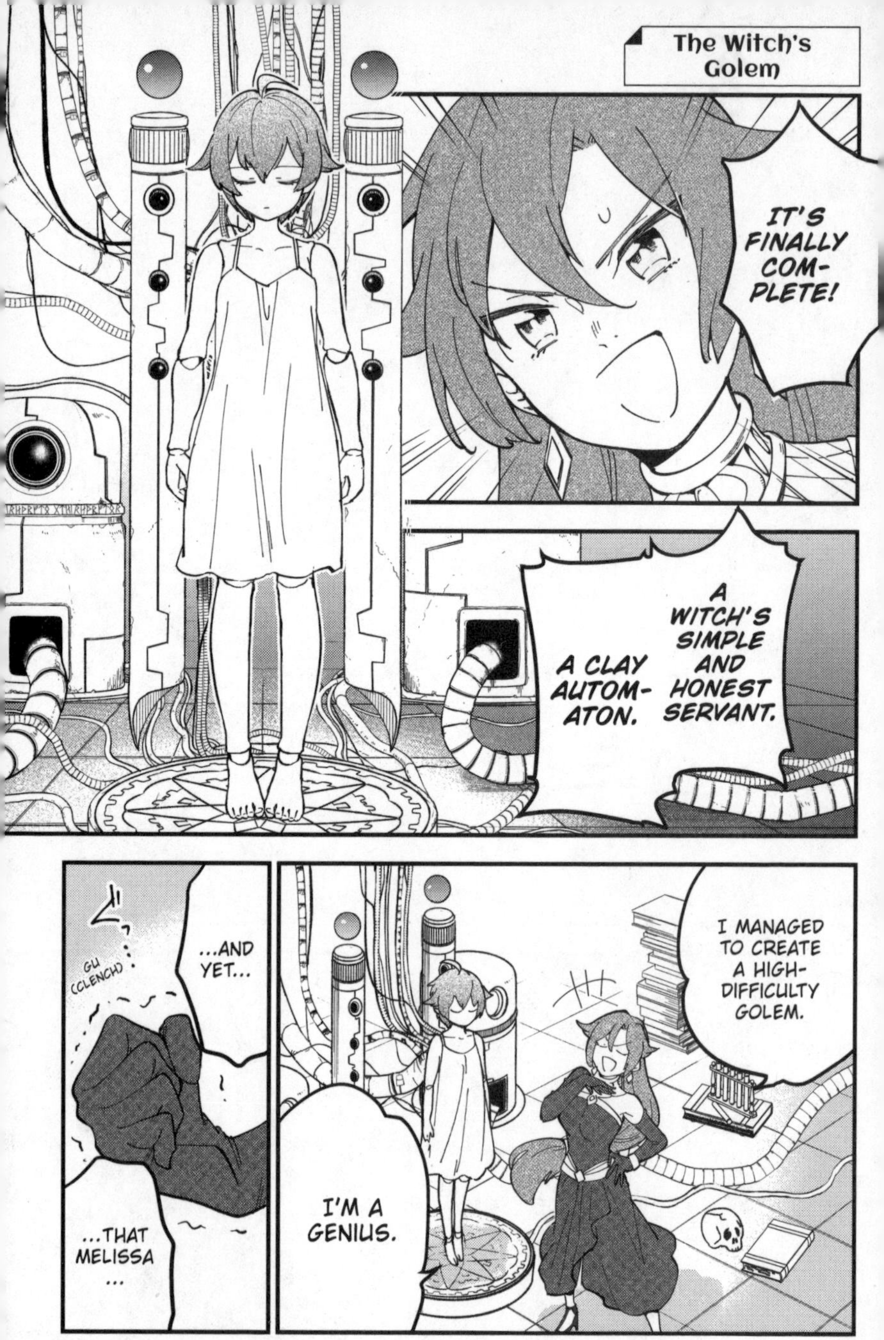

IT'S FINALLY COMPLETE!
A WITCH'S SIMPLE AND HONEST SERVANT.
A CLAY AUTOMATON.
I MANAGED TO CREATE A HIGH-DIFFICULTY GOLEM.
I'M A GENIUS.
...AND YET...
GU (CLENCH)
...THAT MELISSA ...

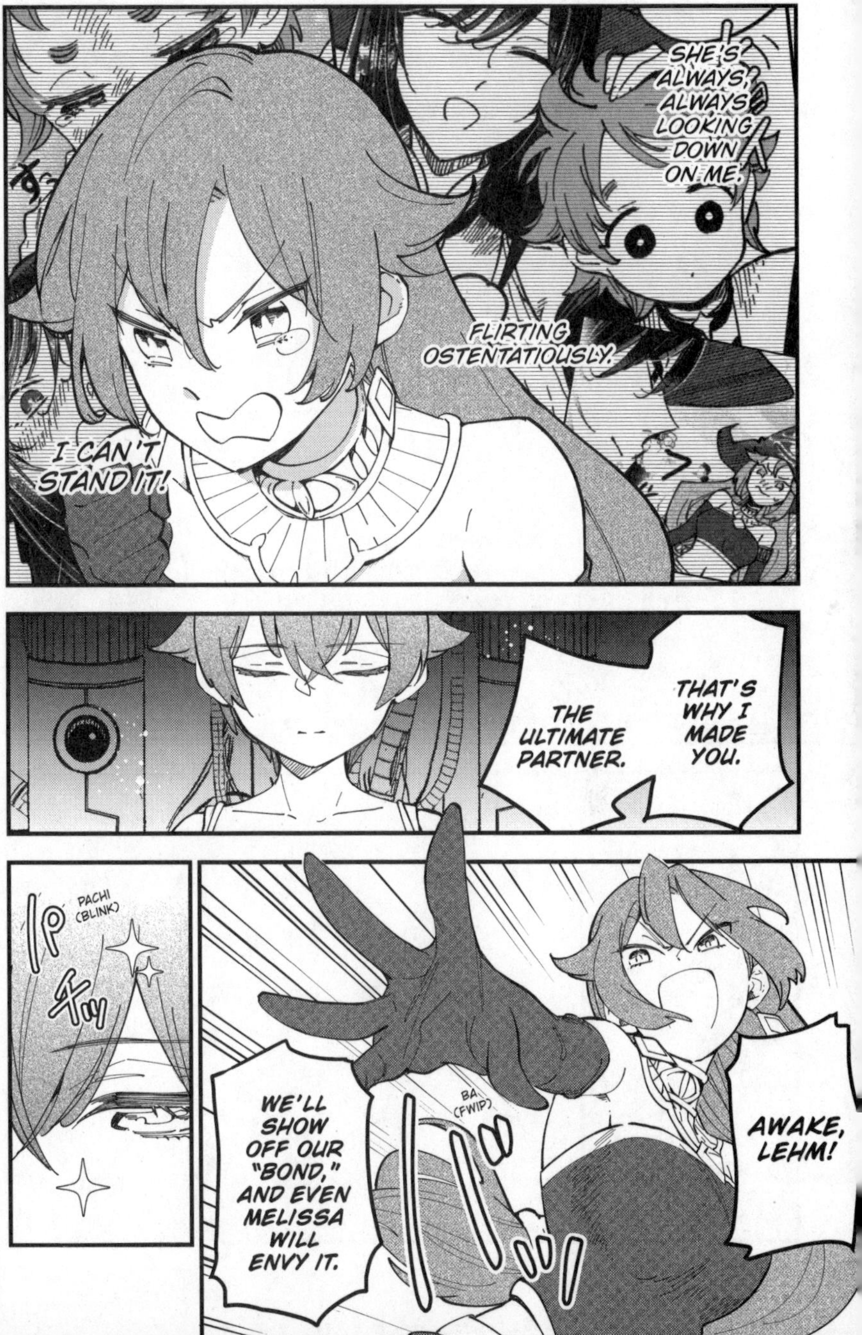
SHE'S ALWAYS, ALWAYS LOOKING DOWN ON ME.
FLIRTING OSTENTATIOUSLY.
I CAN'T STAND IT!
THAT'S WHY I MADE YOU.
THE ULTIMATE PARTNER.
AWAKE, LEHM!
BA (FWIP)
WE'LL SHOW OFF OUR "BOND," AND EVEN MELISSA WILL ENVY IT.
PACHI (BLINK)

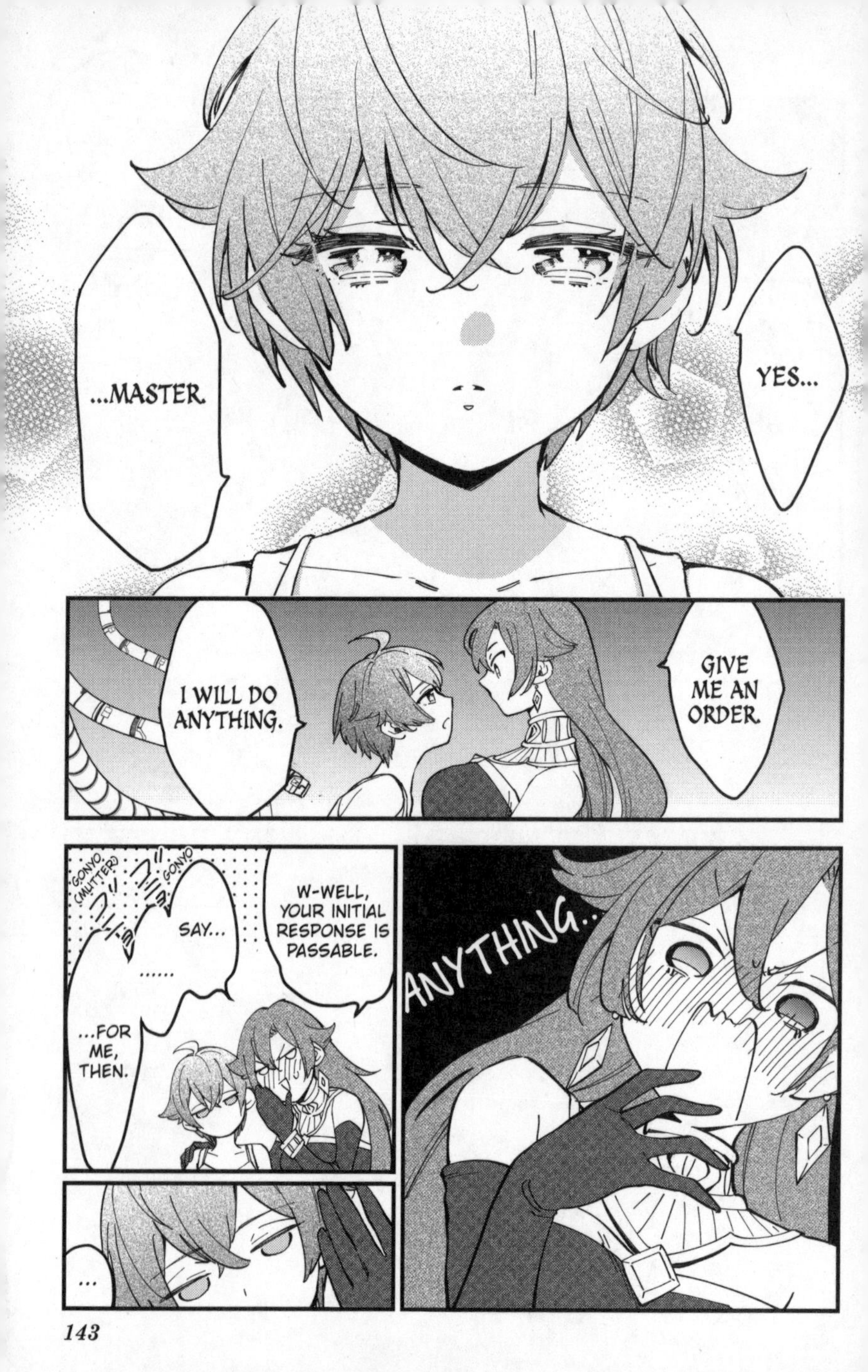
YES...
...MASTER.
GIVE ME AN ORDER.
I WILL DO ANYTHING.
ANYTHING...
W-WELL, YOUR INITIAL RESPONSE IS PASSABLE.
GONYO
GONYO (MUTTER)
SAY...
......
...FOR ME, THEN.
...

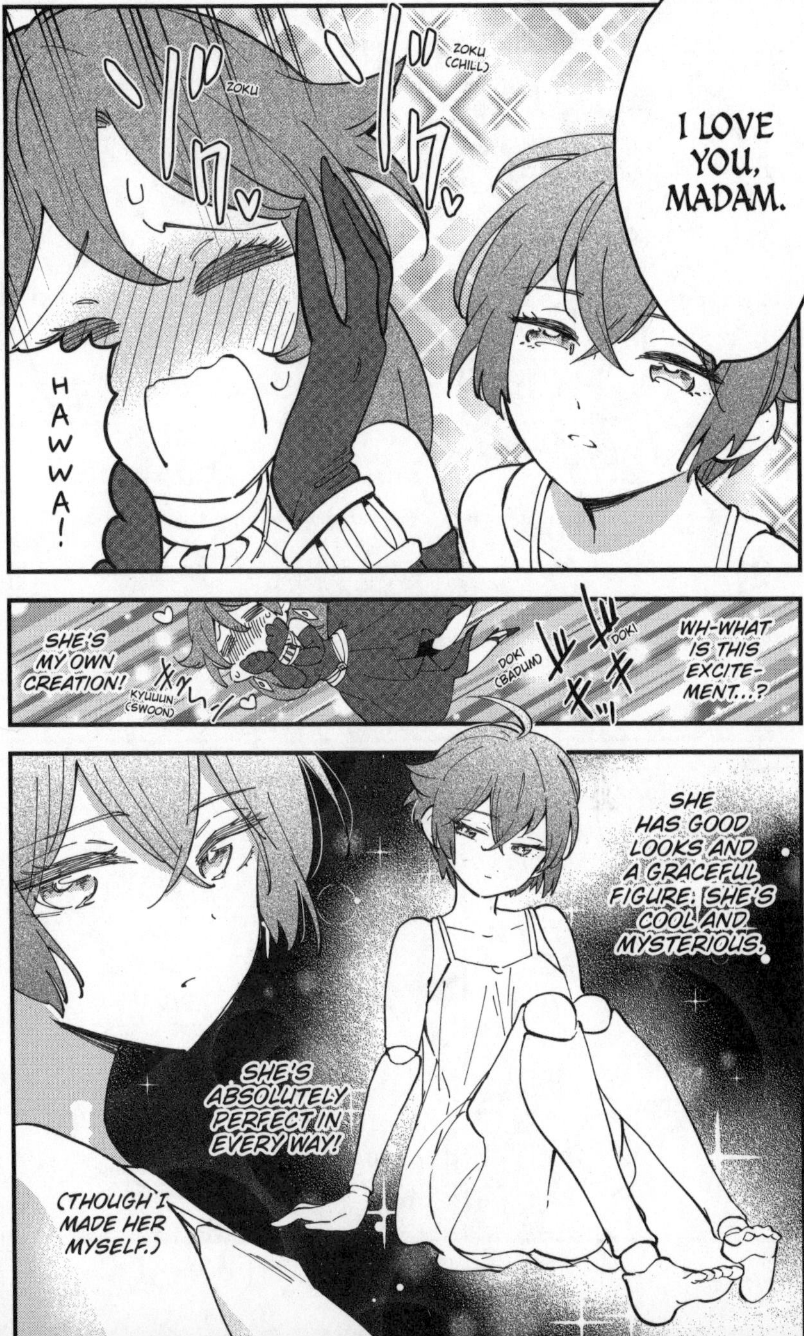
I LOVE YOU, MADAM.
ZOKU (CHILL)
ZOKU
HAWWA!
WH-WHAT IS THIS EXCITE-MENT...?
DOKI
DOKI (BADUM)
KYUUUN (SWOON)
SHE'S MY OWN CREATION!
SHE HAS GOOD LOOKS AND A GRACEFUL FIGURE. SHE'S COOL AND MYSTERIOUS.
SHE'S ABSOLUTELY PERFECT IN EVERY WAY!
(THOUGH I MADE HER MYSELF.)

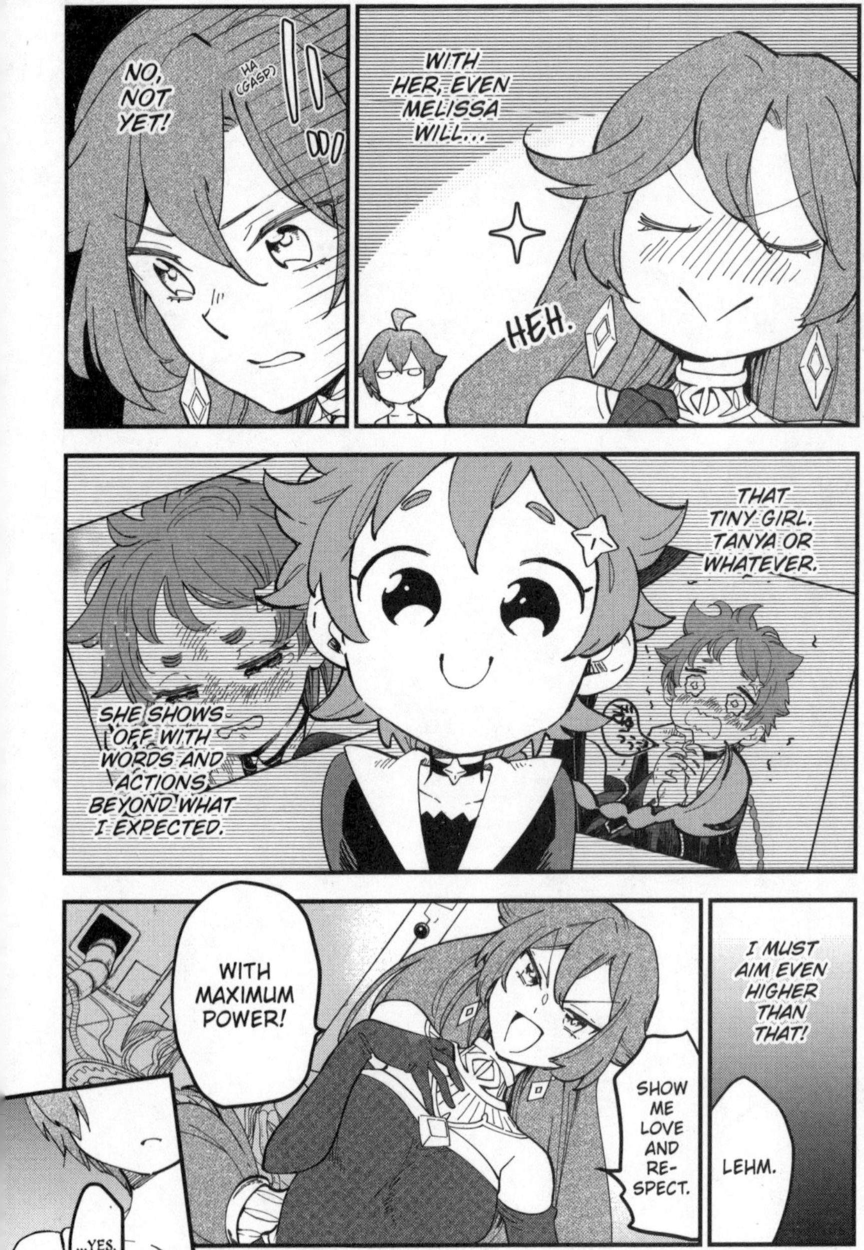
WITH HER, EVEN MELISSA WILL...
HEH.
HA (GASP)
NO, NOT YET!
THAT TINY GIRL, TANYA OR WHATEVER.
SHE SHOWS OFF WITH WORDS AND ACTIONS BEYOND WHAT I EXPECTED.
I MUST AIM EVEN HIGHER THAN THAT!
LEHM.
SHOW ME LOVE AND RE-SPECT.
WITH MAXIMUM POWER!
...YES.

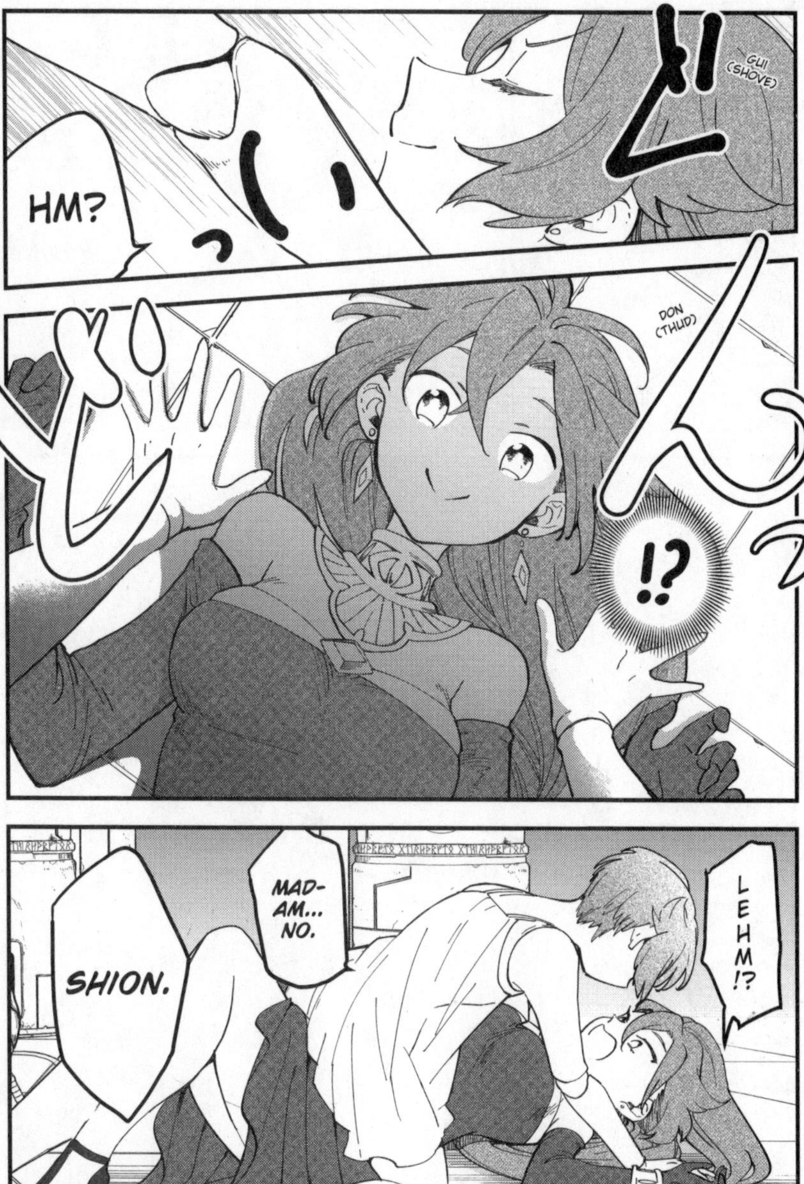
GUI (SHOVE)
HM?
DON (THUD)
!?
LEHM!?
MAD-AM... NO.
SHION.

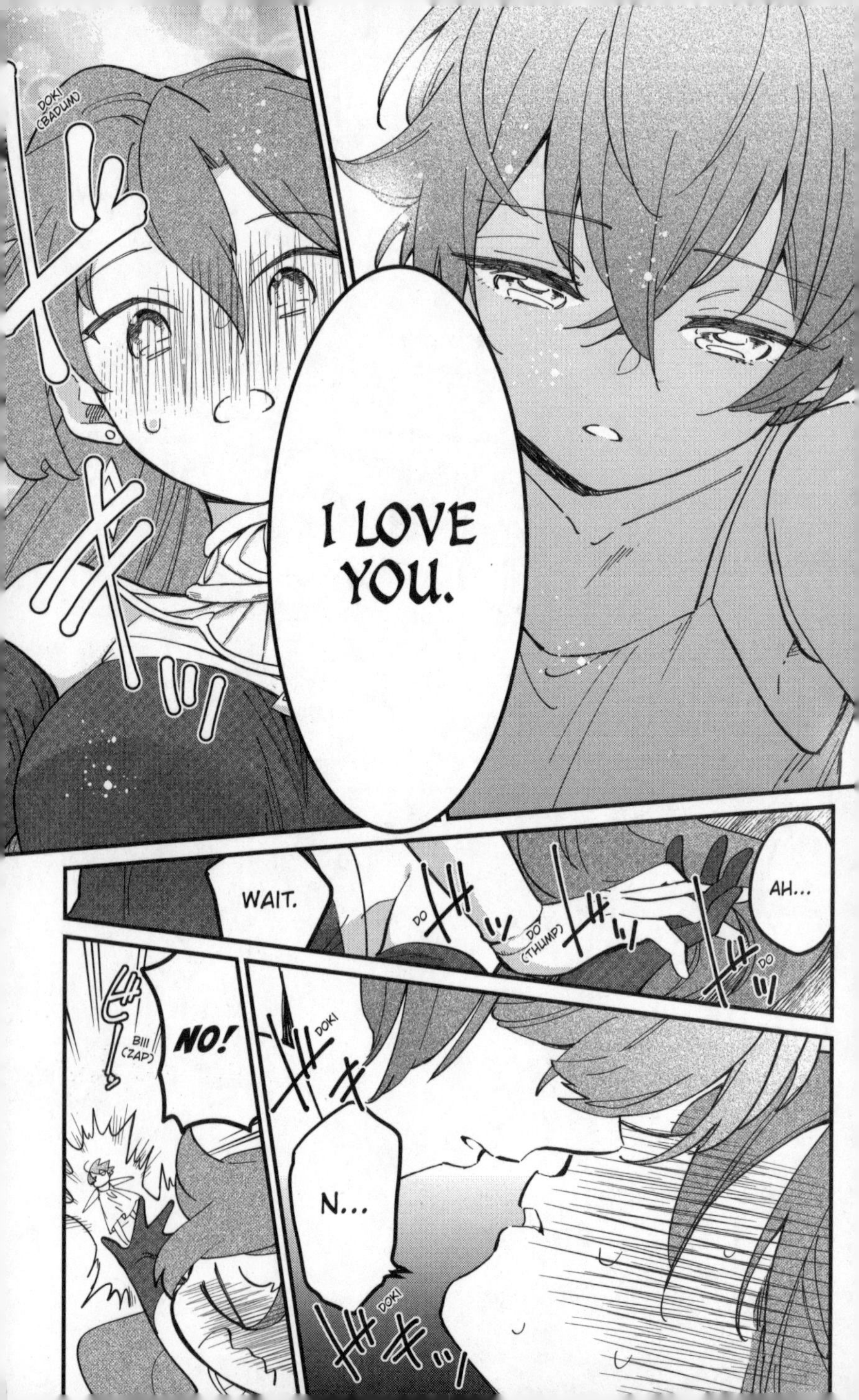
I LOVE YOU.
DOKI (BADUMP)
AH...
DO
DO (THUMP)
DO
WAIT.
DOKI
N...
DOKI
NO!
BIII (ZAP)

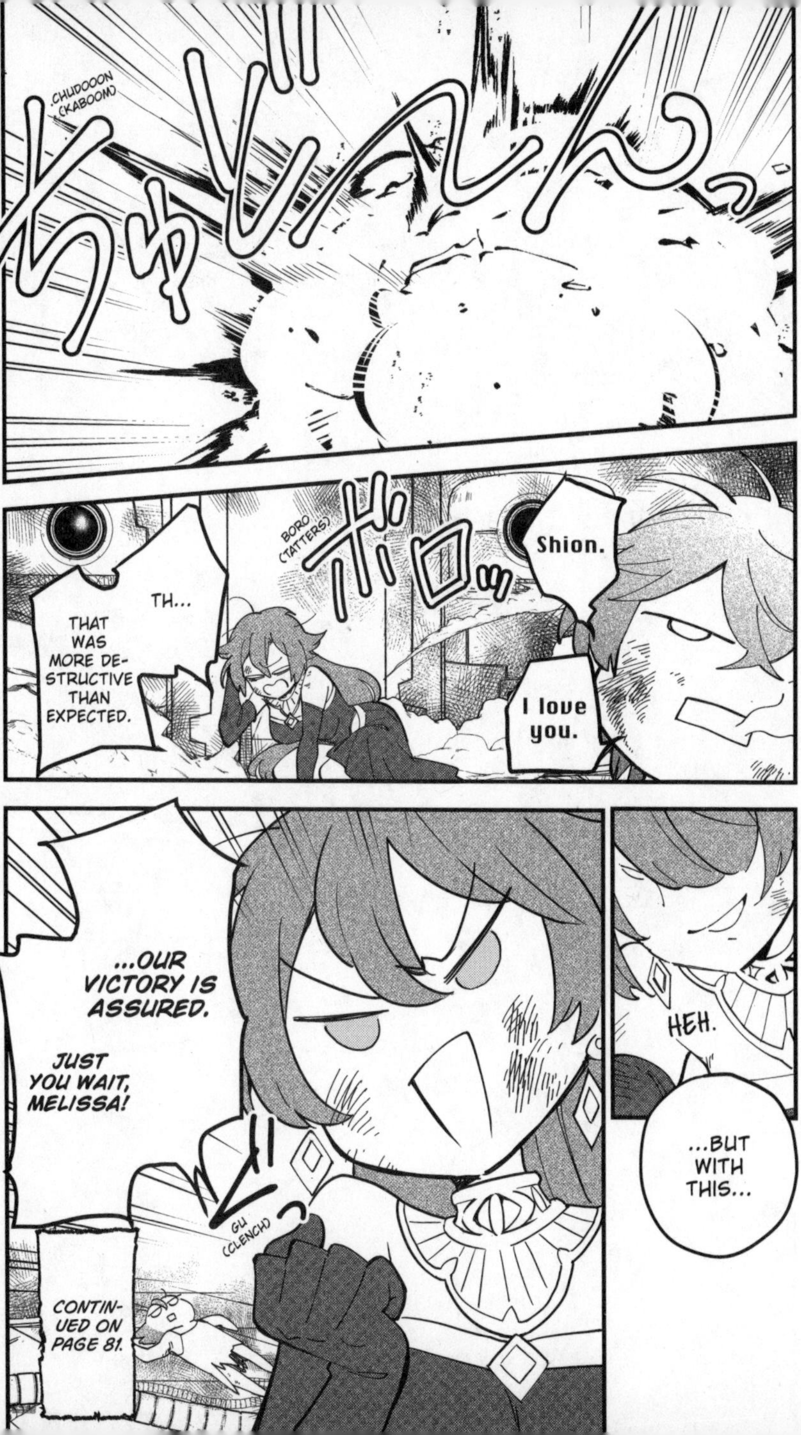
ちゅどーんっ
CHUDOOON (KABOOM)
Shion.
ボロッ
BORO (TATTERS)
TH...
THAT WAS MORE DE-STRUCTIVE THAN EXPECTED.
I love you.
HEH.
...BUT WITH THIS...
...OUR VICTORY IS ASSURED.
JUST YOU WAIT, MELISSA!
ぐっ
GU (CLENCH)
CONTIN-UED ON PAGE 81.

The Witch's Baby

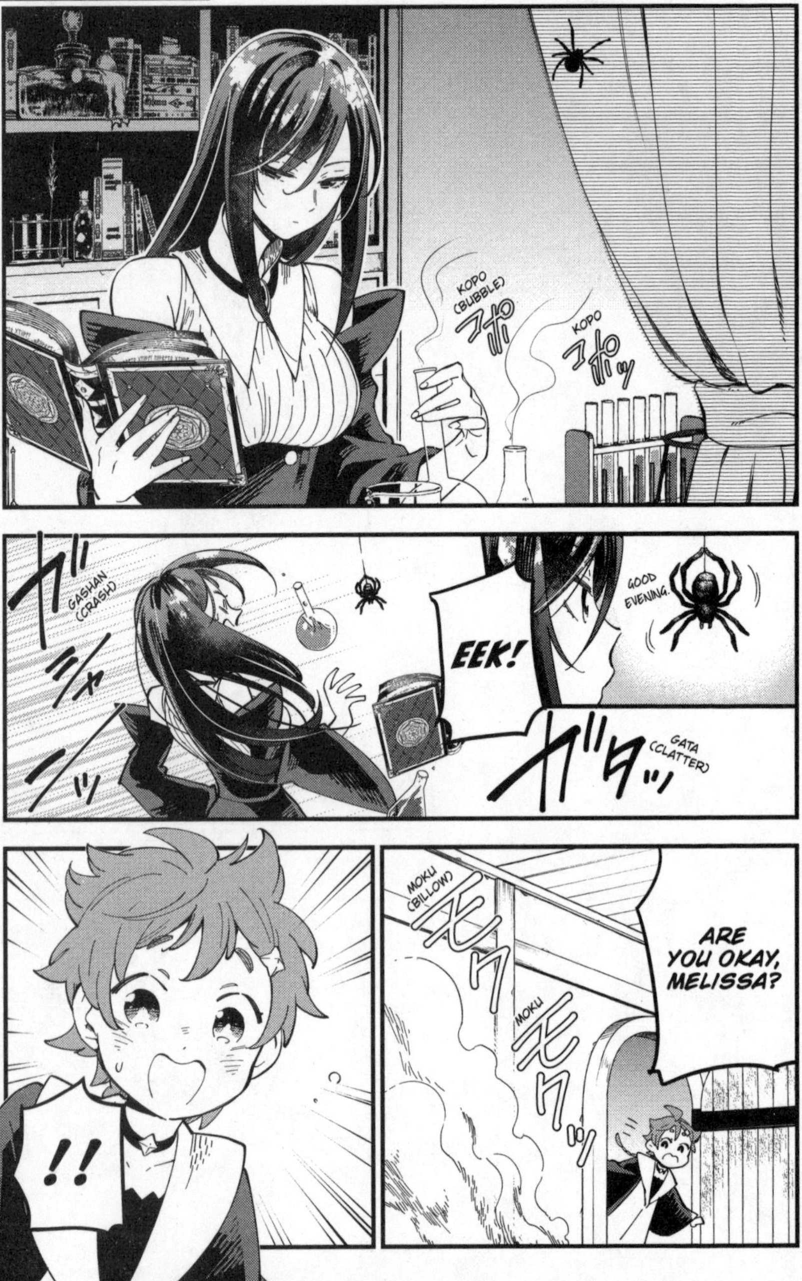
KOPO
KOPO (BUBBLE)
GOOD EVENING.
EEK!
GATA (CLATTER)
GASHAN (CRASH)
ARE YOU OKAY, MELISSA?
MOKU (BILLOW)
MOKU
!!

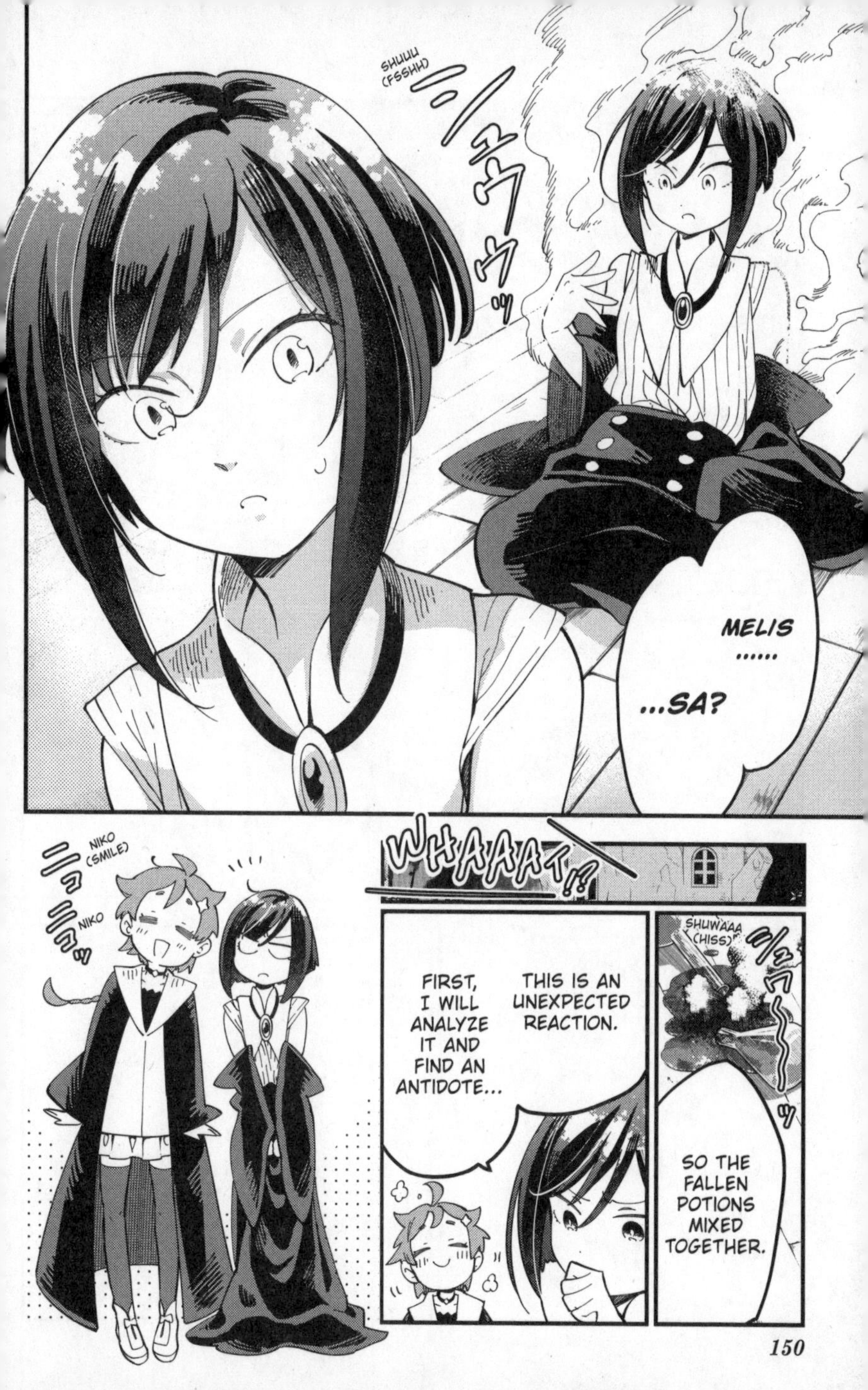
SHUUU (FSSHH)
MELIS ......
...SA?
WHAAAT!?
SHUWAAA (HISS)
SO THE FALLEN POTIONS MIXED TOGETHER.
THIS IS AN UNEXPECTED REACTION.
FIRST, I WILL ANALYZE IT AND FIND AN ANTIDOTE...
NIKO (SMILE)
NIKO

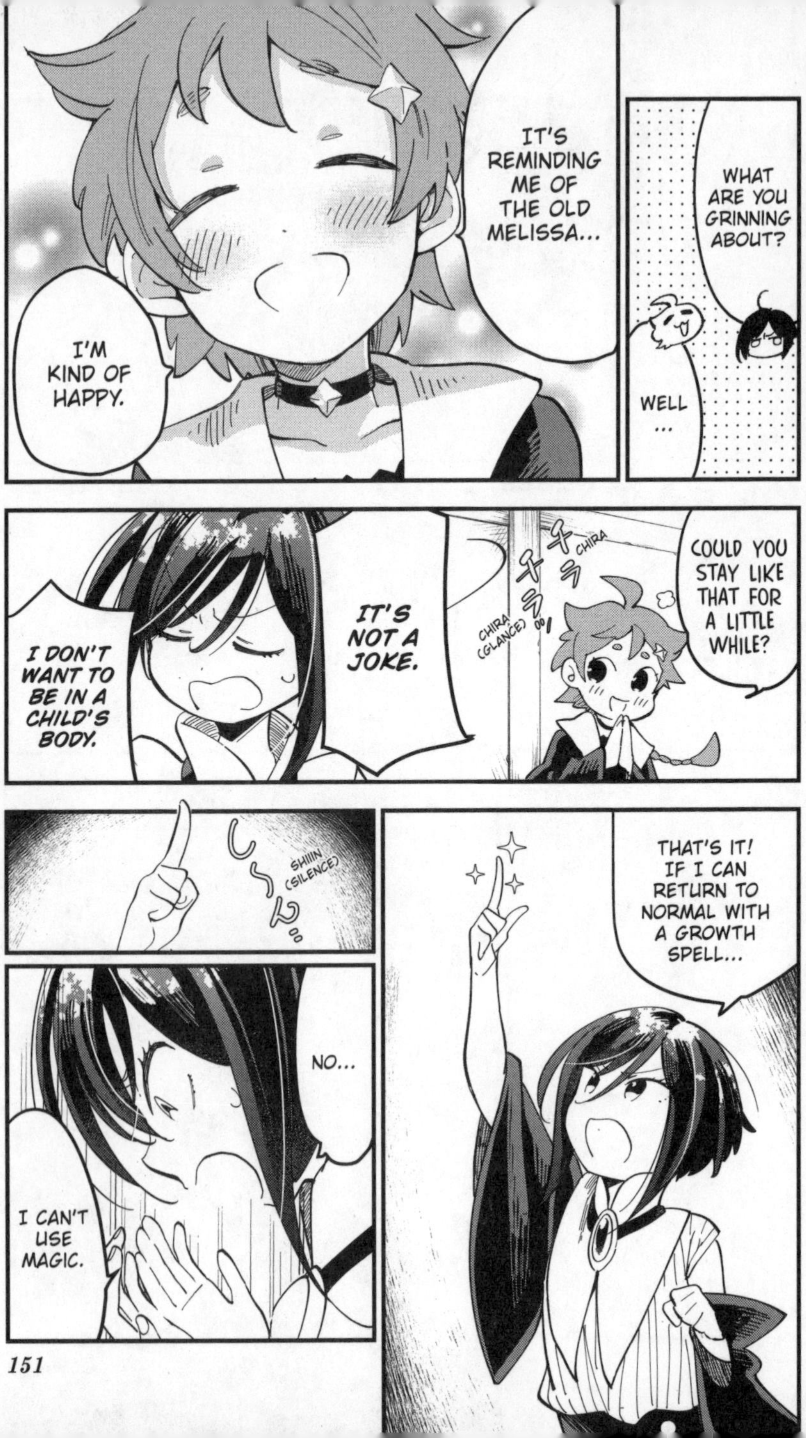
WHAT ARE YOU GRINNING ABOUT?
WELL ...
IT'S REMINDING ME OF THE OLD MELISSA...
I'M KIND OF HAPPY.
COULD YOU STAY LIKE THAT FOR A LITTLE WHILE?
CHIRA
CHIRA (GLANCE)
IT'S NOT A JOKE.
I DON'T WANT TO BE IN A CHILD'S BODY.
THAT'S IT! IF I CAN RETURN TO NORMAL WITH A GROWTH SPELL...
SHIIIN (SILENCE)
NO...
I CAN'T USE MAGIC.

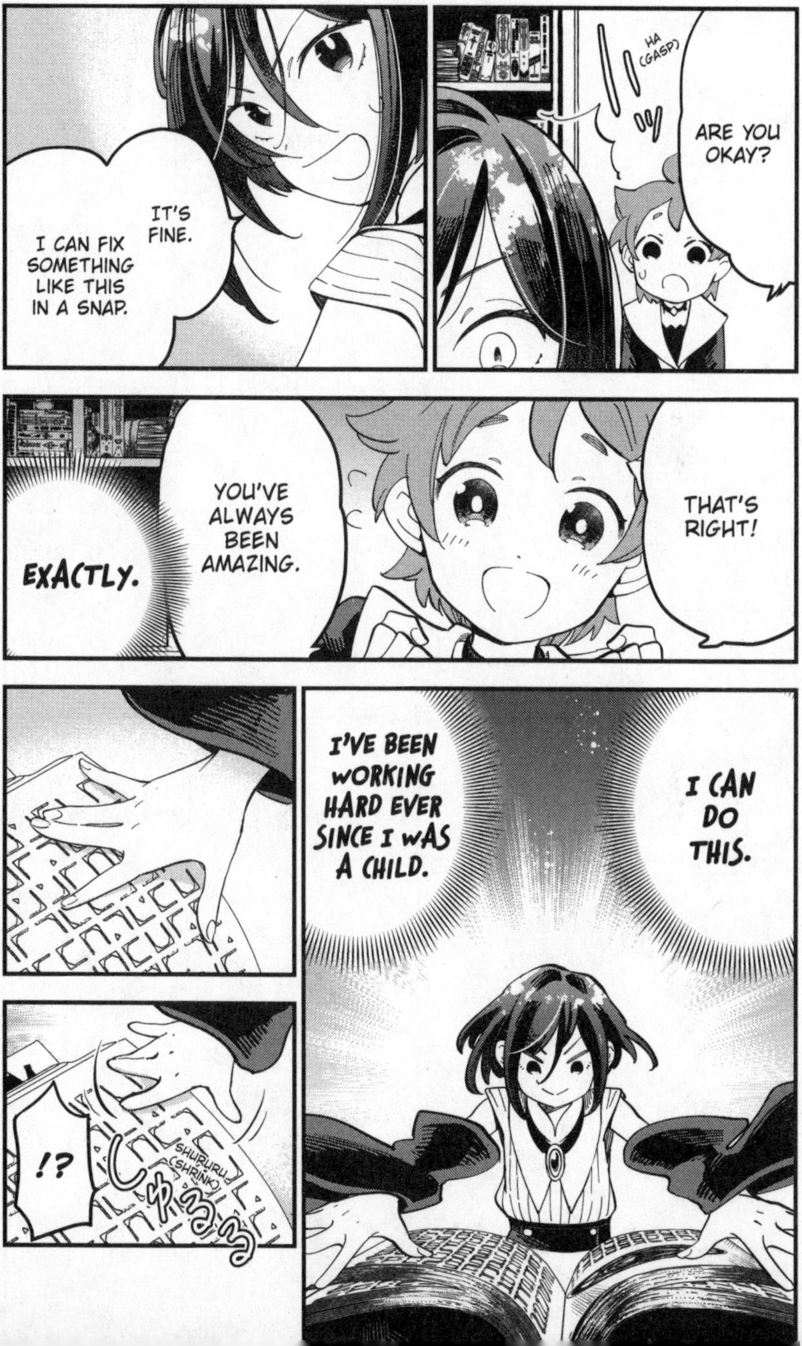
HA (GASP)
ARE YOU OKAY?
IT'S FINE.
I CAN FIX SOMETHING LIKE THIS IN A SNAP.
THAT'S RIGHT!
YOU'VE ALWAYS BEEN AMAZING.
EXACTLY.
I CAN DO THIS.
I'VE BEEN WORKING HARD EVER SINCE I WAS A CHILD.
SHURURU (SHRINK)
!?

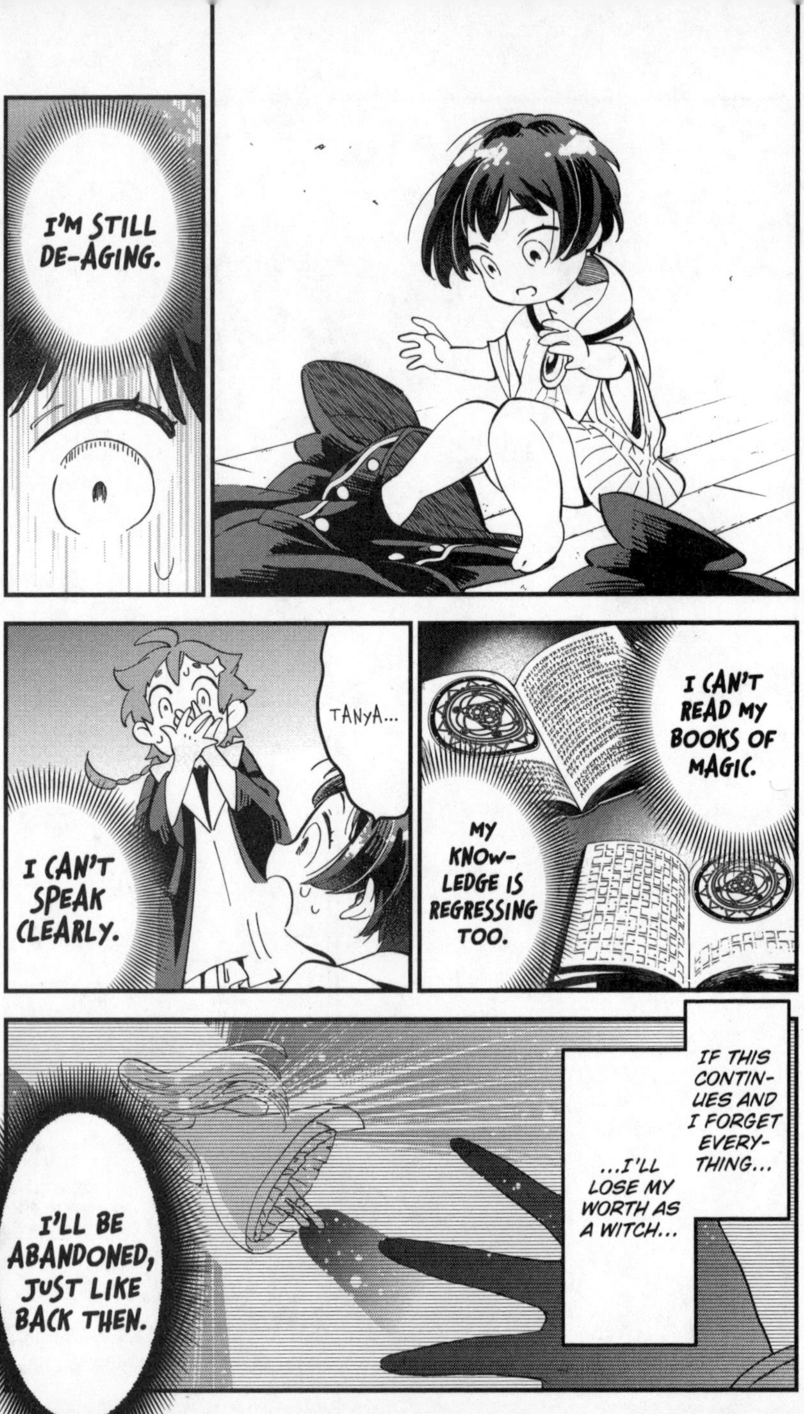
I'M STILL DE-AGING.
I CAN'T READ MY BOOKS OF MAGIC.
MY KNOW-LEDGE IS REGRESSING TOO.
TANYA...
I CAN'T SPEAK CLEARLY.
IF THIS CONTIN-UES AND I FORGET EVERY-THING...
...I'LL LOSE MY WORTH AS A WITCH...
I'LL BE ABANDONED, JUST LIKE BACK THEN.

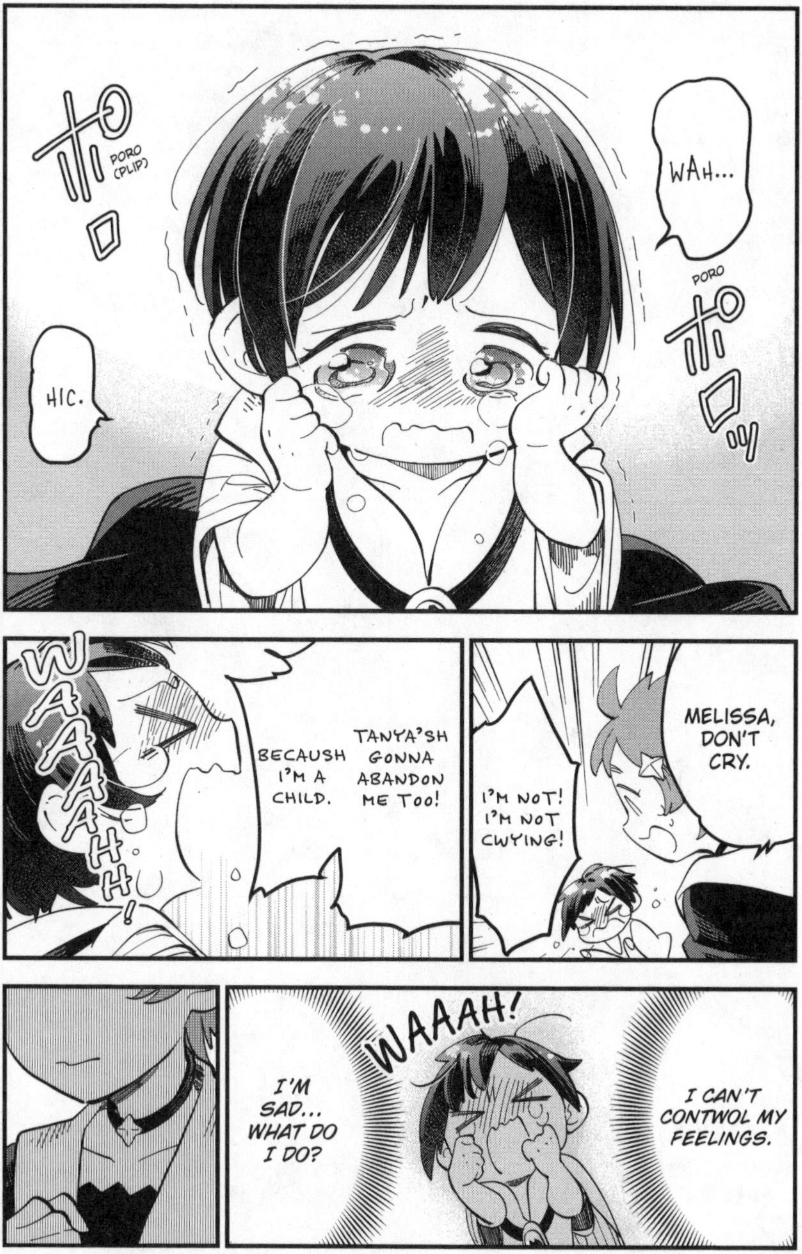
WAH...
PORO
PORO (PLIP)
HIC.
MELISSA, DON'T CRY.
I'M NOT! I'M NOT CWYING!
TANYA'SH GONNA ABANDON ME TOO!
BECAUSH I'M A CHILD.
WAAAAHH!
WAAAH!
I CAN'T CONTWOL MY FEELINGS.
I'M SAD... WHAT DO I DO?

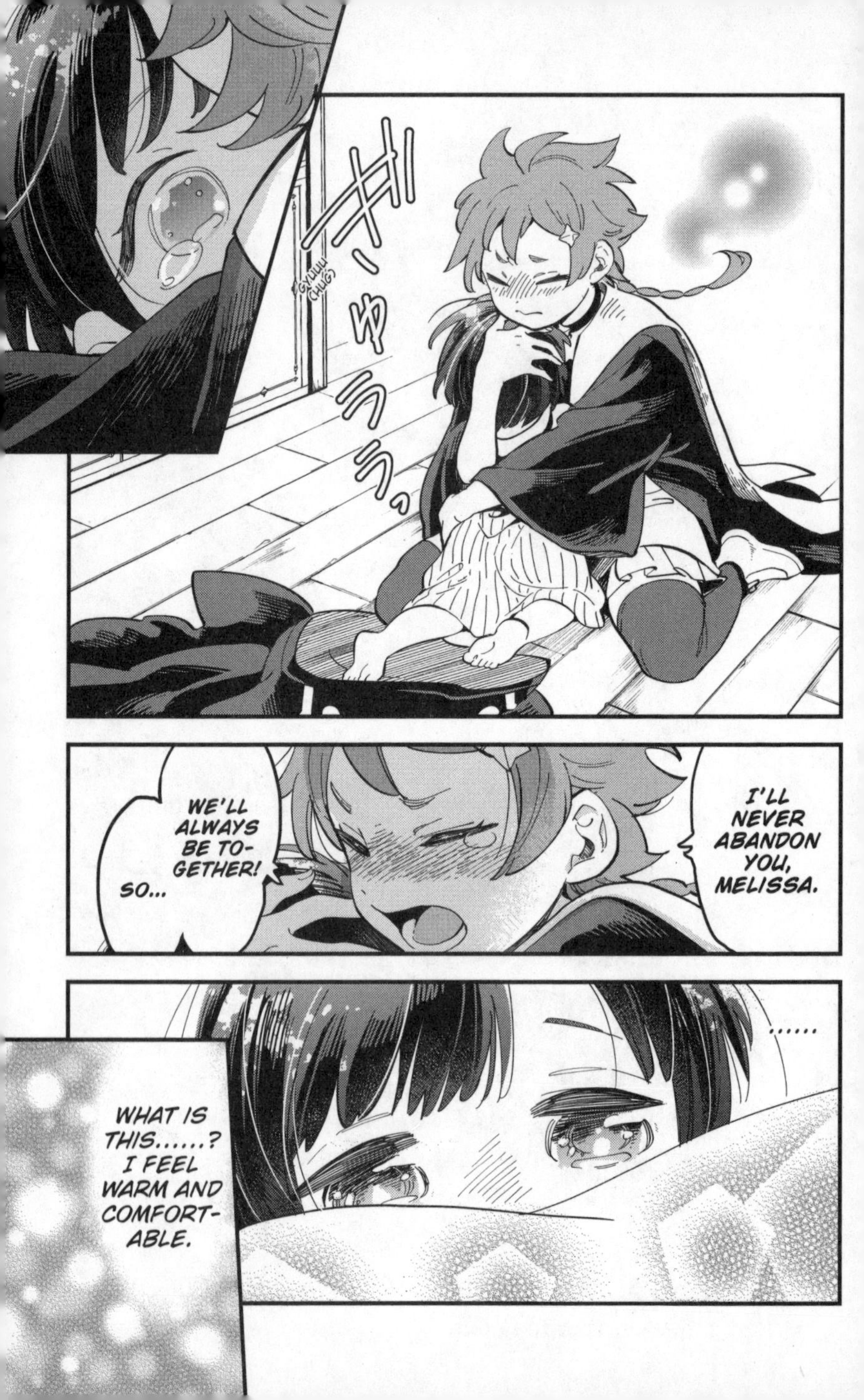
GYUUU CHUG
I'LL NEVER ABANDON YOU, MELISSA.
WE'LL ALWAYS BE TO-GETHER! SO...
......
WHAT IS THIS......? I FEEL WARM AND COMFORT-ABLE.

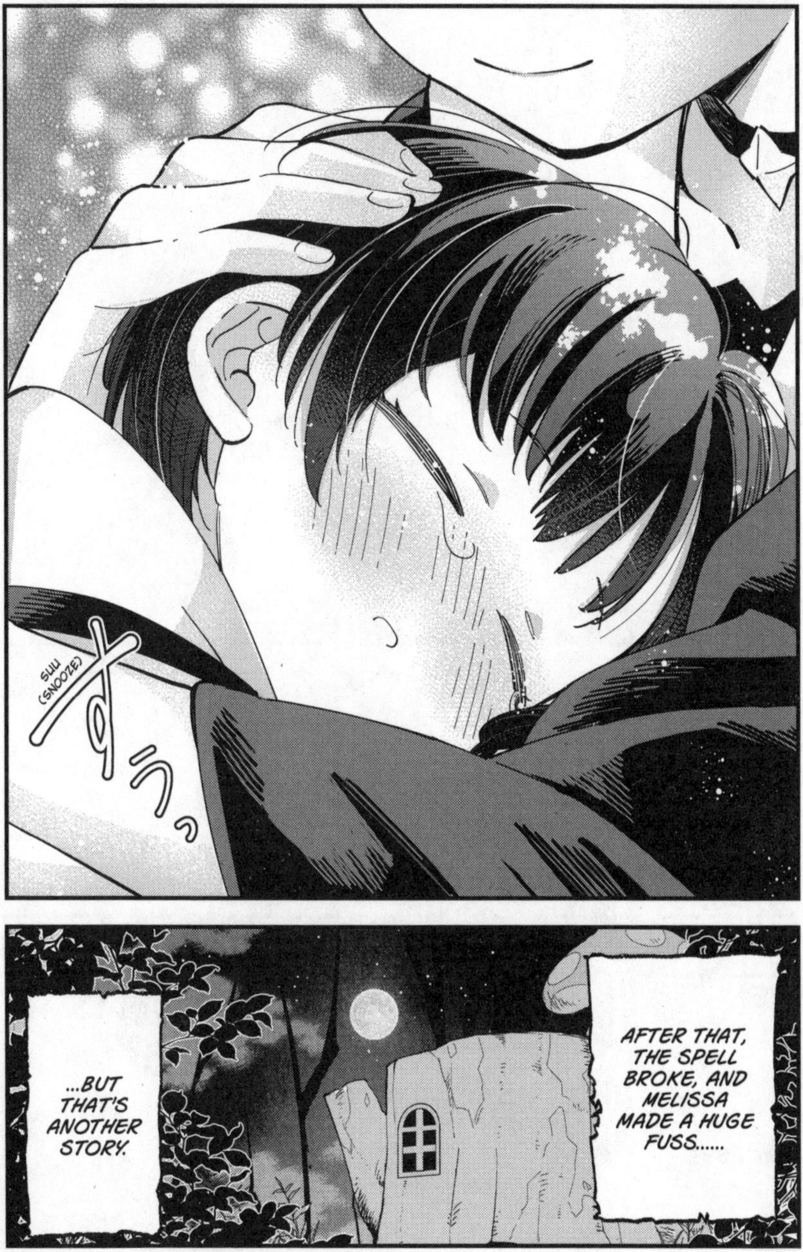
SUU (SNOOZE)
AFTER THAT, THE SPELL BROKE, AND MELISSA MADE A HUGE FUSS......
...BUT THAT'S ANOTHER STORY.

The Witches' Marriage 1 End

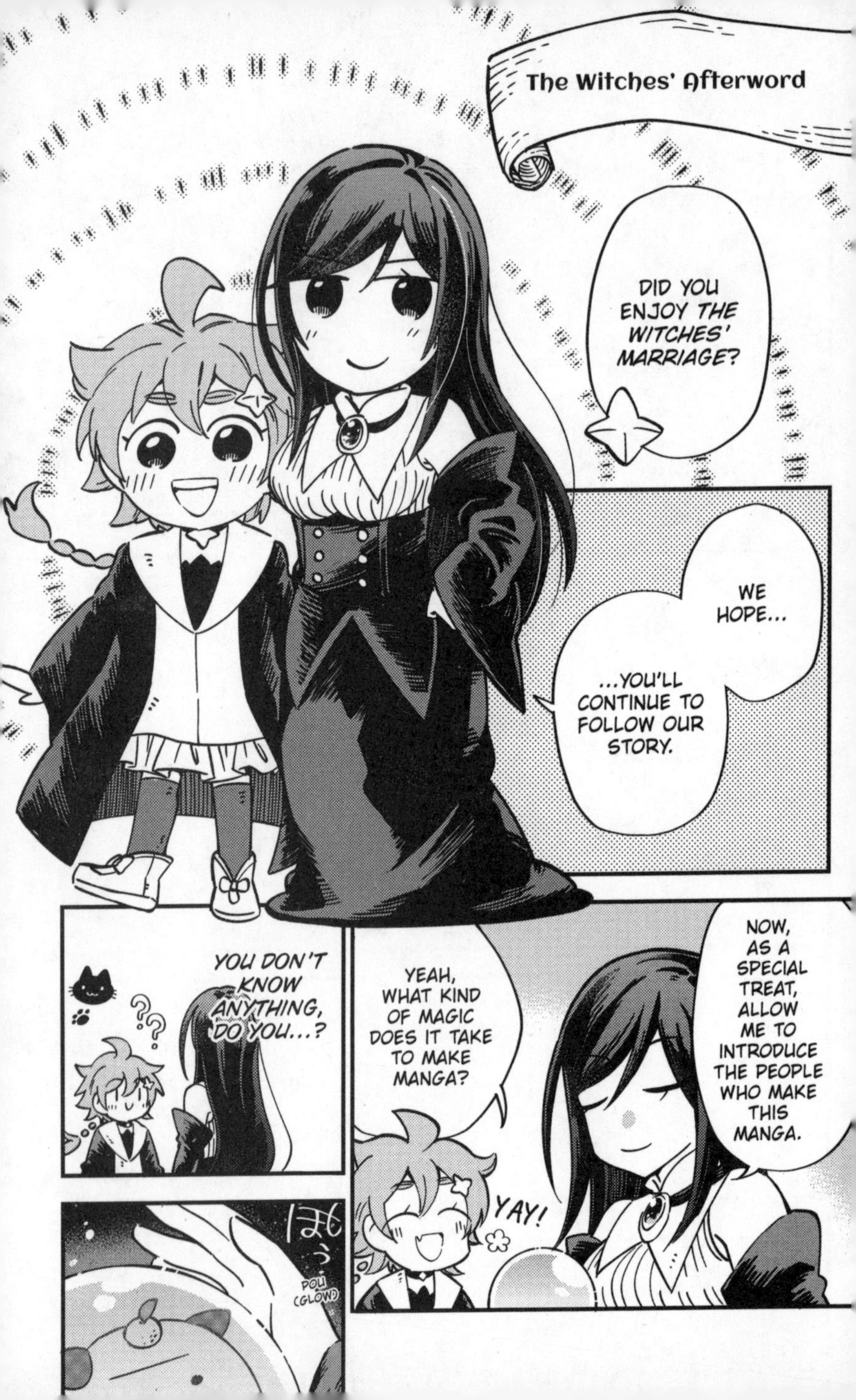
The Witches' Afterword
DID YOU ENJOY THE WITCHES' MARRIAGE?
WE HOPE...
...YOU'LL CONTINUE TO FOLLOW OUR STORY.
NOW, AS A SPECIAL TREAT, ALLOW ME TO INTRODUCE THE PEOPLE WHO MAKE THIS MANGA.
YEAH, WHAT KIND OF MAGIC DOES IT TAKE TO MAKE MANGA?
YAY!
YOU DON'T KNOW ANYTHING, DO YOU...?
POU (GLOW)

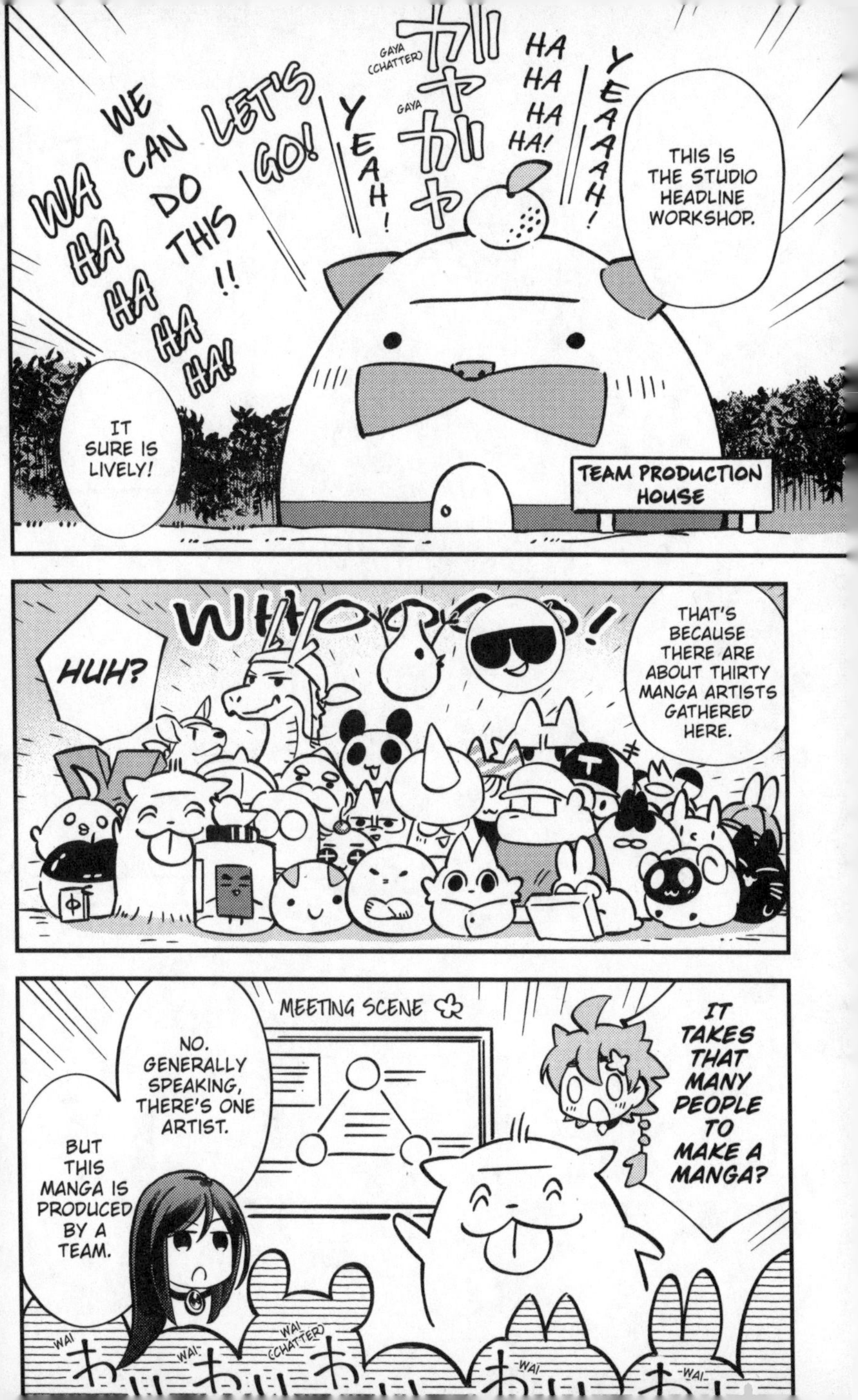
THIS IS THE STUDIO HEADLINE WORKSHOP.
YEAAAAH!
HA HA HA HA!
GAYA (CHATTER) GAYA
がやがや
YEAH!
LET'S GO!
WE CAN DO THIS!!
WA HA HA HA HA!
IT SURE IS LIVELY!
TEAM PRODUCTION HOUSE
THAT'S BECAUSE THERE ARE ABOUT THIRTY MANGA ARTISTS GATHERED HERE.
WHOOOO!
HUH?
IT TAKES THAT MANY PEOPLE TO MAKE A MANGA?
MEETING SCENE
NO. GENERALLY SPEAKING, THERE'S ONE ARTIST.
BUT THIS MANGA IS PRODUCED BY A TEAM.
WAI WAI WAI (CHATTER) WAI WAI

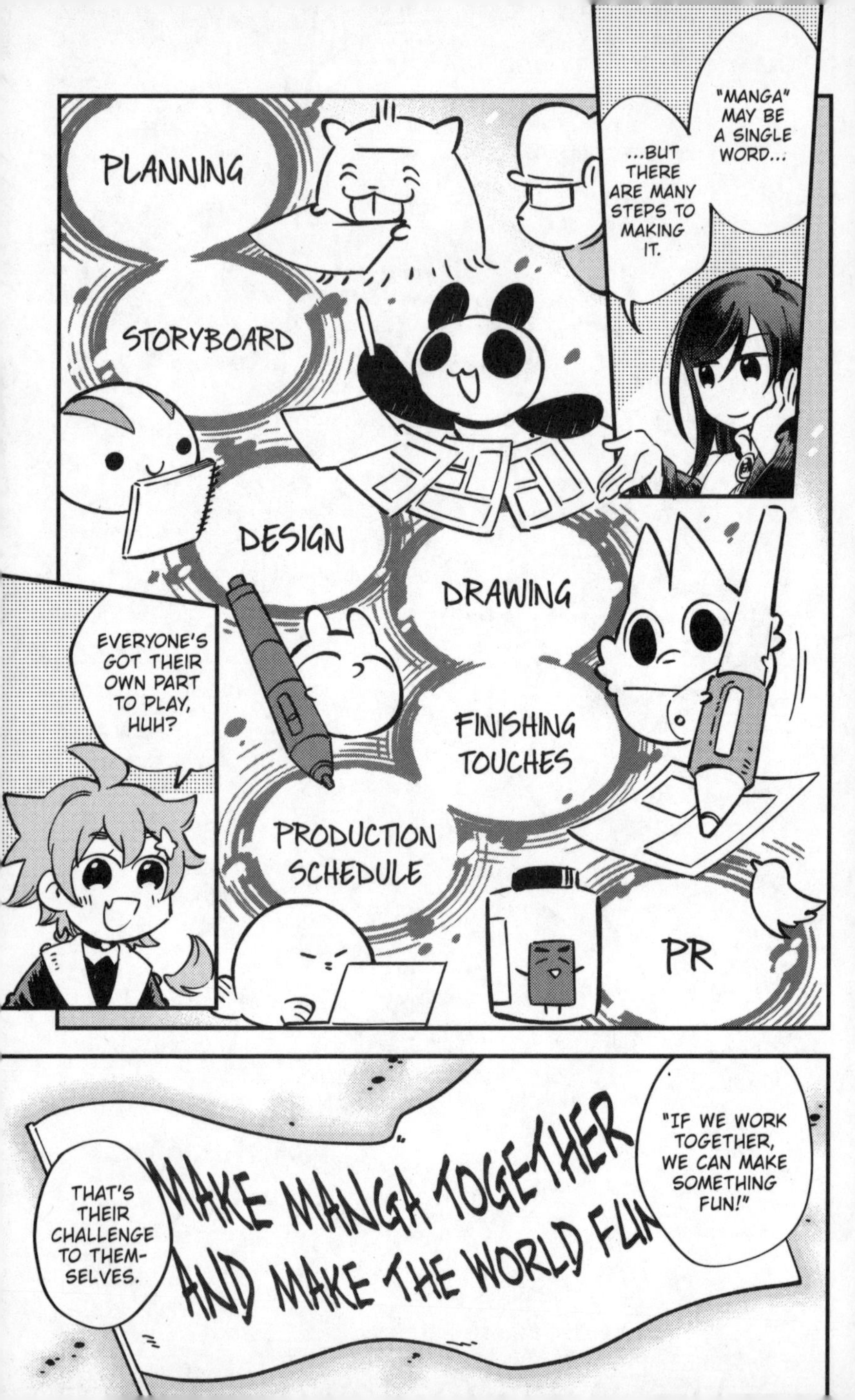
"MANGA" MAY BE A SINGLE WORD...
...BUT THERE ARE MANY STEPS TO MAKING IT.
PLANNING
STORYBOARD
DESIGN
DRAWING
FINISHING TOUCHES
PRODUCTION SCHEDULE
PR
EVERYONE'S GOT THEIR OWN PART TO PLAY, HUH?
"IF WE WORK TOGETHER, WE CAN MAKE SOMETHING FUN!"
MAKE MANGA TOGETHER AND MAKE THE WORLD FUN
THAT'S THEIR CHALLENGE TO THEM-SELVES.

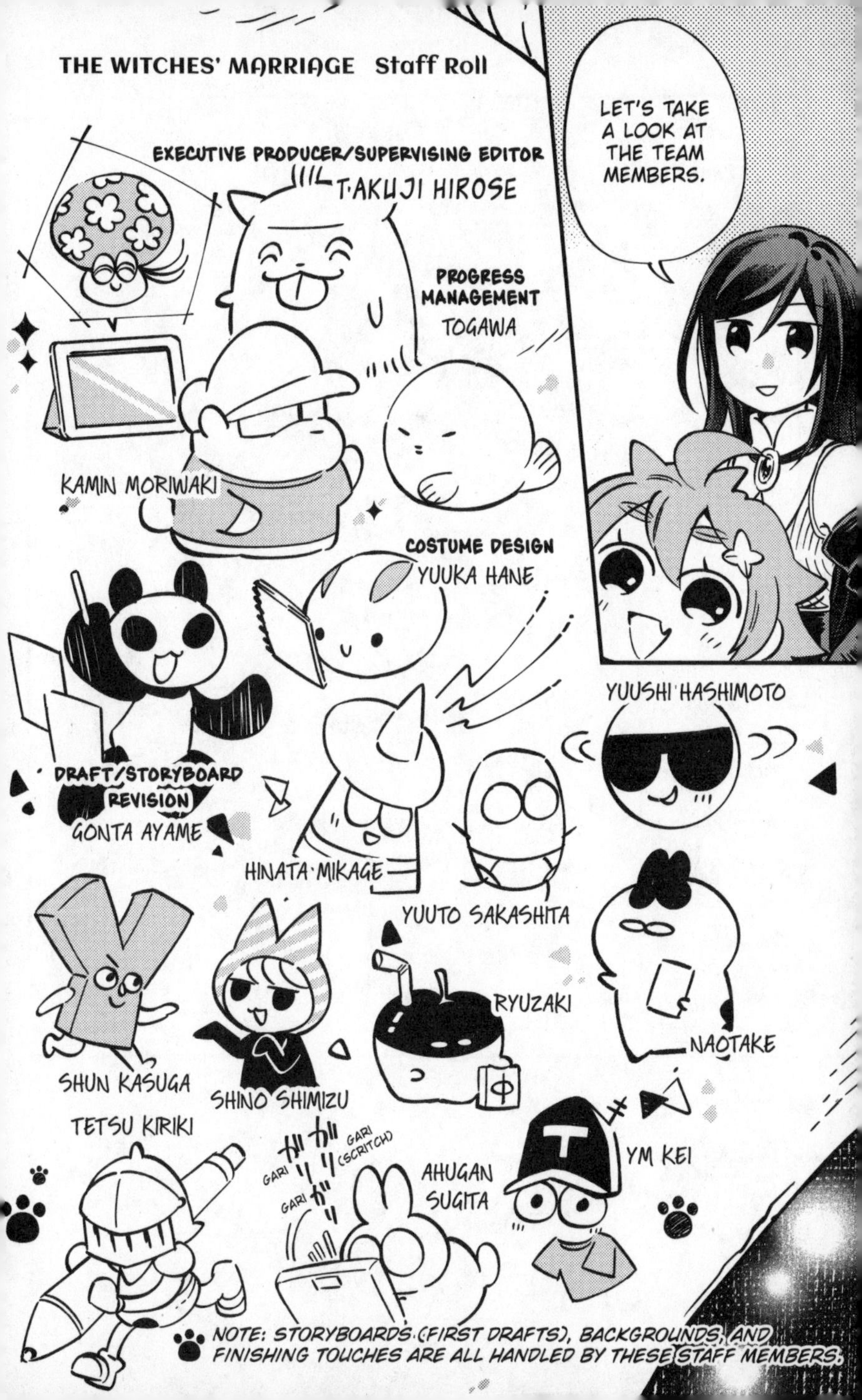
LET'S TAKE A LOOK AT THE TEAM MEMBERS.
THE WITCHES' MARRIAGE Staff Roll
EXECUTIVE PRODUCER/SUPERVISING EDITOR
TAKUJI HIROSE
PROGRESS MANAGEMENT
TOGAWA
KAMIN MORIWAKI
COSTUME DESIGN
YUUKA HANE
YUUSHI HASHIMOTO
DRAFT/STORYBOARD REVISION
GONTA AYAME
HINATA MIKAGE
YUUTO SAKASHITA
RYUZAKI
NAOTAKE
SHUN KASUGA
SHINO SHIMIZU
TETSU KIRIKI
GARI GARI (SCRITCH)
GARI
GARI
AHUGAN SUGITA
YM KEI
NOTE: STORYBOARDS (FIRST DRAFTS), BACKGROUNDS, AND FINISHING TOUCHES ARE ALL HANDLED BY THESE STAFF MEMBERS.

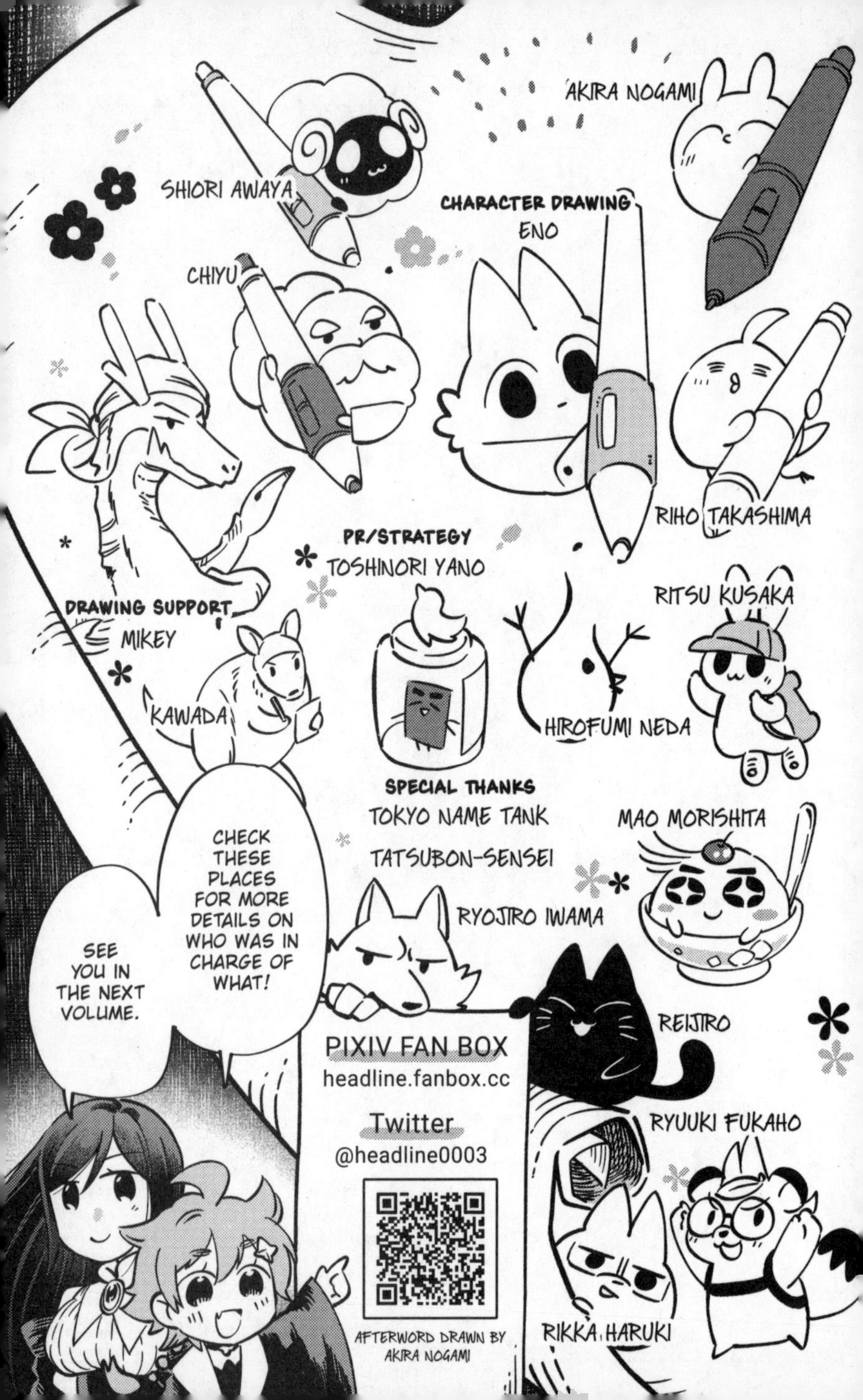
AKIRA NOGAMI
SHIORI AWAYA
CHARACTER DRAWING
ENO
CHIYU
RIHO TAKASHIMA
PR/STRATEGY
TOSHINORI YANO
DRAWING SUPPORT
MIKEY
KAWADA
RITSU KUSAKA
HIROFUMI NEDA
SPECIAL THANKS
TOKYO NAME TANK
TATSUBON-SENSEI
MAO MORISHITA
RYOJIRO IWAMA
REIJIRO
CHECK THESE PLACES FOR MORE DETAILS ON WHO WAS IN CHARGE OF WHAT!
SEE YOU IN THE NEXT VOLUME.
PIXIV FAN BOX
headline.fanbox.cc
Twitter
@headline0003
RYUUKI FUKAHO
RIKKA HARUKI
AFTERWORD DRAWN BY AKIRA NOGAMI

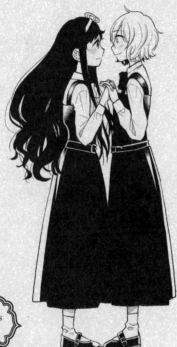
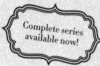
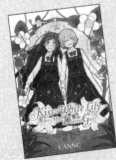

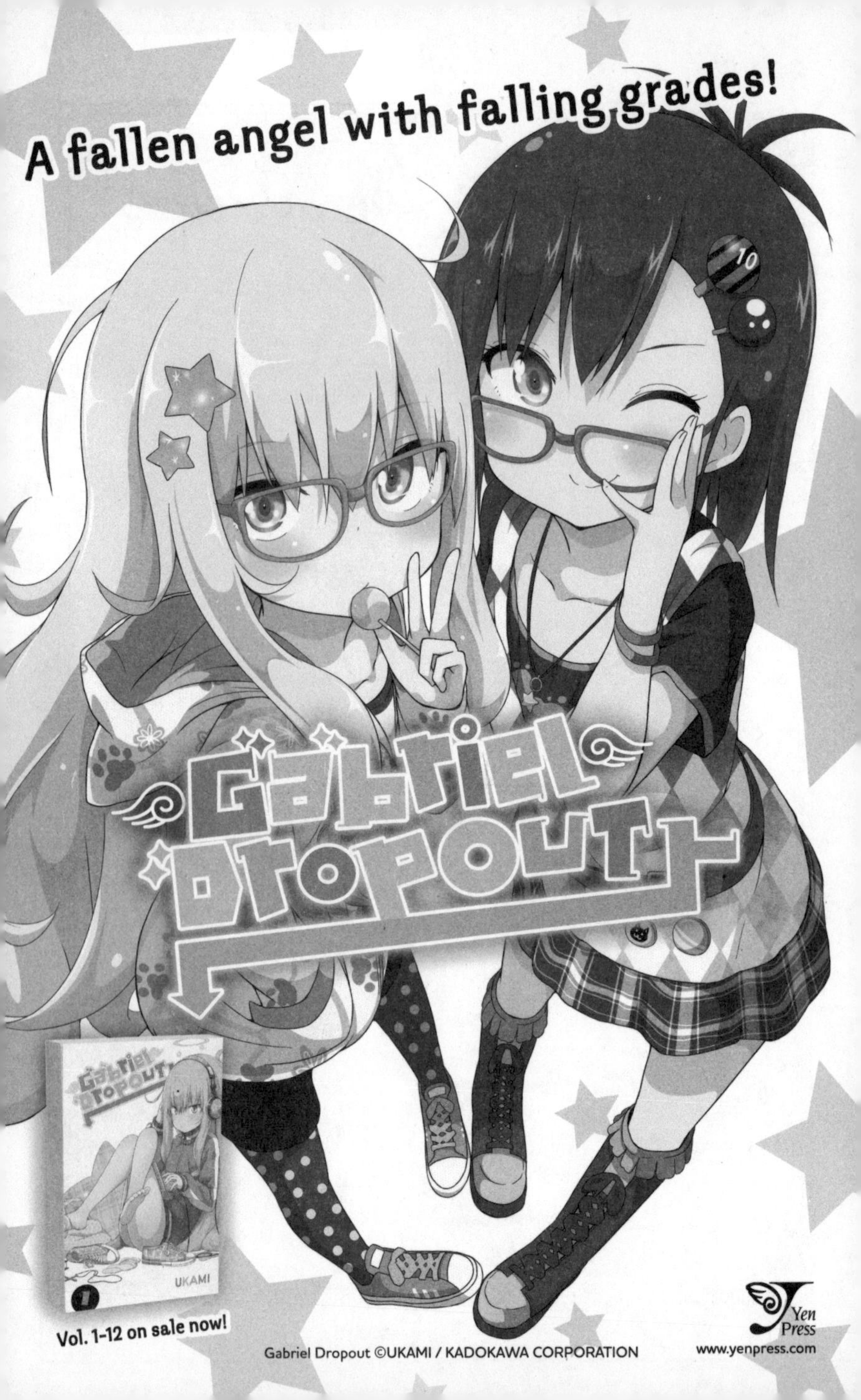

A fallen angel with falling grades!
Gabriel Dropout
Gabriel Dropout
UKAMI
1
Vol. 1-12 on sale now!
Gabriel Dropout ©UKAMI / KADOKAWA CORPORATION
Yen Press
www.yenpress.com

The Witches' Marriage

 studio HEADLINE

Translation: Eleanor Summers ✳ Lettering: Bianca Pistillo

MAJO NO KEKKON Vol. 1
©studio HEADLINE 2021
First published in Japan in 2021 by KADOKAWA CORPORATION, Tokyo.
English translation rights arranged with KADOKAWA CORPORATION, Tokyo,
through TUTTLE-MORI AGENCY, INC., Tokyo.

English translation © 2023 by Yen Press, LLC

Yen Press
150 West 30th Street, 19th Floor
New York, NY 10001

Visit us at yenpress.com
facebook.com/yenpress ✳ twitter.com/yenpress
yenpress.tumblr.com ✳ instagram.com/yenpress

First Yen Press Edition: August 2023
Edited by Yen Press Editorial: Mark Gallucci
Designed by Yen Press Design: Liz Parlett

Yen Press is an imprint of Yen Press, LLC.
The Yen Press name and logo are trademarks of Yen Press, LLC.

The publisher is not responsible for websites (or their content) that are not owned by the publisher.

Library of Congress Control Number: 2023938737

ISBNs: 978-1-9753-6038-2 (paperback)
978-1-9753-6039-9 (ebook)

1 3 5 7 9 10 8 6 4 2

WOR

Printed in the United States of America